BEYOND CUBA:
Latin America Takes Charge of Its Future

Contributors

Luigi R. Einaudi
Michael Fleet
Herbert Goldhamer
Edward Gonzalez
Shane J. Hunt
Richard L. Maullin
David F. Ronfeldt
Daniel M. Schydlowsky
Robert L. Slighton
Alfred C. Stepan

BEYOND CUBA:

Latin America Takes Charge of Its Future

EDITED BY

Luigi R. Einaudi

THE RAND CORPORATION

Crane, Russak & Company, Inc.

NEW YORK

Published in the United States by
Crane, Russak & Company, Inc.
52 Vanderbilt Avenue
New York, N.Y. 10017

Copyright © 1974 The Rand Corporation

ISBN 0-8448-0224-7

LC 73-8644

Printed in the United States of America

"We can no longer afford to import foreign political or economic systems. We must develop, in a profound act of true creation, a social order that reflects the originality and history of our country and our continent."

General Juan Velasco Alvarado
President of Peru
Message to the Nation, July 28, 1969

PREFACE

This volume examines the major forces of contemporary Latin American development, with emphasis on the broad lines of evolution that may be expected in the next several years. The separate essays, therefore, focus on issues of general significance rather than on individual countries. Taken together, they provide a comprehensive and timely interdisciplinary review of Latin American political and economic life, the growth of major institutions, and Latin America's changing world role.

With but three exceptions, the papers collected here were originally presented at a conference on "Trends in Latin America," organized by the Rand Corporation. The conference, held at Airlie House in Warrenton, Virginia, May 12–14, 1972, was attended by some thirty-five analysts from government, business, and the academic community. The discussions these analyses generated were frequently intense, but always constructive, and the authors considered them fully in revising their individual papers, published initially as *Latin America in the 1970s,* R-1067-DOS, The Rand Corporation, Santa Monica, California, December, 1972. For the present volume we have revised most of the original conference papers, and have added new materials to the chapter on Latin America's international relationships, expanded the conclusion to take into account changes in the United States' posture toward Latin America, and included chapters on the Latin American revolutionary tradition and on the evolution of Catholic thought and military perspectives.

The publication of this volume reflects our belief that Latin American problems are of interest to the general reader as well as to the specialist in Latin American affairs. The erosion of the international economic and political balance that followed upon World War II is steadily altering the shape of the world. And Latin America, thanks to the resilience of its governments, its remarkable and continuing economic growth, and the imaginativeness of its cultural and political elites, is a most challenging part of that world. Indeed, it would not be surprising if Latin America, precisely because its societies combine so many elements of tradition and modernity, were to become a touchstone of the economic and political relationships between the "industrialized" and the "less developed" countries, and therefore of progress toward a less divided world.

No effort as broad as that represented by this volume can be undertaken without support. Excepting only the editor's chapter on the revolutionary tradition, all of the papers collected here were originally sponsored in whole or in part by the Office of External Research of the U.S. Department of State. Except for the articles by Daniel Schydlowsky and Shane Hunt, all were written at the Rand Corporation, drawing on Rand's accumulated research on Latin America, much of it self-sponsored. While neither the Department of State nor Rand may be held accountable for the views (and errors) contained in this volume, both institutions deserve credit for the environment that enabled us to pursue our work.

Though it is impossible to mention all those whose encouragement made this volume possible, two persons deserve special thanks. G. Harvey Summ stands out among the many Foreign Service Officers whose criticism and openness to ideas sustained and enriched us all. Geraldine M. Petty's assistance in all phases of our work at Rand was essential throughout to its quality and relevance. Finally, the editor wishes to thank his Rand colleagues, his fellow contributors, and the participants in the Trends Conference itself for their support and encouragement in even attempting so broad a task.

L.R.E.

Santa Monica, California
September, 1973

CONTENTS

CONTRIBUTORS

Luigi R. Einaudi
Social Scientist, The Rand Corporation. Ph.D. in Political Science, Harvard University.

Michael Fleet
Assistant Professor of Politics and International Relations, University of Southern California. Ph.D. in Political Science, University of California at Los Angeles.

Herbert Goldhamer
Social Scientist, The Rand Corporation. Ph.D. in Sociology, University of Chicago.

Edward Gonzalez
Associate Professor of Political Science, University of California at Los Angeles. Ph.D. in Political Science, University of California at Los Angeles.

Shane J. Hunt
Associate Professor of Economics, Princeton University. Ph.D. in Economics, Yale University.

Richard L. Maullin
Deputy Secretary of State of California. Ph.D. in Political Science, University of California at Los Angeles.

David F. Ronfeldt
Social Scientist, The Rand Corporation. Ph.D. in Political Science, Stanford University.

Daniel M. Schydlowsky
Associate Professor of Economics, Boston University. Ph.D. in Economics, Harvard University.

Robert L. Slighton

Economist, The Rand Corporation. Ph.D. in Economics, Johns Hopkins University.

Alfred C. Stepan

Associate Professor of Political Science, Yale University. Ph.D. in Political Science, Columbia University.

I. INTRODUCTION

1. The Scope of This Book

Chapter One

THE SCOPE OF THIS BOOK

Luigi R. Einaudi

This study seeks to identify broad regional trends likely to condition Latin American development during the 1970s. Each essay considers an issue or set of problems central to the interpretation of contemporary Latin American events. The unifying purpose is to provide an intellectual synthesis of the most important directions of change in the major countries and in Latin America as a whole. The goal, in other words, is not the analysis of individual country situations, but rather the illumination of basic patterns in Latin America's recent evolution.

Such an ambitious undertaking is hazardous. Generalizations about a region so complex and varied are inherently dangerous. The inevitable exceptions to even the broadest generalization frequently create doubts about the overall interpretation. The emphasis that many analysts of Latin American affairs currently place on the problems of specific countries constitutes a healthy reaction to past overgeneralization. In-depth country studies will in the long run certainly facilitate sounder comparative judgments.

Despite the difficulties, however, a sensible interim awareness of regional trends is also necessary. All too frequently, the persistence of old and often erroneous images of Latin American development has interfered with the perception of emerging trends—within individual countries as well as in the region as a whole. Partly as a result of common historical experiences and linkages, the individual countries of Latin America share characteristics that invite generalization.

The images most prevalent during the 1960s, for example, tended to picture Latin America as a collection of traditional agrarian societies besieged by problems of population growth, urbanization, and political instability to a point that threatened their orderly transition from semifeudalism to modernity. From this perspective, signs of change were frequently interpreted as indicators of a profound crisis that would bring turmoil and might possibly lead to the emergence of totalitarian societies with which the United States could find little if anything in common.

While such images of revolutionary potential were stimulating the Alliance for Progress, other analysts were pointing out that Latin America was quite resistant to change. Despite surface signs of instability, Latin America's political culture was held to be so inherently conservative and tradition-bound as to defy significant progress. From this perspective, signs of turmoil implied continuity rather than change: *plus ça change, plus c'est la même chose*. Such interpretations provided important correctives to the dominant images of revolutionary explosiveness, but were also of little help in interpreting the sometimes spectacular processes of change visible in many countries.

The papers in this volume challenge both the revolutionary and the conservative images of development in Latin America, while offering an interpretation that combines elements from each. Our central theme is that Latin America's recent political struggles have contributed to the evolution of increasingly stable and sophisticated institutions which, in contrast to the past, are now often providing determined leadership for reform. Latin America continues to modernize, and the modern nation state, in Latin America as elsewhere, while essentially proof against violent social revolution is also capable of change. The struggle for innovation, when it takes place within the framework of substantially developed societies, is not adequately described by the cataclysmic stereotypes of left and right.

From this vantage point, the predominant earlier images of revolutionary explosiveness or stagnation seem to have derived in the main from American fears and experiences in the Caribbean, overlooking the many diversities within the Latin American region itself and, perhaps most importantly, ignoring the many dramatic changes that had already taken place in Latin America during the twentieth century. Two world wars, the depression, and more recent economic policies have helped to accelerate Latin America's industrial development to the point that important modern sectors coexist with the more traditional aspects of Latin American life. Contemporary tensions should thus be interpreted as occurring against a background not of weak, oligarchical societies unable to cope with them, but rather of steadily modernizing societies with important institutions whose interplay will be decisive in shaping future responses to the challenges of development.

Some General Trends

For a region whose history has been studded with the heroics of individual leaders and which has given us the term *caudillo,* perhaps the single most important contemporary fact is the inability of individuals alone to impress their will on the increasing complexity of institutions and social forces that have arisen. Even within the military institutions, a traditional source of individual *caudillos,* the troop commander who can convert armed force and individual popularity directly into national·leadership is present only in the least developed countries. In the major South American countries and Mexico, military leaders operate within a bureaucratic setting, depending on their general staffs and on increasingly well-trained and functioning officer corps. The Church, long a source of legitimacy for organized governments, has become increasingly independent and simultaneously more involved in debates over national goals. Universities, long the refuges of elite elements, have multiplied and broadly expanded their enrollments. National governments, seeking to retain some measure of authority in fluid domestic and international environments, are everywhere expanding their activities and developing national planning institutes and other organisms of central control.

The fluidity of the contemporary Latin American scene is underscored by the rapid growth of Latin America's major urban centers. The inadequate housing occupied by many of the new urban migrants is a convenient symbol for social protests, and the aspirations of migrants and their children constitute a major factor in populist pressures. Less visible, but perhaps more politically important, is the growing strength of previously silent or ineffective middle-class groups who are exploiting the increased availability of higher education to challenge the ruling elites of Latin American societies on their own grounds, frequently by working through established institutions, such as the military, the Church, and the national bureaucracies.

Industrial activity is growing rapidly, and is frequently neither as inefficient nor potentially as dependent as is commonly believed. Brazil's exports of manufactured and semiprocessed goods have quadrupled since the mid-1960s and will soon approach a billion dollars annually. Similar progress in nontraditional exports appears possible at least in Argentina and Mexico, and is spurring efforts at industrialization and integration in the countries of the Andean Group. The growth of these and other modern activities strongly imply that Latin America can no longer simply be dismissed under the label of "underdeveloped."

Some Ambiguities

The complexity of the contemporary Latin American scene is underscored by the fact that these basic trends also contain striking elements of continuity.

The *institutions* that have traditionally dominated Latin American life, demonstrate increased flexibility, but remain largely the same. The military, the Church, and the growing government bureaucracies show no signs of being swept aside by mass forces organized by voluntaristic revolutionaries like Che Guevara or his emulators. Indeed, several of the essays suggest that forces of change are increasingly being expressed through Latin American institutions. This is to some extent a guarantee of change, but it is also an important element of social control and continuity.

Politically, although industrialization and agrarian change have greatly weakened the traditional landed gentry, the destiny of Latin America is still in the hands of relatively small elites engaged in activities from which the masses of the population are largely excluded. But these elites are themselves divided and evolving new values. The Cuban revolutionary experience, as perceived by contemporary Latin American leaders, is ambiguous, encouraging caution as well as new initiatives. Despite authoritarian tendencies and the pressures of modern communications, political parties and elections continue to play an important role in the organizing of governments.

Economically, prospects for overall growth are generally modest and seem likely to be unevenly distributed. The failure of even Cuba to escape from sugar suggests, moreover, that the traditional areas of Latin American economic activity will not disappear despite the growth of new industries. Indeed, though an expansion of nontraditional exports may alter the picture, industrialization has thus far generally depended on the foreign-exchange earnings of mining and agriculture. With the notable exception of some agricultural exports, traditional rural production has failed to keep pace with industry, and thereby contributes indirectly to population pressures and to highly visible social inequalities.

Uneven development, with increased differentiation between workers engaged in modern economic activity and the larger numbers in traditional semiskilled pursuits, is a major source of social unrest. Important elements of the population seem likely to remain largely as they are today, impoverished, underemployed, and excluded from the progress of other sectors of the society. Nonetheless, future political instability seems likely to be checked somewhat by Latin America's growing institutional development. This is not a guarantee that radical changes will not take place, particularly if marginal sectors can enlist the political support of part of the elite. In Cuba, after all, revolution was largely imposed from above, after control of the government was won by an alienated segment of the ruling elite allied with youthful elements of the middle sectors acting in the name of the population at large—but even in Cuba revolutionary success required the conjunction of additional factors, such as exceptional internal leadership and equally extraordinary external opposition and support.

Ambiguity marks even the strongest trends of the recent past: the institutional reorientations of the Catholic Church and of the military. The Church, after moving decisively to accommodate change, has tended to divide into small but committed radical and conservative wings, even as the hierarchies as a whole seem to yearn for a disengagement from active politics. Although no longer the decided support for the status quo of days past, the result is not the prophetic leadership in the battle for social justice envisioned by the more impassioned advocates of the "theology of liberation." The military, also drawn into greater political participation, remain divided behind their monolithic façades of discipline and secrecy. At times the military may act as a force for "historical acceleration," breaking a political impasse. Normally, however, military institutions reflect the uncertainties and tensions of their societies, and participate in frequently shifting coalitions with civilian leaders.

Internationally, despite the growth of nationalism, coming years are likely to witness greater interdependence. The search for new institutional arrangements for foreign capital is spurred not so much by desires to exclude foreigners as by a drive to find less politically and economically costly ways of importing necessary skills and technology in accordance with locally determined priorities. To the extent that countries other than the United States expand their activities, U.S. influence may decrease and opportunities may increase for powers such as the Soviet Union to exploit Latin American conditions to their advantage. Yet Latin America's growth suggests that foreign entanglements as a whole will be moderated by Latin America's own greater development and international weight.

The Structure of This Study

The conclusion expands on these themes and suggests further implications for both Latin America and the United States. But readers are invited to turn first to the individual essays that inspired—but also, because of their richness, escaped—this summary introduction. Before doing so, however, it may be appropriate to consider briefly how this study originated, and how the volume is structured.

Our original task was to analyze major trends in Latin America during the 1970s for the Department of State. When we first considered this problem, we were struck by all that we would have to omit. We agreed from the start to include separate analyses of national leadership patterns, political and economic organization, and international relationships. Indeed, together with a section on institutions, which draws on earlier research for the Department of State, these topics constitute the framework of this volume.

But what about other issues? Discussion of agrarian reform was a characteristic of the 1960s. As a result of events in Peru, Chile, Argentina, and Mexico, debates over worker participation in industry are acquiring similar prominence during the 1970s. And what of population growth, which underlies many contemporary pressures for change? We could not overlook these issues, yet we found as we proceeded that we had difficulty considering them separately. Much debate, for example, went into how to treat the population issue. The work of Paul Schultz on fertility problems in Puerto Rico and Colombia, and of William Butz on Guatemala, and their concern for the implications of demographic theory for economic development, are an integral part of Rand's research perspective. Nonetheless, we ultimately concluded that population growth rates as such would have relatively little impact on the short-term political future, and that the extensive treatment of the issue in most other studies of Latin America would enable us to contribute little new perspective. Discussion of population pressures was therefore integrated into other analyses, such as those of expanded electorates, changing attitudes toward income distribution, and the general problems of uneven development.

Although our original report to the State Department included separate analyses of student politics and of the role of women, these, too, have been omitted from the present volume. Students, traditional political activists, have recently been relatively quiescent. Women, in Latin America as elsewhere perhaps the most important untapped reservoir of talent, seem likely to continue to exercise indirect rather than independent political influence. Neither topic, therefore, seems central to the immediate evolution and uses of power in Latin America, which is our primary concern in the pages that follow.

The volume opens with a consideration of political problems. The first essay traces the political origins of Cuban-type revolutionary pressures in Latin America to the frustrations and divisions within the popular, Aprista-type parties during the mid-1950s. The failure of democratic experimentation after 1945 led to the radicalization of youthful segments of these parties and to a revived nationalist revolutionary militancy which expressed itself in anti-imperialist and anti-American terms. The consummation of this latent division among Latin American revolutionary groups after the Cuban Revolution, together with other changes in the regional and international political contexts, renders repetition of the Cuban experience elsewhere in Latin America improbable, despite the continuing relevance of radical nationalist critiques of the *status quo.*

Prospects for violence are discussed next, and the point is made that even though sporadic violence is likely to continue, guerrilla insurgencies have been largely controlled, and in the process central governments have increased their interactions with isolated rural areas. In addition, the prevalence of violence has led to increased concern over its causes, including uneven development, and domestic and foreign opposition to reform. These themes are reflected in the chapter on changing patterns of leadership, which concludes that Latin

America's leaders are likely to be more independently innovative than in the past, and to seek reform within a nationalist framework. The final chapter in this section reviews the uncertain record of constitutional procedures and elections for resolving political disputes, and concludes that although elections will remain a central feature of Latin American life, they must be understood in a context broader than the liberal democratic model of political competition.

The section on institutions begins with excerpts from two prior Rand studies on changes in the Catholic Church and in the perspectives of the military in Peru and Brazil. These institutional dimensions reveal the depth of the processes of change underway in Latin America, and should constitute an important theme of future research. The treatment of institutions concludes with an essay that raises some important questions about the nature of political processes and institutions in the organization of governments, beginning with the proposition that most governments are neither military nor civilian, but result rather from complex interactions leading to shifting civil-military coalitions.

The section on economics opens with the most technical but also perhaps the most provocative essay in this collection. The argument is made here that major Latin American industries are neither as inefficient nor as inherently dependent as is frequently believed, and that the adoption of export promotion policies could contribute to a major increase in Latin America's nontraditional exports, and hence in Latin America's economic growth. This prescription for growth through aggressive industrialization highlights the trade restrictions of the currently leading industrial countries, and thereby indirectly sets the stage for the subsequent chapter which analyzes changing attitudes toward foreign direct investment in Latin America. Again the conclusion is similar: current tensions derive less from "underdevelopment" than from the growing capacity of Latin American governments to seek new institutional arrangements at lower cost, politically and economically, to national development. Finally, this section concludes with an analysis of the inevitability, given the difficulties of meeting popular expectations through economic growth alone, of measures aimed at income redistribution.

The last two sections focus on Latin America's international role. The expanded activities of foreign powers in the region are matched by increased Latin American interest in international relations and by growing interactions among the Latin American states themselves. A note on U.S. government exchange programs suggests some guidelines that might improve mutual understanding between the two Americas. The conclusion presents an overview of Latin America's development, and describes some of the difficulties of developing a more positive U.S. response.

II. POLITICS

Chapter Two

THE REVOLUTIONARY TRADITION IN PERSPECTIVE*

Luigi R. Einaudi

In 1959 the Cuban Revolution thrust Latin America upon American consciousness, and led to an upsurge of speculation that revolution would spread from the Sierra Maestra to the Andes. Some of the very factors which had induced prior American neglect and complacency about Latin America—the closeness to home (more apparent than real in the case of South America); the seemingly endless succession of comic, sometimes cruel, but always inefficient governments; the picturesqueness of millennial poverty—took on in the light of the successful revolution led by Fidel Castro an ominous appearance of impending collapse, of hungry Indian peasants brandishing machetes and spreading Communist power on our doorstep.

Observers differed over precisely how this would happen. Much debate was expended on the social ingredients of the revolution in Cuba, and on whether it would be the same groups or others that would make the revolution in Latin America. Some had their doubts about the extent to which starving Indians could be mobilized, or about the ease with which, once mobilized, they would fit into the world Communist system. But if it would not be the peasants to rise, then it would be the urban slum dwellers, or the students and intellectuals, or the modernizing middle classes.

The Cuban Revolution is now in its fifteenth year. The remaining countries of Latin America have not eliminated violence or injustice, nor have they attained the higher living standards presumed necessary to avoid repetitions of the Cuban experience. Yet the Andes have not become another Sierra Maestra, and the isolated attempts to make them one have met with dismal failure. Not a single Latin American country has gone the way of Cuba.

Why has the Cuban example, which aroused such expectations, not been emulated elsewhere? This is not, admittedly, the kind of question to which it

---

*This chapter is largely drawn from the author's Ph.D. dissertation, *Marxism in Latin America: From Aprismo to Fidelismo,* Harvard University, Cambridge, Massachusetts, June, 1966. An earlier version was presented before the 1966 Annual Meeting of the American Political Science Association and issued as P-3440, The Rand Corporation, Santa Monica, California, September, 1966.

is possible to provide any easy or definitive answers. We have no way of turning the clock back to any of the innumerable potentially pivotal events of the recent past to determine what would have happened if that event had been different. If Brazil's President Goulart had not undercut his military supporters and had remained in power; if the Peruvian army's crack Rangers had not gone into action at the first sign of guerrilla activity; if the United States Marines had not intervened in the Dominican Republic; if there had been no Alliance for Progress . . . The "ifs" are interminable: within certain broad limits, each of us is entitled to his own list according to his analysis and values.

Nevertheless, the question "Why has the Cuban Revolution failed to spread elsewhere in Latin America?" is still relevant. Speculations, assumptions, and convictions about the answer underlie much, perhaps too much, contemporary political activity and public policy in Latin America. This essay seeks to clarify the nature of revolutionary pressures in Latin America by considering first some matters of definition, and then turning to the intellectual and political origins of the new radicalism exemplified by Cuba's leaders.

Revolution and Violence

If we take the Cuban Revolution to mean a transformation involving the authoritarian imposition of substantial changes in political, social, and economic relations in society, then a historical answer suggests itself at once. Though violent changes in government personnel have been frequent in Latin America, social revolutions have been very rare indeed. The Cuban Revolution, seen in this perspective, was only the third such movement in Latin America (or fourth, if in addition to Mexico and Bolivia one were to add Perón's Argentina). Each of these revolutions, like the one underway in Peru since 1968, has in addition been marked by unique national characteristics, further underscoring the difficulties of generalization.

If we follow the *fidelistas'* own interpretation and preferred means of export, and define the Cuban Revolution as a successful guerrilla movement, the rarity of the phenomenon becomes all the more apparent. Of all the governmental changes produced in Latin America by nonconstitutional means, it is difficult to recognize any, including the Cuban one itself, which conform to the patterns developed in the writings of Che Guevara and other Cuban theorists. Not that violence is uncommon: a compilation by the Department of State identified 106 changes of chief of state in Latin America between 1930 and 1965 by other than constitutional means. I calculate that some 270 changes of chief of state took place throughout the region during this period, which suggests that approximately 40 percent of the changes involved successful oppositional violence. The qualification "oppositional" is used here in distinction to "official" violence, since the State Department list does not include cases of single-candidate elections, *continuismo,* or other successful use of force to ensure the continuation in office of a chief of state or his protégé. Nor does the figure include cases where the functioning of the constitutional process has been obtained by a show of opposition force (for example, a barracks uprising intended less to seize power than to demonstrate that all is not well among the military supporters of the regime).

Traditionally, however, Latin American "revolutions" have rarely led to striking policy changes: limited stakes are disputed among articulate minorities. The pattern of politics in most Latin American countries is normally determined by the interplay of the leadership elements of the political parties and organized labor, the hierarchy of the Roman Catholic Church, the government bureaucracy, the military command, and the spokesmen for the large landowners and local and foreign investors. These groups have many important differences and conflicts: urban-rural, agrarian-industrial, national-foreign, lay-clerical, civil-military, and so on. One of the characteristics of these conflicts is that, although often fought in the name of first principles and sometimes accompanied by violence, frequently with students as a catalyst, they rarely have had immediate repercussions on the structure of society as a whole. The leaders of a victorious "revolution" are absorbed into the system through public offices and private concessions. Issues with broad repercussions not subject to such "individual solutions" are left to be resolved by changed circumstances or to be raised anew by future aspirants to power.

As previously passive mass elements began to acquire political consciousness after 1930, and particularly since World War II, however, the disturbing possibility of "social revolution," of radical change and displacement rather than evolution and assimilation, has increasingly intruded into normal politics. The stakes of political action have grown, as questions affecting the very nature of the economy and the society entered the political arena. The prior development of formal democratic institutions under leaders who were themselves often highly doubtful about mass aspirations, limits the credibility and capacity of existing democratic procedures to resolve the new issues, usually also raised in the name of "democracy." The tendency is thus strong to consider "revolution" a prerequisite for needed structural changes.

The traditional use of violence to resolve limited issues, however, raises serious questions about whether the presence of violence is an indicator of revolutionary pressures. The changing political context does not appear to have markedly affected the incidence of violence related to the tenure of chiefs of state. Between 1959 and 1965, for example, 16 of 37 changes of chiefs of state (43 percent) occurred by nonconstitutional means. As we have seen, this is a gross measure, and quite possibly not the most relevant one; but it suggests that violence remains a secular characteristic of politics in Latin America, and does not appear to be increasing. This particular pattern, in fact, is depressingly stable.

As K. H. Silvert has put it,

If the normal way of rotating the executive in a given country is by revolution and if there have been a hundred such changes in a century, then it is not being facetious to remark that revolutions are a sign of stability—that events are marching along as they always have.[1]

Like other generic factors often associated with revolution (such as racial tensions, economic underdevelopment, or weak and dictatorial governments), the prevalence of violence may arise from a variety of quite different political situations, and is of limited utility in an attempt to analyze the immediate causes and the nature of revolutionary processes.

The Frustrated Revolutionary Tradition

To understand some of the more explicitly political factors giving rise to revolutionary activities in Latin America during the late 1950s and early 1960s, we must examine the specific expectations and perspectives that emerged among Latin American progressives in the period immediately preceding the Cuban Revolution. Until then, the most important organizational and intellectual force on the nationalist left in Latin America was the American Popular Revolutionary Alliance (APRA), founded in Mexico in 1924 by the Peruvian Victor Raúl Haya de la Torre. The *apristas* had become a prototype for indigenous leftist parties and movements throughout Latin America.[2]

The mid-1950s found these nationalist revolutionary movements undergoing a profound crisis. A decade earlier, in the wake of the democratic propaganda and expectations which had characterized the war effort to block

---

1. *The Conflict Society, Reaction and Revolution in Latin America,* New Orleans, Hauser, 1961, p. 20.

2. Robert J. Alexander is the most important American chronicler of Latin America's populist revolutionary parties, most of which issued from the depression, but never shared power until after World War II. See Alexander, *Prophets of the Revolution,* Macmillan, New York, 1962.

Axis penetration in Latin America, the parties of the "democratic left" had found themselves riding the crest of a wave of democratic experimentation. Nowhere was this more in evidence than in Venezuela, with the rise to power of Rómulo Betancourt and Acción Democrática, in Cuba, with the electoral triumphs of Ramón Grau San Martín and Carlos Prío Socarrás of the Cuban Revolutionary Party, and in Peru, where APRA itself was an active participant in a newly-elected parliamentary government, and where Haya de la Torre was maneuvering for the presidency. By the mid-1950s, however, all of these men were in exile. The Venezuelan and Peruvian coups of 1948 and the Cuban coup of 1952 were symptomatic of the collapse of the political expectations of the immediate postwar period.

In discussing the causes of the failure of the democratic experiments, it would seem, particularly to those of us in the United States, that the exiles should have given considerable attention to problems of internal organization and leadership, the analysis of specific local political conditions, and other problems which had prevented either the normal functioning of the overthrown governments or their successful accomplishment of revolutionary programs. So bitter and personal were many of the initial recriminations, however, that relatively few of the ousted progressive politicians engaged in serious discussion of the specific problems and failures of the postwar governments. Instead, they preferred to heap invective on the governments, mainly military, which had inherited the disaster—and on the United States, which was gradually coming once again into focus as the source of all evil.[3] To quote an eminent Venezuelan writing in November, 1954:

Whatever the dominant beliefs in Washington concerning the nature of economic imperialism, in Latin America opinion is practically unanimous that this phenomenon is one of the primary causes, if not the primary source, of such striking evils as the low standard of living of the masses and the resurgence and strength of despotic governments engendered by small privileged groups and based on the pretorianism of the so-called national armies. It is for this reason that attitudes toward imperialism are, among Latin Americans, the touchstone of political and moral positions and an unavoidable aspect of any discussion of political or social matters.[4]

Here was an issue on which all could unite. The struggle against imperial-

---

3. Criticism of the U.S. became particularly pronounced after the 1954 intervention in Guatemala against a government that had become progressively radicalized since the democratic "opening" of 1945, and whose collapse marked the definitive end of the reformist trends ushered in after the war.
4. Gonzalo Barrios, "Seguridad política e imperialismo en la América Latina," *Humanismo*, No. 25 (November 1954), p. 63.

ism focused primarily on an external foreign enemy. Emotional denunciations of the United States and of the brutality of military dictatorships could serve to gratify the piques of leaders and perhaps provide slogans to build eventual popular support. But they bore little practical relation to any return to power or to the development of new programs to alter the course of events. Nonetheless, these appeals were to assume great significance for the future course of radical politics, for they concealed the gradual development of fundamental differences among Latin American radicals.

The growth of major potential differences over revolutionary strategy is clearly apparent in the just cited article on "Political Security and Imperialism in Latin America," published in a journal edited by Cuban, Venezuelan, and Guatemalan exiles in Mexico City.[5] This article addressed itself largely to the tactics required to deal with the influence of the United States in Latin America. It phrased the alternatives as follows:

> Contemporary experience demonstrates that there are two paths of struggle open to subjugated peoples: to obtain the support of the power which is the enemy of the oppressing power, or to reach a political understanding with the potentially similar forces within the oppressing nations.[6]

In the mid-1950s, neither alternative seemed particularly practical, and the debate over these alternatives was inevitably inconclusive. Those who favored turning to the Soviet Union ("the enemy of my enemy") for assistance, had to consider the fact that, as the same article put it:

> The Communist analysis of United States imperialism seems to accept the idea that Latin America is a *politically secure zone* [for the United States] . . . as may be judged by the fact that Communist propaganda and activities do not strike directly at the adversary, whom they *de facto* repute invincible on his own grounds, and are rather limited to secondary maneuvers designed to support the Soviet cause as the center of the opposition to the United States.[7]

---

5. *Humanismo,* which had been founded by a largely Mexican group in July, 1952, had become regional in staff by August, 1953, and became after July, 1954, a virtual house organ for radical debate. Among its editors were the Cuban Raúl Roa (later Fidel Castro's Foreign Minister), the Guatemalan Mario Monteforte Toledo (formerly Secretary-General of Arévalo's Partido Acción Revolucionaria), the Venezuelan Ildegar Pérez Segnini (later an Acción Democrática Senator), the Mexican Senator Luis I. Rodríguez (formerly Ambassador to Republican Spain), and the expatriate Peruvian poet and former Aprista, Alberto Hidalgo, then residing in Buenos Aires.

6. Barrios, *loc. cit.*

7. *Idem.* Haya had used similar arguments against the Communists in the late 1920s and 1930s: Communists are not to be trusted because they are not true revolutionaries.

The "sense of geographic fatalism" was reinforced after the events of 1954 in Guatemala and of 1956 in Hungary, as a result of which many argued that Latin America and Eastern Europe represented comparable, mutually recognized spheres of influence of the two super powers. How, then, could the Soviet Union be brought in as effective support for a new Latin American liberation movement? After all, when Bolívar had obtained British support against Spain, he had not needed to do any convincing. And in any case, relations with the Soviet Union might involve complications, even if they could be obtained.

On the other hand, it was just as difficult to argue that the Democratic Party, the AFL-CIO, or American university students were potentially reliable allies in an anti-imperialist struggle. American labor and students, in spite of Norman Thomas, Serafino Romualdi, and the United States National Student Association, simply looked neither very radical nor very powerful.[8]

Inconclusive as this debate was in the mid-1950s, the positions it revealed reflected a serious element of generational conflict. The older leaders of the established revolutionary parties, Haya de la Torre of APRA in Peru, Betancourt of Acción Democrática in Venezuela, or Grau and Prío of the Cuban Revolutionary Party, inclined strongly to the second solution—that of finding allies within the United States. Two experiences which dated from the 1930s were very important in conditioning their views. They had seen the United States abandon what had seemed in their own early student days to be an internally reactionary and externally imperialist posture. The Marines had been withdrawn in favor of a noninterventionist good neighbor policy, and Franklin Roosevelt had replaced Hoover. They thus felt that the United States was amenable to change, and that within the American tradition there were elements upon which they could rely. Conversely, their experiences with the Soviet Union in the interwar period did not predispose them to optimism. Many of them had traveled to the Soviet Union, only to find that the Soviet Union was in many ways more backward than their own countries, and that there was no significant awareness or disinterested sympathy for Latin America. For these if for no other reasons, the Soviet Union was not a likely candidate for assistance to carry out Latin American revolutions.

---

8. Serafino Romualdi was the Inter-American representative of the AFL-CIO, and became heavily involved in Latin American labor matters after the war. The National Student Association, in which this writer was active in 1955–57, maintained relations with Latin American student federations on the basis of a common struggle against racism, oppression, and ignorance. But this contrasting image of the United States, which might have strengthened the more liberal currents in the debate, was too weak to offset the growing post-Guatemala radicalization, and was later fatally flawed by the revelations of funding provided by the U.S. Central Intelligence Agency (CIA).

Foreign policy, however, was not the only question at issue: what were the internal policies and programs to be followed? The older leaders, from what we might call the "Generation of 1930," had in the early postwar years put their faith in moderation and had gotten nowhere. A counter-thesis was well formulated in 1953, appropriately enough by a spokesman for the 1952 Bolivian revolution, at that time the most promising radical experiment in a continent seemingly engulfed elsewhere by a conservative reaction:

> The inevitable law of every future event in our rebellious and tumultuous America is as follows: any revolution which cuts itself off from the common man, any revolution which permits monopoly and privilege to exist will ultimately destroy itself. Agrarian reform and control of production for the collective good are thus the foundation stones of all national constructions.[9]

This, of course, is just what Haya had meant in 1924 when he made "nationalization of land and industry" a cornerstone of the original *aprista* program. But was it right? The Generation of 1930 had had too many disappointing experiences with the "common man" and too many failures in attempting to implement such a program to think that now, Bolivia notwithstanding, such a "return to the beginnings" was likely to contain the magic answer sought all these years. Younger leaders increasingly disagreed. Before turning to their views, however, it is instructive to consider the course of this debate within the most prestigious, if not always successful, of the established revolutionary parties: Peru's APRA.

The Crisis in APRA

The debate over the state of revolutionary politics hit the leading prewar revolutionary party, APRA, at a particularly difficult moment. Although dominant in Congress after 1945, APRA had been unable to implement its program, an abortive uprising in Callao in 1948 by the party's radical wing had failed, and Peru had come under the rule of General Manuel Odría, who outlawed the party and persecuted the *apristas.* The 1945–48 period, with its final debacle, had left many scars, few of which were visible at the time.[10]

---

9. Fernando Díez de Medina, "Los dos grandes temas de las revoluciones americanas," *Humanismo,* No. 13 (August 1953), p. 31. Díez de Medina, the leading ideologist of the early phase of the Bolivian revolution, leaves no doubt as to the essential neutralism of his approach to foreign policy: "We have taken all that was useful from the civilization of the United States and the experience of Russia." (p. 37)

10. Haya de la Torre had sought political asylum in the Colombian Embassy in Lima in January, 1949. Contrary to all Latin American tradition, however, the Odría government refused him safe-conduct to leave the country, and Haya was not released until

For the first time, however, serious questions were being raised concerning Haya de la Torre's leadership.

That the crisis affected the ideology and program of the party as well as its leadership is demonstrated by the contents of a secret letter addressed to Haya de la Torre in Mexico shortly after his release from the Colombian Embassy. The letter asked Haya, in the name of the remaining Aprista leadership, to submit himself to party discipline and lead the party back to its former revolutionary position.[11]

The immediate cause of this effort to call to order the founder and until then virtually unquestioned leader of APRA was an article Haya wrote for *Life* magazine after his release.[12] The article is a folksy account clearly written for an American audience, and is largely devoted to the banalities of five years of existence cooped up in the Colombian Embassy. A few passages touched on politics, however, and these provoked the storm. In an evident effort to appeal to American opinion, Haya wrote, for example: "I believe that democracy and capitalism offer the surest solution to world problems even though capitalism still has its faults." Other passages reaffirmed APRA's anticommunism, and its policy of "inter-American democracy without empire" (but without any concrete references to the United States). When the article was published in *Life en Español* and distributed throughout Latin America, and the Aprista leaders' letters of inquiry to Haya requesting an explanation or rectification of such "patent journalistic errors" went unanswered, the APRA Executive Committee in Exile resolved to act. Its letter to Haya argued that *"anyone reading the phrase* [on capitalism cited above] *as*

April, 1954, after his stay had provided material for the most celebrated Latin American case on asylum. Haya's prolonged "imprisonment" in the Colombian Embassy led to something of a moratorium on internal criticism.

11. The letter was signed by Manuel Seoane, APRA's most popular and important leader after Haya, acting in his capacity as Secretary-General of the Coordinating Committee of Exiled Apristas, and by Luis Barrios Llona, Foreign Secretary. It is dated June 11, 1954, in Santiago de Chile. The contents of the letter were so frank and went so directly to the core of the internal party differences that only twelve copies were made and sent by messengers under conditions of great secrecy. Víctor Villaneuva, a leader of the abortive 1948 Aprista revolt, published a copy as Appendix 6 of his *Tragedia de un Pueblo y un Partido* (pp. 227–57 of the 2nd edition, Lima, 1956) because even though the document criticized the Callao uprising, its writers accepted Aprista responsibility, blaming the revolt on the development of an "involuntary and subtle, but real, gulf between the masses and the leadership" (*Ibid.*, p. 229), and otherwise supported Villaneuva's account, which was being publicly disowned.

12. "My Five-Year Exile in My Own Country," *Life,* Volume XXXVI, No. 18 (May 3, 1954), pp. 152–56.

it appears in print can only conclude that Aprismo is a liberal democratic party which supports minor social reforms."[13]

On the problem of anticommunism, the letter reviews APRA's "fundamental differences" with both local communism and the Soviet Union, which "arise from Indo-American reality and its national interests," but notes that these "cannot and must not be confused with the anticommunism of the reactionary groups who oppose all social reforms, nor with the anti-Sovietism of empires competing with Russia for world domination."[14] The letter concludes on this point:

Therefore, the respective positions [of APRA and of the United States] vis-à-vis Communism and the Soviet Union, although both hostile, have antagonistic origins and purposes, which must be continually underscored and explained, energetically preventing the confusionist actions of those who favor converting the Party's opposition to communism and the Soviet Union into a means of currying favor and reaching understandings with the reactionary forces of imperialism.[15]

The use of anticommunism as a means of "currying favor," that is, of gaining support in the United States, and of neutralizing conservative internal and foreign opponents, was of course precisely what Haya had in mind. Like the writers of the letter, he believed ideally in the formula "neither Washington nor Moscow." Unlike the writers, he believed it necessary to choose, albeit perhaps only temporarily, and in that light he could only choose Washington.

The letter devotes much space to APRA's position toward the United States. In recapitulating its evolution, the letter cited a 1947 statement of APRA policy which noted that "the radical change given to the relation between the United States and Indo-America by the new policies of President Roosevelt was the basis of a firm and progressive orientation during the war." APRA had therefore supported the Good Neighbor Policy. But, the letter continued:

Circumstances have once again changed. The "new policies" of President Roosevelt have been replaced by the "old policies" of imperialism, sponsored and supported by the Republicans.... Monopolist interests dominate the White House. In these very days, the United Fruit Company, affected by the

---

13. *Ibid.,* p. 253. Emphasis in the original. In view of APRA's historic anticapitalist position ("which you have so well expressed in works like *El Antiimperialismo y el APRA*") the letter continues, "the question arises whether you are perhaps bound by some temporary commitment which limits your public activities."

14. *Ibid.,* p. 241.

15. *Idem.*

Guatemalan agrarian reform, and by Honduran labor demands, is mobilizing its influence to push the government in Washington to provoke an intervention or a fratricidal war to crush our sister popular revolution in Guatemala. It is impossible to speak of democratic inter-Americanism as of a distant dream when reality indicates that imperialism is at its height, when American jet planes fly over Central America bearing arms to assist the repulsive petty tyrants of Nicaragua and Honduras. *No, compañero jefe, let us not avoid with plans for the future the irrevocable demands of a present which requires a frank and combative posture, at the cost of losing the party's position of continental leadership.* [16]

Faced with these signs of incipient rebellion within APRA, Haya met with the dissidents in Montevideo; the results of the meeting were kept secret and he then left for Europe and Scandinavia. Other members of the Generation of 1930, however, put themselves on record, and their views were similar to what could be read into Haya's actions. Vicente Sáenz, a Costa Rican whose thirty years of permanent political opposition and refusal to soften his criticism of the United States had made him Central America's leading polemical anti-imperialist, found time to interrupt his pamphleteering in defense of Guatemala long enough to comment unhappily that radical language was sometimes counterproductive. What had the Guatemalans' "frank and combative" language earned them?

The moderate gains of the movement of October [1945]—much less radical than the definitive conquests of the Mexican revolution—could have been defended with local polemical formulations . . . and had it been necessary to use other languages to resist Anglo-Saxon Cold War hysteria, then use that of the papal encyclicals . . . of the I.L.O. . . . . of the U.N. . . . or even of the "New Deal" . . . Truman. [17]

The fall of the popular-front style government of Colonel Jacobo Arbenz in Guatemala in 1954 had led to an impressive outpouring of anti-American literature. Former President (1945–1950) Juan José Arévalo published three brilliant, wrathful polemics; Guillermo Toriello, Arbenz's Foreign Minister, and Raúl Osegueda, a former Foreign Minister and Minister of Education, did likewise. The criticism of the United States reached unprecedented proportions, and influenced many Latin Americans, including moderates who had had little use for Arbenz. One former Guatemalan Minister (of Finance, under Arévalo) who did not follow the lead of Arévalo and his fellow ex-Ministers in rushing into print to express their solidarity with Arbenz, agreed with Sáenz:

---

16. *Ibid.*, p. 236. Emphasis in the original.
17. Vicente Sáenz, letter to Ildegar Pérez-Segnini, dated July 29, 1955, printed in *Humanismo*, No. 31–32 (July–August 1955) pp. 88–90, citation at 88–89.

A people's freedom is compromised more by gestures of useless rebellion than by the subtleties of a statesman, which in appearance resemble surrenders. A small country must not strut like a drunken mouse defying the cat. [18]

To these counsels of ideological retreat and avoidance of the issues of the Cold War, Rómulo Betancourt added a word of hope about potential changes in the United States policy when he wrote in 1956:

The prolonged nature of the struggle between the two world camps, the West and the East, and the generalized belief that a Third World War is less likely with every passing day, will in the long run remove one of the most solid external props of the Latin American dictatorships and despotisms. In an international climate in which the military Chiefs of Staff will no longer influence as greatly the formulation of the foreign policy of the Western powers, it would seem reasonable to expect the conflict between the United States and Russia to shift progressively towards spheres other than competition in armaments. The controversy will turn more on issues of doctrine and principles, and in such an ideological competition, the Soviets will have a solid arsenal of arguments if the governments of the Western camp continue to publish the speeches of Khrushchev to prove that Stalin was a leader of criminal conduct, and at the same time continue to offer assistance and support to Latin American governments with repressive traits similar to those of the Stalin regime. This basic error in the conduct of foreign policy of their country is the object of repeated criticism by important groups within the United States, led by the powerful unified labor movement, and by periodicals and individuals with much influence on public opinion. It is highly likely that such criticism will lead, in a more or less short space of time, to a shift in United States foreign policy.[19]

At the same time that Betancourt wrote these words, Haya de la Torre authorized from Rome a pact which pledged APRA support in the 1956 elections to Manuel Prado, the man who had kept APRA outlawed during his previous presidency, from 1939 to 1945. In return, APRA would be allowed to organize freely to prepare for the 1962 elections, six years in the future. Haya had won his internal struggle.[20]

The mid-1950s thus found the Generation of 1930, superior in age and experience, using the anti-imperialist and anti-dictatorial litany as a conve-

---

18. Clemente Marroquín Rojas, *La Derrota de una Batalla,* n.d. (c. 1957), p. 9.

19. Rómulo Betancourt, *Política y Petroleo,* Mexico, 1956, pp. 773–74.

20. But his party critics turned out to have been largely right. APRA lost its position of Latin American progressive leadership. By the time the United States, under a new Democratic president, once again adopted a "new policy" and rediscovered the "democratic left," revolutionary leadership in Latin America had passed from the Generation of 1930 and *aprismo* to the Generation of 1950 and *fidelismo.* And in Peru itself, a weakened APRA participated in two national elections, losing ultimately to another upstart, Fernando Belaúnde Terry, young enough to be Haya's son.

nient tool of opposition politics, but simultaneously moderating their programs and aspirations in the hope of attaining power in their lifetime.

The New Radicalism

The pragmatic responses of the Generation of 1930 were not shared by its younger followers. Those who had graduated from the universities in the postwar period, and whom we might call the Generation of 1950, had experienced neither Soviet irrelevance nor the acceptance of reforms, such as the Mexican oil expropriation, by the United States. To them, the main problem of the times could be identified as imperialism; and its solution, as it had once been for the Generation of 1930, was revolutionary intransigeance.

Since the original revolutionary formulations had never been formally discarded, they provided a roof under which two groups speaking similar languages temporarily coexisted. The older generation had become essentially liberal. Their younger followers, however, were rapidly becoming Leninist.

The process of radicalization began with the reformulation of the problem of imperialism along the lines which Haya had developed in the 1920s, and which had typified the thinking of the Generation of 1930 prior to the coming of the New Deal and the Good Neighbor Policy. Whereas Haya had ultimately resolved the issue along reformist lines à la Kautsky, the intervention in Guatemala provided the basis for a return to a more orthodox Marxist-Leninist interpretation. Unlike Haya, who had in effect proclaimed that *imperialism was a policy,* and one which could be changed or reversed, as had happened with the Good Neighbor Policy, the new generation redefined the Good Neighbor Policy as a *policy of imperialism.* In early 1955, a young Aprista defined the Good Neighbor Policy as "a change in the forms of United States policy to avoid [Latin American] susceptibilities but in no way affecting fundamental problems."[21] From this perspective, the Good Neigh-

---

21. Ezequiel Ramírez Novoa, *La farsa del panamericanismo y la unidad indoamericana,* Editorial Indoamérica, Buenos Aires, 1955, p. 47. Ramírez Novoa's book is interesting in its own right as a review of the inter-American system by a young member of the Generation of 1950. Ramírez, however, also had an interesting personal history. Secretary-General of APRA university youth, he also was President of the National Student Federation of Peru (FEP) in the early 1950s. As a young lawyer in exile, he met Juan José Arévalo in Montevideo in early June, 1954, when Arévalo was attempting to rally Uruguayan opinion behind Arbenz. His book, with a prologue written by Arévalo, is an excellent example of the process of radicalization which took place within the non-Communist left as a result of Guatemala, and which remained initially unperceived by most observers because its exponents were youthful members of the increasingly liberal traditional parties. In July, 1959, after the APRA National Plenary refused

bor Policy had been a tactic designed to deceive Latin Americans, and had ultimately led to greater imperialist penetration. Those who were taken in by this tactic had been unprepared for "Operation Guatemala," and had thus refused to face reality. This reality was that the United States had accepted the Mexican land reform and oil expropriation only because of the need to maintain hemispheric unity in the face of a coming Second World War. Even so,

If Mexico had not paid [compensation], General Enríquez would have been provided with arms and staging areas to overthrow Avila Camacho, just as these had been made available to Madero against Porfirio Díaz, to Pascual Orozco and Huerta against Madero, to Carranza against Huerta, to Villa against Carranza, etc.[22]

Guatemala taught, therefore,

that the popular and nationalist struggles for the integral independence of our countries must face this aggressive and imperialist policy which has come once again to dominate the United States, and which is supported by the continental satraps who prosper in its shade.[23]

And a "correct" analysis of United States relations with Latin America showed that this was inevitable, that U.S. policy was not a policy but a tactic, and that any Latin American movement which affected imperialist interests would necessarily face United States hostility, as had been the case in Guatemala.

Interestingly, the younger and the more radical exiles also objected to exclusive concentration on the United States:

To pretend to sum up everything in imperialism, or in an even more precarious analysis, in the Republican Party of the United States, demonstrates a lack of political sense and bourgeois conformism . . . insufficient even if illuminated by a fervent nationalism . . . To create hopes overlooking the essence of imperialism is . . . also to fail to accept our own internal contradictions, to avoid the class struggle, nationally as well as interna-

---

to adopt a *fidelista* program, Ramírez and several other youth leaders walked out, forming initially the "28th of July Movement" (after Peru's national independence date), then the APRA Rebelde (which at one stage in 1960 virtually coincided with APRA youth), and then, finally, the Movement of the Revolutionary Left (MIR), which was virtually wiped out when it engaged in guerrilla activities in 1965. Cf. also Ezequiel Ramírez Novoa, *El proceso de una gran epopeya: La Revolución Cubana y el Imperialismo-Yanqui,* Editorial "28 de Julio," Lima, 1960.

22. Clemente Marroquín Rojas, *op. cit.,* p. 15.

23. Guillermo Toriello, *La Batalla de Guatemala,* Cuadernos Americanos, Mexico, 1955, p. 204.

tionally, in its multiple implications, to locate oneself on metaphysical grounds.[24]

We have already identified, fully, the forces of aggression. We can identify their behavior, their instruments, their strategy. We must now examine, critically, the forces responsible for the defense.[25]

To the small groups of exiles in Mexico and elsewhere, this was a fundamental question, since it focused directly on the problem of power. More important yet, it raised the question of the retention of power. The Generation of 1930 had already given its answer: power was difficult to attain, and once attained, it should not be squandered by needless provocations of the United States. Implicit in this view was at least a partial abandonment of earlier revolutionary dreams.[26] To the Generation of 1950, full of revolutionary zeal, with attitudes akin to the optimistic revolutionary voluntarism of the Marx of 1848, the problem was not how to attain power—that would come easily enough; it was not even what to do with it—that, too, was easy, for the point of revolution was to remove the sources of exploitation by "nationalizing the lands and mines" (as Haya had put it in 1924) and giving the popular majorities of peasants and workers a chance to develop freely; the problem was rather how to keep power and ensure the carrying through of the revolution.

In Guatemala, when the time had come for the confrontation with the invading forces, Arbenz had fled. To the extent that the Generation of 1930 commented on this, either Arbenz should have stayed and fought, or he had no choice but to yield to superior power.[27] Neither option yielded much light on the policies that would have ensured a successful outcome of the struggle, or that could be applied in future revolutions. Furthermore, to suggest the inevitability of the triumph of imperialism through superior

---

24. Luis Cardoza y Aragón, *La Revolución Guatemalteca*, Cuadernos Americanos, Mexico, 1955, p. 154.

25. Antonio García, letter to Ildegar Pérez-Segnini, dated June 10, 1955, reprinted in *Humanismo*, Nos. 31–32 (July–August 1955), pp. 67–70, citation at p. 69.

26. Though usually without the candor of a Peruvian member of the Generation of 1930 who confided to this writer in 1964 that, looking back, he was rather relieved that he and his fellow activists within APRA had failed to seize power in 1948.

27. The most complete and explicit debate on Guatemala is in Ildegar Pérez-Segnini, "Lo inexplicado en el Caso Guatemala," *Humanismo*, No. 29 (March 1955), pp. 31–44, in which the young author refuses to accept the silence generally maintained on certain key questions, including Arbenz's resignation, and invites debate. The responses, reprinted with commentary in "Debate Sobre lo Inexplicado en el Caso Guatemala," *Humanismo*, Nos. 31–32 (July–August 1955), pp. 60–94, constitute a fascinating and extremely important source for the thinking of the period. Despite the challenge, the

power was to preclude the existence of such policies and to assume a defeatist position. The Generation of 1950 preferred Toriello's explanation:

> The betrayal by a few high chiefs of the Guatemalan army, which had been sought for a long time, apparently unsuccessfully, in the halls of the American Embassy, gave the United States at the last minute the unexpected card of triumph for the United Fruit Company-Department of State-C.I.A. consortium. Thanks to them [U.S. Ambassador] Peurifoy rescued Castillo Armas from disaster.[28]

The postwar democratic governments had all fallen to military coups. As we have seen, the revival of anti-imperialism already had strong anti-military overtones. Out of the Guatemalan affair, however, came a new formulation: the problem was less the evil of military dictatorship than it was the potentially counterrevolutionary nature of the military, now seen as an obstacle not only to the seizure of power but also to the carrying out of the revolutionary program. Confident of his support in the army, Colonel Arbenz had left it untouched; the army had remained like a Trojan horse within the revolution, ready to destroy it. That this was indeed a key aspect of the problem was further indicated by the Bolivian revolution, which had crushed the traditional army and initially replaced it with peasants' and workers' militias under the control of the Nationalist Revolutionary Movement (MNR).

> The great triumph of the Bolivian revolution does not consist merely in the fact that it is distributing the land—with an intensity and pace unknown and undreamed of in Guatemala—or that it has nationalized the tin mines, but that it has built the two interrelated weapons of revolution: a party and an army.[29]

Fidel Castro was the first to put these perceptions to the test. When his forces marched triumphantly into Havana, he was initially satisfied to leave most government posts, including the presidency and the premiership, to the older generation. The post he reserved for himself was that of Commander in Chief of the Cuban armed forces. And he placed his brother and his key guerrilla commanders, most of whom had participated in the exile debates in Mexico, in charge of restructuring the Cuban army. Only then, when he had

---

members of the Generation of 1930 still generally refused to comment on internal problems within the revolutionary family; the Guatemalan Arévalo actually writes rather pointedly that he expects the Venezuelan Pérez-Segnini will now open a second debate on "the unexplained in the Venezuelan case." (Letter of July 19, 1955, at p. 92).

28. Toriello, *op. cit.,* p. 183.
29. Antonio García, *loc. cit.*

insured himself against internal counterrevolution, did he turn to the agrarian reform that became the symbol of the revolution "many times promised, and as many times betrayed."

The Changing Context of Revolution

The seizure of power in Cuba by the radicalized younger generation brought the latent schism between the Generation of 1950 and that of 1930 to a head. Throughout Latin America, as the United States blindly prepared to apply its Guatemalan policy to Cuba, the Generation of 1950 rejected the leadership of the Generation of 1930. In Peru, Venezuela, and Colombia, guerrilla warfare was undertaken not by the old Moscow Communist parties, but by youthful former followers of Haya, Betancourt, and Gaitán. The net result, however, was not only the proliferation of new revolutionary movements of varying insignificance, but the political and occasionally physical decimation of the non-Cuban *fidelistas* and other radicalized nationalists and leftists who followed them to the hills.

Why? Why did the *fidelistas,* who were so successful in seizing power in Cuba, and who correctly foresaw many of the problems they would face, fail so miserably in their attempts to bring revolution to other countries? This question, with which this essay opened, can now be answered by saying that the events surrounding the Cuban Revolution radically altered political conditions in a manner eminently unfavorable to the *fidelistas* and their would-be emulators. Some of the changes, as might be expected, were due to the Cuban Revolution itself. To some extent, at least, the Cuban Revolution could not be repeated because it had already happened. In addition, the reformulation of revolutionary nationalism in Marxist terms was both accelerated and limited by the coming of the Cuban Revolution, making the political context of revolutionary activity after 1961 very different from the context of the late 1950s.

The fall of Batista on January 1, 1959, was the culmination of a period interpreted by many as the twilight of the tyrants and as the affirmation of democracy in Latin America. The fall of Perón in 1955, followed in 1956 by the withdrawal of General Odría of Peru and the assassination of President Somoza of Nicaragua, and in 1957 and 1958 by the overthrow of Rojas Pinilla in Colombia and of Pérez Jiménez in Venezuela, had all seemed to augur a renewed period of democratic experimentation in Latin America. Everyone's heart seemed on the left; dictatorships were out of style. In this atmosphere, large numbers of Cuba's upper and middle classes had turned against Batista (assisted, it must be noted, by Batista's tendency to include "decent people" in the "torturable" class). Younger Cuban military officers, headed by Colonel Ramón Barquín, refused to support a military junta against both Batista and Castro, and instead placed the regular army at the disposal of the triumphant Castro. Few looked for a "safe" democratic alternative to Castro in Cuba, first because "safety" seemed less of a factor, and secondly, because Castro seemed to be a democrat. No post-Cuba *fidelista* is likely to find a similar reception. The desire for class and institutional survival makes similar developments elsewhere virtually out of the question. The realization that revolution is not a "promenade under the palms" is very different from the optimistic vision of a coming Utopia.

The conversion of the Cuban revolutionary elite to Marxism-Leninism once it was in power further limited the revolution's appeal. The early radicalization of the Cuban revolutionaries had been initially concealed from outside observers partially because Castro realized that, as Martí had put it in 1895, "there are things which must be hidden if they are to be obtained" (itself a commentary on what might have happened even under the favorable conditions of 1957–1961 if the radicalization had been known). Because the split between the two generations had remained hidden, the *fidelistas* had been shielded by the verbal radicalism, oppositionist policies, and organizational structure of the old revolutionary parties. The course of the Cuban Revolution removed this prop by bringing the Cuban leadership's conflicts with the Generation of 1930 into the open. The increasing sectarianism of the Cuban leadership, culminating in espousal of Marxism-Leninism and alliance with the Soviet Union, further weakened its nationalist Latin American credentials. In roughly parallel fashion, it also destroyed any possibility of support from liberal opinion in the United States. The Generation of 1930, which, during the mid and late 1950s, had been reduced to a defensive position, counseling patience and the need to obtain United States support, was enabled to take a more offensive stance after 1961. The increasing communization of Cuba and the initiation of the Alliance for Progress gave astute and vigorous politicians like Rómulo Betancourt arguments with which to hold the support of groups who otherwise would have been more vulnerable to the *fidelista* line.

The course of the Cuban Revolution also revealed a number of major analytical weaknesses in the new radicalism. Guerrilla warfare had been only one aspect of the Cuban insurrection, which received both urban support and substantial international acquiescence. The *fidelista* theorists, however, particularly Guevara, elevated guerrilla warfare into the central means of revolutionary struggle. Yet every attempt to "replicate" Guevara's theory failed. In 1965, for example, Haya's nephew, Luis de la Puente Uceda, a young radicalized ex-*aprista* who had been with Guevara in Mexico in 1954, attempted to start a guerrilla movement in the Peruvian Andes. De la Puente had visited Cuba and followed the Guevara prescription minutely, but obtained no local support and was killed with most of the few who had followed him. Most other would-be guerrilla revolutionaries met similar fates. Together with Guevara's own death in Bolivia in 1967, their failures suggest that the attempt to universalize from the Cuban revolution was a misunderstanding if not of the Cuban experience itself, then at least of conditions elsewhere in Latin America.

But Cuban foreign policy had had an even more resounding prior failure. Guevara had correctly anticipated that the U.S. would attempt to apply the "Guatemalan solution" to Cuba.[30] In considering their response, the Cubans concluded that it would be "impossible to liquidate the Cuban sugar quota."[31] The United States, enmeshed in its own imperialist system, would attack Cuba politically and militarily, but not economically. From this perspective, which carried economic determinism to absurd lengths, the Cuban leaders felt they had an economically based guarantee of independence from the Soviet Union, even while seeking its support against the United States. Unlike Arbenz, the Cubans would fight: as Guevara quoted an unidentified member of the Cuban government: "They may attack us for being 'Communists,' but they are not going to wipe us out merely because we were stupid."[32] Cuba would arm, while the U.S. stood helplessly by, impaled on the contradictions of its own system.

But Cuba won one battle and lost another. When the sugar quota was indeed eliminated, Cuba, which Sartre had dubbed the "diabetic island," became vulnerable to Soviet pressure. Cuba's leaders placed their remaining hopes for independence in a reverse form of "geographic determinism" (their distance from the Soviet Union), hoping that revolution elsewhere in Latin America (or at least Venezuela) would give them a continental base which

---

30. The Epilogue of Guevara's famous Handbook on Guerrilla Warfare, entitled "An Analysis of the Cuban Situation: Its Present and its Future," and prefaced with the comment that "everything that follows is the opinion of the leaders of the rebel army with regard to Cuban policy," is surely one of the most fascinating and least understood documents to have issued from the Cuban revolution. Its prediction that the U.S. would apply some "aspect of the Guatemalan variant" was written some months before President Eisenhower secretly authorized the C.I.A. in March, 1960, to prepare a contingency plan for an exile invasion similar to the one which had toppled Arbenz in 1954.

31. The quote is from page 78 of the edition *Ché Guevara on Guerrilla Warfare* published by Praeger in 1961.

32. *Ibid.*, p. 80.

would enable them to move out of the Soviet wake. But none of this materialized, and although Castro did obtain personal political control (the elimination of an independent Cuban Communist party) in return for his declaration of Marxist-Leninist allegiance, Cuba remains now and for the foreseeable future tied to the Soviet Union. And this is clearly contrary to Latin American nationalism; even, as the missile crisis plainly indicated, to Cuban nationalism.

The Cuban leaders had misunderstood the sources of U.S. opposition, and thereby contributed to a mistake which ultimately bound Cuba to the Soviet Union, and isolated it from the mainstream of Latin American nationalism, perhaps the major source of radical strength. Nationalism in Latin America almost inevitably is revolutionary and Marxist in mood. The nationalist believes in the necessity of developing a strong nation in which the Indian and other marginal elements will be integrated. There is almost a Rousseauan sense in which the traditional ruling classes are seen as separated from and alienated from "the people" who make up the real nation. In an age of imperialism, the essence of nationalism lies in revolution against the imperialists and their local lackeys in the traditional ruling classes. Depending on the situation, members of the "national" bourgeoisie, that is, local entrepreneurs, and representatives of government bureaucracies, including the military, may participate in the struggle.

But no matter how great its "Marxist" tone, Latin American nationalism remains opposed to "dependence," including new forms of dependence on Communist as well as "capitalist" powers. Most Latin American radicals envisage a form of neutralism in world politics, hoping that, to use Arévalo's imagery, the sardines can find room between the sharks to swim safely. The Cuban sardine, closely pursued by the American shark, sought safety in the wake of the Soviet shark—and was swallowed. It seems likely that Cuba will prove indigestible in the long run, and will return to the Latin American (if not the "Inter-American") fold. It is already regaining diplomatic acceptability among the more nationalist governments. But Cuba is clearly no longer the wave of the future, although Castro will probably continue in power as long as Cuban nationalism has no clear alternative.

The Generation of 1950 in the rest of Latin America, however, will retain revolutionary unity even less than did the Generation of 1930. Not only is it finding the insurrectional path to power blocked, but it is being subjected to a fragmentation born out of the sudden lack of definition of nationalism (whom will it serve: itself, Latin America, Cuba, which retains a claim for its support, the Soviet Union, China . . .?), and the emergence of still other formulations (like radical Christian Socialism, Peronism, or even military populism) which seek to reconcile primitive Marxism, nationalism, and revolution with opposition to Communist as well as Yankee imperialism.

Since this essay was first written, in 1966, the relative importance of the superpowers in Latin America has decreased noticeably. Although the Soviet Union has continued to expand its formal relations with Latin America, it has had no spectacular successes, and may have actually declined as a potential ally against the United States. This is partly due to the passing of the exaggerated prestige enjoyed by the Soviet Union in the late 1950s, when Sputnik, the "missile gap," and the U.S.S.R.'s rapid industrialization gave Soviet Communism an aura of ascendancy. It is also due to the establishment of clear limits on Soviet power following the 1962 missile crisis. President Kennedy's acceptance of defeat at the Bay of Pigs had implied lack of power as well as moral and political self-restraint. This missile crisis, and the Dominican intervention of 1965, underscored the continued power of the U.S., which was exercising it in other ways as well. The Alliance for Progress, though full of internal contradictions, represented tangible proof of concern for Latin American development. More recently, the downgrading of the Alliance under the "low profile" has had positive side-effects in lessened interventionism. Castro has occasionally complained that Latin America has profited because the United States has learned from his movement; in doing so, he is implicitly recognizing the historical roots and limits of the *fidelista* phenomenon.

But the most important developments in recent years have been in Latin America itself. Continuing economic growth, changing elite perspectives, and the translation of the impulse toward change into the programs and activities of central governments have given a new vitality, strength, and sophistication to the region's politics. These are the subjects of the essays that follow. Together, they make up the substance of nationalism in Latin America, which absorbs the energies of many who would earlier have been confident *fidelistas*. Latin America has moved beyond Cuba, and though many similar issues remain, it is rapidly taking charge of its own future.

Chapter Three

PROSPECTS FOR VIOLENCE

David F. Ronfeldt and Luigi R. Einaudi

Latin American governments are frequently portrayed as under attack from revolutionary and radical elements with national and international interests and objectives. During the past generation, political struggles in Latin America took many violent forms, varying from simple assassinations of political leaders, attempted coups d'état, and rural and urban insurgencies, terrorism, and subversion, to the peaceable but potentially violent mobilization of radical movements and organizations.

Among the violent threats to the stability of governments, rural and urban insurgencies have recently received greatest attention.[1] Indeed, during the early 1960s, *fidelista* revolution was popularly forecast for Latin America, and foreign-supported guerrilla insurgencies did beset a number of regimes. By 1970, however, rural guerrilla bands had been defeated or contained throughout the hemisphere. Rural insurgency, though capable of provoking continuing trouble in countries with long traditions of internal violence,[2] no longer appeared to be a viable or appealing revolutionary strategy. Moreover, it had become quite clear that the conditions for a successful violent revolution on a national scale did not exist and could not be readily created even by determined bands of rural guerrillas.[3]

---

1. Most of this attention has been polemical rather than scholarly, beginning with Ernesto Guevara's own handbook, *Guerrilla Warfare,* 1960, and continuing with the Brazilian Carlos Marighela's *Minimanual for Urban Guerrillas,* 1969, both of which have appeared in numerous editions. Among the more recent treatments by outside observers, Luis Mercier Vega's account, *Guerrillas in Latin America: The Technique of the Counter-State,* Praeger Publishers, Inc., New York, 1969, is a useful synthesis, while Richard Gott, *Guerrilla Movements in Latin America,* Doubleday, Garden City, N.Y., 1971, and the SORO Casebook Series provide differing perspectives on individual situations.

2. This correlation between traditional violence and the longevity of attempted revolutionary violence is established for Colombia by R. L. Maullin, and for Guatemala by C. Sereseres. See Richard L. Maullin, *Soldiers, Guerrillas, and Politics in Colombia,* Lexington, Mass., D. C. Heath and Co., 1973, and Caesar D. Sereseres, *The Impact of Military Aid to Guatemala,* Ph.D. thesis, University of California, Riverside, July 1971.

3. Realization of this possibility, which contradicted Guevara's early theories, is at the heart of much of the writing by Régis Debray, who nonetheless also sought initially to explain away failure.

What successes rural guerrillas had achieved occurred mainly in physically isolated regions with impoverished populations that were becoming independent of the old hacienda system of life but not yet effectively linked into the national economic markets and government bureaucracies. One of the political consequences of the lack of national integration was the transformation of some such areas into bases for insurgent revolutionaries. Throughout history peasant revolts have typically occurred in post-feudal societies that are just beginning to undergo a centralization and bureaucratization of political power and authority. However, as the Latin American experience is again demonstrating, such regional rebellions or insurgencies are neither long-lasting nor capable in themselves of stimulating national revolutions.

What forms of violence seem most likely during the 1970s? And what will be their likely political impact? This essay, after examining the present prospects for revolutionary violence (which it deems poor) and the likelihood of continuing nonrevolutionary violence (which it estimates to be high), concludes that the military containment of revolutionary violence during the 1960s has contributed to channeling pressures for change into "traditional" authoritarian institutions. As a result, during the 1970s government bureaucracies and religious and even military forces will manifest considerably greater flexibility and political diversity than in the past, occasionally accepting previously illegitimate movements (such as Peronism) or ideologies (such as socialism).

The Challenge of Urban Insurgency

Despite (or perhaps because of) the many failures of rural insurgents, persistent revolutionaries resorted after 1967 to new strategies and tactics of urban guerrilla warfare, in order to create the conditions for revolution if not the revolution itself. As a result, incidents of urban terrorism, kidnapping, robbery, and propaganda abounded during the late 1960s, and urban insurgents acquired credibility as internal security problems in such countries as Argentina and Uruguay. Thus, what rural insurgency failed to accomplish during the 1960s, it is feared—or hoped—that urban insurgency may achieve during the 1970s.

In practice, however, urban insurgency is now proving to be less of a threat in Latin America than was rural insurgency during the previous decade. Incidents of urban terrorism sometimes appear to be quite numerous, impressive, and worrisome. Yet, incidents alone—even in large quantities—need not in themselves add up to a real threat to government institutions. Indeed, despite the volume of violent terrorist tactics, the revolutionary insurgents do not appear to be gaining a strategic advantage for themselves, whether measured by organized populist support, elite fragmentation, or institutional collapse.

Politically, of course, the very persistence of urban terrorism may have profound consequences, despite the failure of insurgents to seize power themselves. Institutional disruption, as in Argentina and Uruguay, may affect both who uses power and how, by influencing the formation of political coalitions and the directions of some government policies.

Militarily, however, insurgents will probably continue to fail to seize power in urban settings because:

a. Overall, the Latin American urban sectors are generally not revolution-oriented.[4]

b. Government institutional capabilities for control and responsiveness are generally stronger in urban than in rural areas.[5]

c. Many—though not all—of the insurgents started as romantic intellectuals and students who lacked discipline and competence in acts of violence, and who are now frequently too isolated to be effective despite their increased experience.[6]

d. The insurgents have failed to develop a rural component to complement their urban strategy, whereas historically urban insurgency alone has never succeeded militarily without rural support.[7]

---

4. A growing body of political participation studies show convincingly that recent peasant immigrants to cities tend to behave conservatively. See William Mangin, *Peasants in Cities*, Houghton-Mifflin, Boston, 1970. Joan Nelson also argues that the perception that the urban masses might be a revolutionary threat is chiefly attributable to middle-class fears, given the relatively modest aspirations of migrants and their capacity to vent frustration through political channels. See her *Migrants, Urban Poverty and Instability in Developing Nations*, Harvard Center for International Affairs, Occasional Paper No. 22, September 1969.

5. This is probably true despite the persistence of notorious problems of competition and absence of coordination among most Latin American police, military, and other security forces. Even in Uruguay where they have frequently made the authorities look like fools, the *tupamaros* can only aspire to seize power by political, not military, means. This conclusion is supported by Robert Moss, "Urban Guerrillas in Uruguay," *Problems of Communism*, Vol. 20, No. 5, September-October 1971, pp. 14–23, who nonetheless also argues that the very presence of urban terrorists threatens democratic institutions.

6. The exceptions are chiefly to be found in "traditional violence" situations where radical causes were grafted onto banditry. For one example, which can also be applied *mutatis mutandis* to Venezuela, Guatemala, and Mexico, see R. L. Maullin, *The Fall of Dumar Aljure, A Colombian Guerrilla and Bandit*, RM-5750-ISA, The Rand Corporation, November 1968.

7. Evidence for this general argument is presented by L. Gann, *Guerrillas in History*, The Hoover Institution Press, Stanford, California, 1971.

These points may on occasion work at cross purposes to other processes. Thus the relative technical inefficiency of youthful radicals must be balanced against the political advantages of a continuing renewal and recruitment of leadership in tune with recent grievances. Nevertheless, the cumulative weight is clear: urban insurgency certainly has no greater prospects for success than did rural insurgency.

The Decline in External Support

Not only do internal political-strategic considerations not favor seizure of power by urban insurgents, but the external environment is no longer as supportive of violent revolution in Latin America as in the recent past. The Soviet Union, although occasionally resorting to subversion, generally gives greater weight to peaceful struggle, and both the Chinese and the Cubans have diminished their former active support of armed struggle. Fidel Castro now appears to favor a two-sided policy of normalized relations with some progressive Latin American regimes, combined with the encouragement of violent revolution in certain other countries. However, in all but one or two countries, the effective support for such revolution has receded to the level of rhetoric; Cuba's export of men, materials, and money has dwindled to the point that the insurgent remnants frequently criticize Cuban inaction.[8] Simultaneously, the lowered U.S. profile in Latin America may also be defusing much of the symbolic target useful to insurgents, even as U.S. military assistance programs may have already contributed to increased local counterinsurgency capacities. Moreover, foreign participation in insurgencies, even when at the higher level of the 1960s, has been rarely, if ever, decisive in determining the outcome.[9]

Permanent Violence

To say that revolutionary violence and insurgency will probably not constitute a serious internal security threat during the 1970s is not necessarily to

---

8. Despite occasional rhetorical statements to the contrary, the Allende government in Chile did not provide much effective encouragement to armed insurgents in neighboring countries, at least partially because good relations with these countries were important to Chile's international posture.

9. This last point is forcefully argued by Jack Davis in his *Political Violence in Latin America,* Adelphi Papers No. 85, International Institute for Strategic Studies, London, 1972, pp. 25 ff.

say that nonrevolutionary violence will abate in Latin America. Instead, domestic political conflict will probably continue unceasingly—and in some countries it might even increase. The kinds of violent disturbances which can be expected are familiar, including

1. Peasant revolt and rural social banditry;
2. Workers' strikes and riots;
3. Student rebellions and demonstrations;
4. Political strife among racial, ethnic, and immigrant factions;
5. Political conflicts involving the Catholic Church or religious leaders;
6. Populist, multi-class demonstrations and disturbances, often over electoral or economic issues;
7. Military revolts and coups d'état;
8. Assassinations or murders of political leaders; and
9. Criminal violence associated with the smuggling of narcotics, drugs, arms, and consumer goods.

These are the most durable forms of domestic political violence in Latin America. Where they exist, these activities may be regarded as internal security threats by particular regimes or authorities. Nevertheless, it is not clear that such problems necessarily threaten Latin America's prospects for development, or, for that matter, Latin America's relations with the United States. Indeed, it is doubtful that development and modernization can proceed without occasional domestic violence.

Far from being abnormal, some domestic political violence is frequently a natural and even unavoidable adjunct of such processes as: bids by marginal social sectors to secure the resolution of popular grievances and to increase their participation in the established institutions; the emergence of new, modernizing elites and power contenders within the nation; and—often overlooked—efforts by the government to establish and centralize institutional authority over isolated and unruly rural areas of the national territory. The presence of violence, therefore, should not necessarily be considered a sign of disorder or inevitable decay. It is virtually impossible for governments to rid their societies of violence; and complete pacification might require such violence-laden suppression as to induce stagnation and be counterproductive.[10]

---

10. This, of course, is the argument of Catholic radicals, who have introduced the term "institutional violence" to characterize a state so organized. For a general discussion of Catholic attitudes, see the essay "The Changing Catholic Church" in this volume.

Past Assumptions and Unexpected Consequences

These forms of "permanent" domestic violence make it increasingly clear that several assumptions need to be modified and put into larger perspective, if not rejected as erroneous. Emerging as counterpoints to analyses that Latin America was on the verge of explosive revolutions, these are the interrelated assumptions that

- domestic political violence can necessarily have only bad consequences for national and hemispheric security and development;
- the lower the level of domestic violence the better necessarily the prospects for development;
- and therefore that nations and governments need to be automatically "shielded" against violence and violence-induced instabilities if they are to proceed with effective development.

Some commonly cited examples of the potentially bad consequences of violence and instability are: heavy budget allocations to military rather than to economic development, the disruption of foreign investment, the deterioration of already-weak political institutions, and the proliferation of anti-democratic tendencies.[11]

These, however, are neither the only nor even the necessary consequences of violence. The presence of regionally circumscribed violence—even including insurgency—may actually help foster continued development by challenging the ruling institutions and elites to govern and perform in more responsible and productive ways. To the extent that the governments in various countries met the challenges in the 1960s, official responses to problems of violence included:

- greater attention to rural needs and demands, including some agrarian reform;
- the strengthening of new institutions and organizations for channeling and responding to popular needs and interests;
- greater integration into the national political and economic processes for isolated and unruly areas;
- improved military institutionalization and capabilities.

---

11. These last assumptions, characteristic of the Alliance for Progress plans, are ably presented in a recent book, *The Alliance That Lost Its Way,* by Jerome Levinson and Juan de Onís, Twentieth Century Fund, 1971.

Thus, depending on the government's capabilities and intentions and on the characteristics of the violence itself, unsuccessful insurgency may stimulate salutary as well as adverse effects on national development. In particular, the threat of increased violence can motivate government leadership to undertake important innovations. The Peruvian revolution of 1968 was in part a delayed response to problems highlighted by the 1965 insurgency but left unresolved once the immediate insurgency problem abated.[12] Indeed, even where the violence was considerable, as in Venezuela, the salutary consequences of the government's responses to insurgency may, over the long run, outweigh the temporary adverse effects.[13] Such relative optimism does not seem warranted for Guatemala and the Dominican Republic, where institutional fragility and political violence have persisted at high levels over prolonged periods of time. Yet even in those countries there have been effects (primarily relating to institutional and rural development) other than the purely negative outcomes hypothesized earlier.

Future Complexities

To say that domestic political violence, whatever its purposes, will probably not pose a serious internal security threat to Latin American development during the 1970s is not to say that the pressures and opportunities for radical change and reform will abate or cease during this decade. Rather they will likely increase: the Latin America of the 1970s may well become more politically radical than the Latin America of the 1960s, with particularly profound consequences for landholding elites and for U.S. economic interests.

In part, the pressures for radical change will continue to emanate from insurgent revolutionary elements. Violent measures can change political conditions; and where political instability is combined with economic difficulties and stagnation, some groups may be particularly inclined to turn to violence. Yet, rather than military victory or even political support for the insurgents, a

---

12. See Luigi R. Einaudi, "Revolution from Within? Military Rule in Peru Since 1968," in David Chaplin, ed., *Peruvian Nationalism: A Corporatist Revolution,* Transaction Books–E. P. Dutton, New York, 1974. Further analysis of the Peruvian case appears in Lt. Col. John G. Waggener, "La Convención, 1962–1963, A Classical Stability Operation in Latin America," U.S. Army War College Student Essay, 13 November 1967.

13. Some general relationships between agrarian problems and government policies in Venezuela are discussed in John Duncan Powell, *Political Mobilization of the Venezuelan Peasant,* Harvard University Press, Cambridge, Mass., 1971.

primary effect of violence may well be the unintended mobilization of new political leaders and groupings—of rightist and leftist as well as moderate persuasions—who prefer institutional politics. These countervailing groups may seek electoral victories, or may even combine their institutional politics with "white terror" tactics of violence. However, these are political processes, and do not mean that the insurgents in themselves constitute serious military threats to governmental security. In some cases, governing groups may be disposed to adopt limited radical programs, if only in an attempt to preempt the insurgents and end the violence.

One striking feature of the 1970s, the above discussion suggests, is that the containment of revolutionary violence is leading to additional pressures for political change within the established institutions. In that sense, the violence of the 1960s succeeded rather than failed in fomenting change. Persons who previously might have resorted to guerrilla activities are now turning to more traditional forms of activity *within*, not outside, the constitutional political processes. Political and economic change, therefore, will originate not so much from elements operating outside the established policy-making institutions, but from the emergence of more nationalistic elites and perspectives within the established institutions, including the state bureaucracies as well as the military and the Church. Some of the pressures for change will also come from members of the established order who feel the past violence has demonstrated the need for social improvements other than better repressive techniques.

If the institutionalization of political reform struggles becomes associated with bitter divisiveness among elite factions, the contest for institutional control may naturally produce some coalition instabilities and succession crises. Moreover, such intra-elite power struggles within the established institutions may help generate some violent incidents at the mass level. Yet even under such extreme conditions, social revolution seems less likely than other potential outcomes, such as institutional disorganization, the establishment of technocratic radical reformist regimes, or even some version of fascism.

When U.S. interests seem threatened, therefore, U.S. policy makers may increasingly find that the source of a presumed threat is a government itself rather than revolutionary elements who may be classified as military internal security problems. Indeed, Latin American perceptions of just what constitutes an internal security threat are also changing. Concepts of national internal security that focus not simply on revolutionary insurgents, but more generally on economic development and social backwardness as the central problems and causes of violence, are increasingly appealing to nationalist elites, including military leaders. Under this broader conceptualization of internal security, threats are perceived to come not only from left-wing extremists but also from foreign interests and local elites who, it is felt, dominate the economic structure, commit economic aggresssion, or create national dependency on foreign powers and markets.[14] Accordingly, certain U.S. economic interests may come to be regarded as inducing internal security threats by limiting prospects for national development; and thus traditional U.S. notions of internal security may increasingly clash with nationalistic interpretations that are spreading among rising elites.[15] The ITT documents relating to Chile were, for example, published in Chile in a "translation made by specialists of the Armed Forces General Staff."[16]

Violence and Future U.S. Policy

In summary, the following points stand out from this discussion, as they relate to the conditions likely to be encountered by U.S. policy makers during the coming decade:

- Revolutionary insurgencies, whether rural or urban, are not likely to constitute major internal security threats, though they may continue to create some internal security problems.
- Foreign support for revolutionary violence has diminished, particularly if compared to the early and mid-1960s.
- Nonrevolutionary domestic political violence will not necessarily prove inimical to Latin American development or to U.S.-Latin American relations.
- The most effective sources of radicalism will increasingly be found within rather than outside established institutions, as a new generation of elites assumes power.
- Internal security problems may increasingly be seen by Latin American leaders as deriving not only from revolutionary insurgents, but also from the unchecked activities of foreign interests.

---

14. Changes in threat perceptions are discussed below in the essay "Changing Military Perspectives in Peru and Brazil."

15. And socialist critiques may similarly find acceptance in nationalist circles. Salvador Allende sought to achieve this linkage by claiming violence is the historic weapon of the political right, and democracy the precursor to socialism. See his *Mensaje al Congreso,* Santiago, May 23, 1971.

16. *Los Documentos Secretos de la ITT,* Fotocopias de los documentos originales y traducción completa del inglés, Santiago, Abril 3, 1972, p. 5.

Chapter Four

NEW PATTERNS OF LEADERSHIP

Edward Gonzalez and Luigi R. Einaudi

The politicians who held power in Latin America during the 1950s and 1960s are being displaced by new political actors. Latin America's new military and civilian leaders still frequently differ ideologically and institutionally from one another. Some of the new leaders subscribe to the values, goals, and political style of their predecessors. But many among them—as clearly evidenced in countries as different as Peru, Chile, Brazil, Argentina and Panama—differ markedly from previous patterns. Latin American leaders currently seem to perceive fewer internal and international constraints on their actions, and therefore tend to be more innovative than were most of their predecessors.

Despite significant differences of approach, an increasing number of governments share the common attributes of assertive nationalism and support for economic development and social reform. Unlike the radical left as well as anti-Communist politicians of the 1960s, however, Latin America's contemporary leaders will probably be thoroughly eclectic in choosing among alternative diplomatic, political, and economic formulas. They are as likely to reject the indiscriminate adoption of the Soviet or Cuban models of communism as they are certain to resist the wholesale emulation of the American way of life for their societies. In particular, Latin American nationalists are drawing on the negative as well as positive lessons to be gained from the *fidelista* experience in Cuba. The drive toward economic and social reform will thus be tempered by a desire to avoid the high costs paid by the Cuban revolutionaries, particularly those associated with close alignment with the Soviet Union, economic mismanagement, and political repression.

We believe these characteristics typify a leadership style likely to predominate among political leaders assuming positions of power and influence during the 1970s. This leadership style, we believe, is demarked less by age than by a break with past beliefs and patterns of elite behavior; and the change cuts across both military and civilian elites.

This essay seeks to explore some of the sources, particularly at the level of values and political experiences, for the behavior of Latin America's emerging

45

leadership groups. Though less extreme than the *fidelistas*, Latin America's current leaders may prove just as taxing for U.S. policy. Latin American elites are determined to reduce their countries' patterns of dependency by seeking to exploit new opportunities in the changing international environment. The open issue is what forms this evolving Latin American assertiveness and nationalism will adopt, and with what consequences for inter-American relations.

The New Elites in Historical Perspective

Latin America has been governed in recent decades by local political elites who were philosophically allied with the United States or who frequently responded to U.S. pressures and cues even when they were not in ideological agreement. These elites ranged from the extreme right to the democratic left, as exemplified by such diverse national leaders during the 1960s as Alfredo Stroessner, Humberto Castelo Branco, Arturo Frondizi, Carlos Lleras Restrepo, Rómulo Betancourt, Fernando Belaúnde, and Eduardo Frei. Institutionally, they, or others like them, controlled the military, the ruling political parties, the Church, much of the trade union movement, and the major domestically owned business enterprises.

Though frequently differing with Washington on some issues, these leaders nevertheless tended to align themselves initially with the United States on major global questions or to respond ultimately to U.S. inducements and pressures. Hence, Latin American governments supported the United States on such vital Cold War issues as internal Communist subversion, relations with the Soviet bloc, and admission of China to the United Nations. During the 1960s, moreover, they joined with the United States in isolating Castro's Cuba and in repelling the *fidelista* guerrilla and Soviet strategic threats to the hemisphere. Ready U.S. access to these political elites combined with the economic dependence of many of their countries to facilitate the exercise of U.S. influence in Latin America throughout the 1950s and most of the 1960s.

Several developments suggest that the characteristic susceptibility of Latin America to U.S. blandishments has already lessened significantly. This is partially the result of the emergence of a highly fluid environment that makes prediction and identification of elite attitudes seem particularly difficult. Viewed domestically, the spread of communication within Latin American societies has done a great deal to erode the frequently complacent foreign orientation of capital cities and governing elites. Nationalist assertiveness, including the rejection of foreign influences through restrictive measures limiting foreign ownership of communications media and the presentation of foreign movies or television programs, increasingly reflects a desire to value or develop local cultural traditions as a basis for national self-confidence. Nationalist and modernizing values have also had a major impact on organized forms of political expression. During the late 1960s new political parties with modernizing social and economic programs, like the Christian Democrats in Chile and Venezuela, succeeded in winning power from established parties, while the populist ANAPO threatened the viability of the National Front in Colombia, and young politicians and labor leaders swelled the ranks of Argentine Peronism.

A new openness to social change and international experimentation also permeated two of Latin America's oldest institutions, both of which were historically closely allied with conservatism. Reformist and even militantly leftist wings developed within the Catholic Church, long considered an automatic legitimizer of established authority and the *status quo*. As discussed in a later essay in this volume, Catholic leaders are differentiating between contemporary and desired social relationships by emphasizing a "prophetic mission" of independent moral criticism of temporal injustice. Meanwhile, military forces in a number of countries have displayed a growing interest in national security doctrines that make national development a virtual prerequisite to security. Disillusioned with the uncritical importation of U.S. military assistance, the military throughout Latin America have turned increasingly to Europe for the purchase of military equipment. More importantly, military leaders and institutions have supported nationalist and reformist initiatives with considerable frequency.

These changes have had direct consequences for governmental actions, frequently in novel directions. The Panamanian military regime in power since 1968 has repeatedly reaffirmed Panama's total sovereignty over the Canal Zone, and has moved toward improved relations with Cuba. After seizing power in October, 1968, Peru's revolutionary military government moved swiftly to adopt industrial reforms affecting foreign and domestic capital, undertook Latin America's most thorough agrarian reform since Cuba, and sought diplomatic relations with all nations, including Cuba, countries of the Third World, and members of the socialist bloc. At the same time, Brazil's military-led authoritarian regime, in power since 1964, attained unprecedented economic growth by attracting foreign private investments, but deliberately sought to reduce dependence on the United States by greatly expanding economic ties with Japan and Western Europe. Nor have countries under "civilian" rule been unaffected. In Mexico, President Echeverría has brought younger leaders to his government and has supported progressive agrarian policies and a multilateral foreign policy. Chile's experiment with socialism was interrupted by a military coup in September, 1973, but only after many innovations had been introduced, several with bipartisan support. Significant changes also began during 1973 in Argentina, though their nature remained uncertain at this writing.

These multifaceted and sometimes contradictory developments reflect more than just the perennial flux of Latin American affairs, or the mere rhetorical adoption by local "establishments" of many of the banners of the disintegrating extreme left. Instead it is becoming evident that reformist and even some radical leaders are acquiring the institutionalized bases of power and legitimacy previously denied to the *fidelista* guerrilla movements of the 1960s, and may implement major changes from within governing institutions under essentially nonviolent conditions. Of course, the failure of the Allende government's "peaceful road to socialism" in Chile shows that there are limits to this hypothesis. As we shall argue below, however, Allende's tragic fate should not blind observers to the generalized spread of innovative attitudes in Latin America.

Latin America's leaders face the 1970s with a general mandate to produce major reforms. The status quo has few defenders, even among conservatives. Most government leaders now come from middle-class groups, including military officers, civilian politicians, technicians, and entrepreneurs.[1] Presently underrepresented groups, including women, peasants, and unorganized labor, are not likely to increase their influence except through multi-class, populist organizations like Colombia's ANAPO, Mexico's PRI, or Peru's SINAMOS, all of which are led by middle-class elements. In addition, the focus and direction of government concerns are shifting under the impact of new generations of leaders and professionals with modern values. To a large extent, of course, this process merely reflects the greater familiarity with the modern world and its productive forces that is to be expected of men educated since World War II, as was already true in 1970 for men in their mid-forties. By 1980, of course, this subministerial generation of today will occupy most ministries and other top governmental posts. On the other hand, in contrast to the *fidelista* movement in Cuba, which was led by a closely knit youthful inner core, the very institutional and coalitional character of the new leadership seems likely to act as a self-regulating mechanism on the new regimes, thereby imposing limits on radical experiments of either the left or the right.

---

1. A similar argument is developed by Víctor Alba, "New Alignments in Latin America," *Dissent,* July-August 1970, pp. 363–67.

The intrinsic makeup of the emerging elite combinations, therefore, may simultaneously impel the new Latin American leadership toward greater experimentation at home and abroad, and yet restrict its range of policy alternatives. The particular choice of regime types and policy mixes will not, of course, hinge only on the leadership's composition, ideology, and goals. The choice of options will also depend upon the new leaderships' perceptions of the domestic and international environments, and upon its reading of the experience of the 1960s. The net effect, we believe, will be to reaffirm contradictory tendencies—toward greater boldness and innovation than their predecessors, yet toward greater moderation and caution than the *fidelista* revolutionaries. These contradictions may be examined, first by exploring the contrast between the Chilean and Peruvian experiences, and then by considering the lessons of Cuba.

Peru and Chile: The Inclination toward Bolder Postures

As the 1970s began, Peru and Chile stood out among countries whose governments had moved aggressively to remake their respective societies and to assert their independence from the United States. Peru represented a military, technocratic, and non-Marxist approach, while Chile under Allende posited a civilian and socialist alternative in a country with a long democratic tradition. As of September, 1973, Peru's experiment could be considered a success, Chile's experience a failure. What do these experiences tell us about the prospects for change in Latin America?

President Velasco and the late Salvador Allende were poles apart in their respective ideological commitments, institutional affiliations, and willingness to mobilize society politically. Yet both were committed to the goals of strengthening national independence, promoting economic development, and restructuring society in behalf of previously excluded or underrepresented popular sectors. As Peruvian and Chilean events suggest, such goals, if they are to be attained at all, imply the strengthening of governmental regulatory capacity over both domestic and foreign interest groups, and may also entail conflict with the United States on specific nonstrategic issues.

At this level of generality, of course, such attitudes are widespread in Latin America today. Readiness to assume the risks of change may be as much a function of frustration with the present as of intensity of commitment to the achievement of a specific future. Support for change is often strengthened by the perception—partially based on recent social science as reflected in such concepts as the Alliance for Progress—that Latin America is condemned to a stagnation or perhaps even anarchy in the absence of radical departures. From this perspective, American-style democracy and free enterprise may come under fire from conservatives as well as from resurgent Latin American nationalists, if they feel that the United States is not really interested in supporting the principles of change they are now—often rather belatedly— coming to espouse. Regional autarchy and authoritarianism are increasingly preached by political and military leaders seeking efficient paths to development.

Agrarian reform, nationalization of foreign and domestic enterprises, and greater state intervention are not likely to be favored by political elites merely as measures for promoting economic and societal development, however. Structural reforms may be advocated also as political weapons for breaking the entrenched power of traditional domestic oligarchs and powerful foreign interests. Peru's agrarian reform in the rich coastal area and Chile's nationalization of the copper mines clearly responded to political as well as economic motivations. Nationalization of foreign enterprises, though a frequently treacherous undertaking, provides politicians a striking means of demonstrating, to their respective societies and to foreign audiences, that they do in fact possess a nationalist commitment and a regulatory capacity over private interest groups. Hence, in deliberate contrast to the delaying tactics of the Belaúnde government, the Peruvian military moved immediately against the International Petroleum Company (IPC) after seizing power, while the Allende government did not hesitate to use its full constitutional powers in expanding the state sector of the economy, and including in it the previously U.S.-owned copper mines. Similar attitudes were partly responsible for the restoration of diplomatic and trade relations with Castro's Cuba,[2] moves toward closer economic ties with the Soviet bloc as well as Western Europe and Japan, controversies over the amount of compensation (if any) for nationalized foreign enterprises, and claims to extensive territorial waters and exclusive jurisdiction over fishing rights.

Internally, the institutional bases of legitimacy and power characteristic of reformist leaders in the 1970s may at first engender or reenforce a perspective that society is malleable and that opposition forces can be neutralized effectively. Military governments, in particular, perceive themselves as encum-

---

2. Thus, the restoration of relations with Cuba, and Castro's visit to Chile in late 1971, may be interpreted in terms of Allende's domestic strategy for coping with the extreme left. In particular, the aim of Fidel's lengthy visit and his carefully chosen statements may have been to bestow socialist legitimacy on Allende and Chile's "revolutionary process" at a time when the government was under increasing criticism by the MIR.

bered by fewer external constraints and are more likely to feel they possess force to impose structural changes. Even if they are lacking in such coercive powers, however, civilian leaderships can compensate for this weakness by mobilizing popular support through appeals to nationalism and social justice, and attacks upon the "oligarchy"—a course of action which, as Peru demonstrates, is also open to the military. Ranking officers in the Velasco government are contemptuous of Peru's traditional upper class, viewing it not only as a former ruling class left powerless since 1968, but as parasitic and superfluous to the modern nation to which they aspire. Peruvian leaders, however, give a high priority to preserving the institutional unity of the Peruvian armed forces, thereby creating internal but nonetheless regularized constraints on policy-making. Able professionals staff public agencies, such as Petroperú, the new national oil company, the National Planning Institute, and the reorganized ministries, thus providing substantive support to the government's policies.

The exercise of government power is, of course, no guarantee of either moderation or success. In Chile, Salvador Allende was dedicated to democratic principles and had long experience in Chile's highly developed constitutional system. Yet as President Allende sought to implement the Popular Unity program, enormous stress was placed on Chile's institutions, and violence became commonplace. Beginning in 1968, Peru's military leaders introduced dramatic changes amounting to a national revolution. But they did so in a context and with an institutional base that precluded significant opposition and allowed considerable flexibility in implementation.

Chilean conditions between 1970 and 1973 were strikingly different. President Allende never had complete control of the machinery of government. The Chilean congress had extensive powers, including the capacity to dismiss government ministers, and was dominated by groups hostile to the Popular Unity coalition. Allende, moreover, was a minority president. Elected in 1970 with 37 percent of the vote, essentially the same proportion of votes which had led him to lose in 1958 and 1964, Allende's partisan identification severely handicapped his efforts to introduce socialism and preserve democratic procedures in the face of uncompromising extremes. Personally flexible and humane, he was subjected to intense pressures from political parties both within and without his coalition. In 1972, Allende attempted to alleviate these pressures by bringing military officers into the cabinet. But even this unprecedented move proved insufficient to restore the government's national credibility. In his last months in office, Allende appeared to have lost control of events. The constitutional legitimacy of the Popular Unity government was finally overwhelmed: social dislocation, economic chaos, and breakdowns in industrial discipline polarized the political community and led to mounting opposition by key civilian elements and ultimately to intervention by the armed forces.

This final outcome, so damaging to Chile, should not be considered representative of the prospects for future change in Latin America. True, the Chilean military ultimately intervened in a fashion reminiscent of the conservative military coups elsewhere in Latin America in the late 1940s and early 1950s, leading many observers to conclude that genuine change remains impossible without violent revolution and the abandonment of democracy. Yet there are also signs that Allende was victimized by the specific characteristics of Chile's political system at the time he assumed office. Chilean democracy, based on ideologically-defined and class-oriented political parties, had been increasingly characterized by immobilism. Even the Christian Democrats, frequently considered a modern, "programmatic" party with a national base, had become virtually paralyzed by conflicts between their progressive ideals and their fearful middle-class electorate. The parties of the left, based on coalitions of trade unionists and middle-class radicals, were themselves bitterly divided, and had never had a chance to rule on their own. When that chance came because of their opponents' even greater divisions, they were ill-prepared. Most professionals, even those with leftist sympathies, were independents, and remained outside of the government.

That the Popular Unity government lasted as long as it did under these circumstances is a tribute to Allende's coalition-building skill—and to the willingness of many Chileans outside the government to accept major reforms. Whether Allende's successors will be more successful in harnessing these forces seems doubtful, given the specific historical context, but it would be unwise to draw too many hasty extrapolations from the Chilean experience.

One additional clue to the Chilean tangle, however, may lie in the formalized patterns of Chilean politics. One of the authors first visited Chile in 1955, and was struck by the parallels in party organizations and programs there to those of France in the Fourth Republic. To the extent that Latin America is today forging its own consciousness and patterns of development, Chile's European-style polity may have been an exception if not an anachronism. Salvador Allende was sixty-five when he died. He had first become a minister in 1939, in a Popular Front government. His outlook was heavily influenced by European socialism as well as Chilean history. His downfall was brought about by the dogmatism of unbending adherents of economic liberalism as well as by utopian would-be emulators of revolutions elsewhere. From this perspective, the Chilean experience may come to symbolize the dangers of attempting to import foreign solutions for Latin America's problems.

The Peruvian government, with its blend of assertive nationalism, technocratic paternalism, and pragmatic insistence on developing a society that is "neither capitalist nor communist," appears to be far more representative of the eclectic nature of the leadership patterns now emerging among Latin America's military as well as civilian elites. Yet even the disappointing institutional crisis in Chile was brought on by the challenge posed by the growing consciousness of Chile's working and professional classes. And no one acquainted with the resilience of that lovely land can say that its leaders will remain behind for long. One thing is certain: whatever the labels, Latin America is not static.

The New Elites and the Lessons of Cuba: The Inclination toward Moderation

Notwithstanding their commitment to change, the new military and civilian elites are not likely to emulate the *fidelista* foreign and domestic policies except on a selective basis. To begin with, Castro's most direct and profound influence waned after the mid-1960s. Even then, the appeal of Cuba had already become largely limited to the most radicalized sectors of Latin American youth willing to take up the armed struggle. Caught up in their own countries' problems, contemporary leaders will inevitably adhere primarily to their own political methods, values, and objectives. Indeed, however much some of them may respect the Cuban leader personally, the Cuban revolutionary process may well appear to them as a form of tropical *caudillismo* peculiar to the Caribbean, if not to Cuba alone. In short, most Latin American leaders seem likely to reject the Cuban example on intellectual, cultural, and institutional grounds, as well as for nationalistic reasons.

This does not mean, however, that Cuba is likely to be irrelevant in the years ahead. The Cuban revolutionary process has been a seminal experience in the political formation of Latin American leaders over the past decade. The lessons of Cuba, both negative and positive, are likely to be incorporated into the values and outlooks of future leaders throughout the hemisphere.

Significantly, many aspects of the Cuban revolution seem likely to repel the new Latin American leadership. A number of respected foreign specialists and observers have been outspokenly critical of the Cuban economy in recent years—most notably the former Chilean economic adviser to Havana Alban

Lataste, the French agronomist René Dumont, and the European journalist
K. S. Karol.[3] Their accounts have detailed the dysfunctional consequences
for the Cuban economy of overly centralized state administration, excessive
personalistic rule by Fidel, ill-conceived planning, and reliance on moral
incentives. Additionally, Castro's failure to achieve his much-vaunted goal of
a ten-million ton sugar harvest in 1970, along with the serious setbacks
produced in other sectors of the economy by the concentration on the
harvest drive, have emphasized the uncertain and frequently wasteful character of the Cuban approach to planning. Hence, even if they lean toward
socialism and statism, the new generation of elites most certainly will want to
avoid duplicating the costly and adventuristic aspects of Cuba's economic
experience.

Moreover, precisely as a result of the Cuban experience, the new elites are
likely to be more cautious than was the *fidelista* leadership in pushing radical
socioeconomic reforms. Partly because of Cuba, Latin American leaders have
entered a "post-Utopian" phase, with vastly decreased expectations. Agrarian
reform or collectivization seems likely to be implemented on a more gradual
and systematic basis in order to avoid precipitating crises in agricultural
production similar to those which plagued Cuba throughout most of the
1960s. Similarly, the ideological and moralizing zeal of the *fidelista* leadership
in creating a new socialist-communist order most probably will be avoided as
excessive by the new elites if only because of its disruptive effects. The
development models now emerging in Latin America, whether in Brazil or
Peru—and probably even Chile—aim generally at some form of mixed economies in which the private sector will continue to play a vital and needed role
alongside public enterprises. Most leaders, themselves of bourgeois and professional extraction, seem unlikely to want to pay the high price incurred by the
fidelistas in losing valuable technical and entrepreneurial talent among the
more than 600,000 Cuban exiles who fled as a result of the regime's policies.

On the international front, the Cuban regime has also paid a high price for
its foreign postures which most likely will discourage emulation. Castro
indeed successfully detached Cuba from the "Colossus of the North," but
only at the heavy cost of becoming economically and militarily dependent
upon the Soviet Union—and increasingly subservient since 1968 to rising
Soviet influence in its own domestic affairs. Ironically, Castro's Cuba has now
become the only state in Latin America (and the world) where the two super

---

3. Lataste, *Cuba—hacia una nueva economia politica del socialismo?,* Editorial Uni-
versitaria, Santiago, 1968; Dumont, *Cuba est-il socialiste?* Editions du Seuil, Paris, 1970;
and Karol, *The Guerrillas in Power,* Hill and Wang, New York, 1970.

powers might be said to operate naval bases—the United States in Guantánamo Bay, and the Soviet Union with its Cienfuegos submarine servicing facility. Notwithstanding the more than three billion dollars in Soviet military and economic assistance to Cuba, therefore, the new Latin American leadership may seek only to play off the Soviet Union against the United States as a foreign policy option far preferable to aligning their respective states with the Soviet bloc. This does not mean that opportunities for Soviet penetration will not increase—for that seems inescapable given the Soviet Union's prior virtual exclusion from the area—only that the impact of Soviet activities is likely to be limited somewhat by the initiative, desires, and capabilities of the Latins themselves.

Not all of the Cuban experience has been negative, and some *fidelista* policies seem likely to have considerable appeal to the new Latin American leaders. This might be particularly true of the Castro regime's efforts to promote mass education for purposes of accelerated economic development and societal modernization, its programs to improve public health, and its drive to transform the countryside and remove social injustices. Moreover, the mobilizational capacity of the *fidelista* regime, with its impressive capability for channeling manpower and resources to development programs and national defense, may also be attractive to those regimes that attempt rapid revolutionary change and are under threat from within or without. Depending upon their feasibility under local conditions, such regimes might attempt to develop mass organizations along the lines of Cuba's Committees for the Defense of the Revolution.

As suggested above, however, the direct transfer of the Cuban model to the rest of Latin America in the 1970s is not likely owing to the character of the new elites, and the *fidelista* model's foreign and domestic failures. In fact, the Cuban experience will probably become most relevant for its negative lessons. Apart from developmental strategy, the new leaders seem likely to differ markedly from Castro in their foreign policy toward the United States. Unlike the youthful Castro in the 1959–1961 period, in other words, the new leadership generation will probably seek to avoid a precipitous break with the United States that would close off needed capital and markets for their developing countries.

Indeed, the Cuban experience appears to have been a sobering one even for Castro himself, as he reportedly advised President Allende on his assumption of power to avoid breaking economic ties with the United States. Radical experience thus reinforces nationalist tendencies to avoid challenging the security interests of the United States through any form of military subordination to the Soviet Union. These, as demonstrated by the Cuban experience itself, are the most vital interests to the United States. Instead, new leaders are likely to test constantly the limits of U.S. power by deviating on economic and ideological issues, yet staying within the prescribed boundaries of the "inter-American community" on matters related to security. The nature of this inter-American community, by 1980, will thus continue to depend heavily on the U.S. responses to these Latin American initiatives. With new leaders on both sides, inter-American relations may come to reflect greater mutuality than in the past.

Developments in the international arena, however, may in the short run dispose Latin American leaders to bargain sharply with the United States. The emphasis on "dependency" is perhaps as much a product of subjective distortions as it is of objective economic conditions. But in any event, the era of Latin America's greatest dependency upon the United States—with its resulting vulnerability to U.S. pressures—may be coming to a close. Much of Latin America has already been purchasing arms from Western Europe, expanding its trade with Europe, Japan, and the Soviet bloc, and seeking developmental capital from Japan and Western Europe. Even if most Latin American states remain significantly enmeshed economically with the United States, these alternative international markets and sources of supply and finance should provide improved opportunities to manipulate the developed countries to maximum advantage, as has been implicitly attempted by the Peruvian government under its new mining and industrial laws. The availability of such international alternatives will simultaneously make the new elites less fearful of U.S. economic reprisals or threats.

The new elites may increasingly suspect that the United States is unwilling to bring its power to bear on defiant regimes or at least unable to inflict intolerable damage. Cuba has survived more than a decade of embargo by the United States. Soviet military as well as political presence is on the ascendant again in Cuba and the Caribbean. Outside of the Cold War context, Latin America has had considerable leeway in pursuing policies that clashed with traditional U.S. interests. The Hickenlooper amendments were not imposed on Peru. Despite the pressures of I.T.T., the Allende government generally escaped official reprisals for being hostile to U.S. private capital, and its ultimate fall should be attributed largely to domestic factors. On a global scale, the United States disengagement from Vietnam, and growing American preoccupation with domestic problems, tend to indicate that the Administration, Congress, and public alike are turning away from venturesome foreign policies.

President Nixon's policies toward Latin America have also encouraged the perception that Washington has abandoned the activist interventionism of the

Kennedy-Johnson years. With its attempt to deal with Latin American states "as they are," the Nixon Doctrine's overall effect has been to grant the Latin American community a wider latitude for national diversity and international maneuvering than at any time since the Good Neighbor Policy. The political, economic, and social experiments now under way in Latin America are unlikely to be radicalized by U.S. governmental opposition. In the long run, U.S. acceptance of diversity may be reflected, perhaps sooner than currently believed possible, in new tolerance toward U.S. policies. In the short run, however, Latin America's leaders, of whatever partisan persuasion, will remain profoundly skeptical of entanglements with the United States.

Chapter Five

ELECTIONS AND THE POPULIST CHALLENGE

Richard L. Maullin and Luigi R. Einaudi

Elections, which are a fundamental feature both of American life and of the ways in which Americans view other societies, have had a difficult history in Latin America; they face strong challenges from expanding electorates, new means of communication, and a growing body of political opinion that regards them as marginal—if not counterproductive—to the solution of Latin America's problems. This essay will consider the place of elections in Latin America in the years ahead by examining their history, uses, and some forces affecting their conduct and outcomes.

Elections and Constitutional Debate in Latin America

The election of national authorities is a political process that derives its legitimacy from the concept of popular sovereignty. The constitutional documents of Latin American states, written by advocates of republican government, embrace popular sovereignty as the fundamental principle for political organization and incorporate electoral systems as the basic technique for the selection of legitimate political leadership. As any student of Latin American politics and history knows, however, the election-based political processes embodied in Latin American constitutions have frequently been imperfectly implemented. Up to the mid-nineteenth century, one cause of the failure of election systems was the existence of politically influential groups and individuals who supported monarchist or other authoritarian political orders that rejected the concept and paraphernalia of popular sovereignty. More importantly, however, since the beginnings of Latin American independence, serious division has existed over fundamental rules for and definitions of a republican form of government among those who have supported it in principle.

Generally speaking, both liberal and conservative views developed within nineteenth-century Latin American political elites. The liberal view interpreted the concept of popular sovereignty in such a way as to require frequent elections to select leaders for most levels and branches of government. Further, the liberal view promoted notions of individual enterprise and individual merit. While this viewpoint often served as a rationale for limiting government intervention in economic and social affairs, it also tended to support an expansion of the voting franchise and government protection of what we in the United States know as First Amendment rights. In short, the liberal viewpoint argued for fewer and less rigid tests for the individual to qualify as an elector of political authority.

Speaking quite generally again, the conservative viewpoint sought to use the electoral process sparingly and to limit the extension of the voting franchise only to those who met quite rigid tests. Property and literacy tests were those most commonly applied to would-be electors. As is well known, these tests have often been used to prevent certain social classes or racial groups from participating in politics and thus having a direct influence on national affairs.

One of the most important characteristics of Latin American constitutional history throughout the nineteenth century was the failure of either the more conservative or the more liberal constitutional viewpoints to establish a prevailing political order. After the demise of anti-republican forces, mainly through their absorption into the conservative sector of the republican elites, liberal-conservative civil wars dominated the politics of the late nineteenth century in all but a few Latin American states. As a result, constitutions providing for quite open or closely restricted electoral systems often succeeded one another as the basic law in many Latin American states. In addition to constitutional instability, liberal-conservative civil wars facilitated *caudillismo*—the extraconstitutional seizure of political power by militarily supported leaders. Combined with the failure to reach a constitutional consensus, *caudillismo* has historically provided one of the most serious impediments to the full establishment of the electoral process as the means for selecting political leadership. One aspect of *caudillismo* that has been especially detrimental to the election process is that a caudillo, by applying violence for purposes other than simple self-aggrandizement, could claim to be executing the popular will and thereby characterize his behavior as the expression of popular sovereignty.[1] In this way, *caudillismo* has served as an alternative to elections for selecting the people's leaders.

---

1. The Venezuelan Laureano Vallenilla Lanz, writing just after World War I, characterized this process as "democratic caesarism."

Through the first decades of the twentieth century, however, adherence to more liberal constitutional norms gradually gained wider acceptance in practice as well as in public ideology.[2] This acceptance seemed to accelerate after the mid-1950s, when the regular use of elections to choose national leadership and extensive popular participation in elections appeared well established in a majority of Latin American countries, especially the most populous and industrially developed.[3] By the early 1960s, several important Latin American countries with long histories of irregular and fraudulent elections or lengthy periods of military rule, or both, seemed to have found a broad consensus for reasonably fair elections. Elections seemed finally to prevail in Argentina, Brazil, Peru, and Venezuela, as well as in Chile, Colombia, Costa Rica, and Uruguay where electoral traditions had taken root earlier.

The Anti-Liberal Challenge to Electoral Politics

In addition to an extension in scope by the 1960s, regularized election procedures had acquired a new ideological twist. Elections had come to be seen as an integral part of the processes of economic and social development. In answer to the radical and authoritarian revolutionary formula espoused by Fidel Castro, proponents of liberal and social democratic politics argued that regular elections allow for the necessary articulation of popular demands for reform and development in a rational manner. Furthermore, according to this view, electoral procedures assured the existing elites that they would have a forum in which to defend their interests and seek equitable adjustments to reformist desires. Thus a liberal political order based on elections offered a means by which national understanding might be reached and the destruction of existing economic and social leadership avoided. The rhetoric of the Alliance for Progress also endorsed this view of elections.

General agreement on liberal democratic politics proved short-lived, however. By the end of the 1960s, the apparent consensus among politically important elites to take their chances in an election-based political process had vanished in many important countries. In Brazil in 1964, Argentina in

---

2. Although two thirds of Latin America's constitutions had by then come to include provisions authorizing military interventions, typically to safeguard the constitution and the nation against disorder and executive abuse.

3. An optimistic interpretation along these lines was provided by Tad Szulc's book, *Twilight of the Tyrants,* Henry Holt and Co., New York, 1959.

1966, and then Peru in 1968, the military, on whom the civilian political elites had depended for social control, rejected election-based political systems and established military governments.

Election-based liberal constitutional orders have lost ground in recent years elsewhere besides in Argentina, Brazil, and Peru. Even Uruguay, long considered a "model democracy," has seen its parliament dissolved. Indeed, the challenge to liberal constitutional procedures has been increasingly articulated even by groups following the rules of the electoral game as constitutionally established. In Chile, Colombia, Uruguay, and Venezuela, major political parties or movements have sought to use the procedures of the liberal political system to gain sufficient power to eliminate it, or to drastically reduce its importance.

The rationales for authoritarian politics found in the left electoral movements such as Chile's *Unidad Popular* and Uruguay's *Frente Amplio,* as well as among the populist parties of the former generals, Rojas Pinilla in Colombia and Pérez Jiménez in Venezuela, are similar to arguments advanced by military leaders in Argentina, Brazil, and Peru: When elimination of underdevelopment and special privilege are the primary national goals, liberal participatory politics with frequent competitive elections are simply too awkward to produce strong national leadership. The liberal election system, this view would argue, is likely to produce more political compromise than economic development. To the critics, electoral processes allow manipulative politicians to exploit public opinion, build popular expectations greater than the national economy and society might be able to satisfy, and undermine the discipline needed to achieve a national goal such as a high rate of industrial investment.

In short, electoral processes founded on liberal constitutional principles have both conservative and populist detractors who would prefer to direct the state and select its leaders by authoritarian means. From a conservative perspective, elections raise the specter of previously excluded social and economic classes gaining control of the policy-making organs of state and instituting processes of socioeconomic changes highly destructive of established interests. From a populist viewpoint, the liberal election system is a cynical device used by the established order to create the illusion of popular sovereignty while assuring that established elites continue to benefit from the direction of government policy.

Strong supporters of liberal political systems continue to be found in virtually every Latin American polity. Competitive elections guided by liberal democratic political philosophy are nonetheless in considerable jeopardy. A critical variable for the longer-term survival of this method of leadership selection and the type of political system it symbolizes—with its characteristics of regularity, relative honesty, broad franchise and inclusion of a wide range of political viewpoints—is the existence of consensus among politically relevant groups and individuals on the rules of the electoral game. The most critical rule, of course, is that the electoral results be respected. Perhaps the second most critical rule is that coercion not be used to influence votes. Consensus on these points appears to be on the wane, not merely because some feel they are not attainable goals but because others feel they are not even desirable.

Elections can be expected to be held with both regularity and order only if they are contests between parties and individuals that are essentially in agreement on the basic definition of the society and the economy. Examples of such contests in Latin America include the rivalries between the *COPEI* and Democratic Action Parties in Venezuela, the Colorados and Blancos in Uruguay, and the Liberals and Conservatives in Colombia. In contrast, in Uruguay, Chile, and even Colombia, the *Frente Amplio, Unidad Popular,* and *ANAPO (Alianza Nacional Popular)* electoral movements represent different attempts to take power through a liberal democratic system which these movements intend to modify once victorious. Such competition must be distinguished from that between parties in agreement on the basic order of society.

Where a party offers not a new program within the present liberal social order but a rejection of the old in favor of something new, many of the principles underlying elections are themselves challenged. In Latin America today, the new order most commonly advocated is collectivist or corporate in nature, and usually involves the supplanting of individual interests with those of a particular class or group that would be interposed between the state and the individual. Individual interests would then be mediated only by the membership of the individual in that particular class or group. A peasant, for example, should be treated as a peasant, but not as an individual. In such a system the society's basic laws would favor class rights over individual rights or claims.

When parties espousing such anti-liberal views compete, elections are likely to be excessively competitive and policy outcomes highly unstable. Each contestant is likely to believe that the other would impose policies that are impossible to accept. If, as occurred in Colombia with the creation of the National Front, the dominant political elites load the procedural dice in their favor (as was also done in postwar Europe, where electoral laws were devised for the specific purpose of denying full representation to parties of the far left or the far right), then an element of imposition has been added, and the degree of coercion has grown, possibly inviting the growth of insurrectional violence and its military repression. In either case, the viability of liberal principles is very much open to question.

Political Uses of Elections

Despite the forces inhibiting regular elections, the authors believe that elections will continue to play a central role in Latin American politics during the coming decade. While it is true that constitutional forms often seem unrelated to practice, Latin American political leaders (like successful politicians everywhere) generally come to terms with the constraints and opportunities born from their countries' political traditions and adapt them to serve their purposes. No matter how poorly observed, the electoral processes contained in the basically Western constitutional systems of Latin America provide opportunities for the exercise of power.

The concrete political purposes of elections, however, are often overlooked. Most U.S. analysts have concentrated on determining the number and relative size of political parties contesting elections. Out of such analyses have emerged classifications characterized, for instance, by the greater or lesser competitiveness of elections in certain countries over time.[4]

In our view, it is most important to focus on the political purposes and uses to which elections are put. From this viewpoint, it is clear that the alternation of public officeholders is but one of the functions of elections in recent political practice in Latin America. Three major functions stand out in our view of elections:

- as a means of changing public officials who differ little over fundamental issues;
- as a means of endorsing power holders and what they represent in office;
- as a means of enabling authorities whose positions have weakened to turn power over to someone else who may be able to preserve essential elements of a sociopolitical system.

---

4. Useful and up-to-date reviews of some English-language literature on Latin American elections generally are found in John D. Martz, "Democratic Political Campaigning in Latin America; A Typological Approach to Cross-Cultural Research," *The Journal of Politics,* No. 2, Vol. 33, May 1971, pp. 370-398, and Ronald H. McDonald, *Party Systems and Elections in Latin America,* Markham, Chicago, 1971.

Elections as a Means of Changing Public Officials

Such elections come closest to the competitive elections in the Anglo-Saxon tradition, with alternation of the political elites holding office a serious possibility. The key element underlying this type of election is basic agreement by a sufficient number of actual and potential holders of power that the election process produces an expression of popular will and respectable national leadership acceptable to most contestants. In some Latin American countries, probably a decreasing minority, elections of this nature are and seem likely to remain a mechanism for real choice among competing political elites. During the past generation, for example, this has certainly been generally true of Chile, Colombia, Costa Rica, Uruguay, and Venezuela, although even in these countries electoral systems are now being challenged by the rise of mass movements whose leaders advocate replacing liberal with collectivist values.

Elections as a Means of Endorsing Power Holders in Office

This form of election is held to endorse or ratify a series of political decisions arrived at by nonelectoral means. In Mexico, for example, political leaders consult within the national elite, including important private and public figures and organizations, construct a political agreement leading to a new president, and then hold the election to endorse their choice. Such an election represents symbolic national adherence to participatory democratic values and popular sovereignty, without risking the uncertainties of majority rule. Another variant of the endorsing election is the national referendum, such as the one held in Colombia to sanction the beginning of the National Front system.

Although it cannot affect directly who holds office, the numerical margin of victory for the "endorsed" candidate (calculated sometimes with such refinements as the number of abstentions) may affect the direction of policy or the balance of power. On another level, the very holding of an election may serve as an outlet for popular discontent. Such elections have been typical of electoral patterns in Mexico since 1940, and those which appear to have evolved in Brazil since 1964.

Elections as a Means of Getting Out of Office

This electoral pattern, like that of March, 1973, in Argentina, we may typify as an "escape election." Such an election typically comes after a political group has attempted to reorder society by authoritarian techniques, yet decides, for whatever reasons, that it is important to give up the task and get out of office. While such a group may no longer be in a position to rule effectively, it is probably still capable of resuscitating some semblance of political life, holding an election, influencing the results, and turning over office to the electoral winners. Although differing in motivation, this pattern is clearly related to the "endorsing election" discussed above.[5]

These are not, of course, the only uses of elections. For example, elections perform an important communications function when they serve to politicize previously marginal populations. Local union or municipal elections serve to communicate popular opinion to the government. Nor is any given election held for only one purpose. We have just described "abstract types," whose characteristics will inevitably be mixed in practice, even should one type predominate. All elections, for example, are to some extent "endorsing elections," as we have defined them, at least to the extent that voters are offered a choice among candidates who have been previously chosen without direct consultation with the electorate or even with party followers. Even so, there is still a fundamental difference between an election among several candidates who are more or less genuinely competitive with each other and who will respect the results, and an election with a single candidate, or in which opposition candidates are known in advance to have no chance of winning.[6]

Factors Shaping the Elections Process: Electorates, Communication Techniques, and Political Parties

The purposes elections are likely to serve are, of course, not the only variables affecting the role of elections in Latin American political life during the coming decade. Future "surprises" cannot all be identified or allowed for in

---

5. Because of the explicit alternation between authoritarian and electoral legitimacy, this pattern frequently is part of a vicious circle in which authoritarian rulers turn over power to political parties so weakened by the intervention that their elected representatives are unable to rule and therefore contribute to a nonelectoral "solution" before the end of their period in office.

6. Thus, for instance, the outcome of the 1966 and 1970 elections in Guatemala, though largely fashioned without the participation of the electorate and to some extent "behind its back," were nonetheless quite different from the Guatemalan elections of 1931 and 1935 or even that of 1957, which were essentially plebiscites. Indeed, in the more recent elections, despite the fact that the distribution of votes among parties remained similar, shifts in electoral alliances led to a major left to right shift in the presidency.

advance, but the characteristics of electorates—as affected by demographic factors, the continued change of legal qualifications for elections, and the impact of modern communications technology on electoral behavior—allow us to identify additional ways in which elections are likely to evolve.

Changes in Electorates

Reflecting the population boom deriving from improvements in health care and the subsequent decline in infant mortality registered after World War II, Latin American electorates are in the short term likely to continue to grow, to become somewhat younger, and to become increasingly urban. The spread of health care, leading to increased life expectancy, seems likely, however, to counterbalance the "baby boom" and to stabilize the age distribution of the population. Population growth rates, among the highest in the world in the 1960s, may well not continue unchecked, and are unlikely in any case to affect the ten-year future.[7]

The most important demographic variable affecting Latin American electorates, therefore, is the rapid rate of urban growth due to rural-to-urban migration. Sociologists and political scientists are currently engaged in both a methodological and polemical argument over whether the growth of urban areas has created an explosively radical stratum of poor people. However, all evidence marshaled for and against the thesis of the radical urban poor acknowledges that the urban condition increases greatly the numbers of potential voters (as well as rioters or revolutionaries) exposed to a wider variety of political communication media and to an increasing diversity of political messages.

As cities continue to grow in the 1970s at rates above 5 percent annually in many cases, greatly increased numbers become available for political mobilization. As a result, the expression of mass political attitudes, whether through voting or other forms, will require much sophistication for purposeful direction or control.

Urban population growth, however, may not be the most significant new factor in shaping Latin American electorates in the 1970s. One could argue that Latin American cities had already overtaken the countryside a decade ago as the center of mass politics, whether electoral or not. Rather, the incorporation of the already existent urban masses into the potential elec-

---

7. Paul Schultz, in his *Demographic Conditions of Economic Development in Latin America,* P-3885, The Rand Corporation, Santa Monica, California, July 1968, underscores the lack of predictive demographic theory as well as the presence of factors, such as increased urbanization and industrialization, historically associated elsewhere with declines in birth rates.

torate may prove to be the most significant change in the electorate and, in turn, may provide the electorate's greatest influence on the survival and form of electoral politics.[8]

Two additional factors may lead to the incorporation of expanded numbers into the potential electorate in the 1970s: the removal of restrictive qualifications for becoming a voter and the sensitizing of previously non-participating peoples to the personal relevance and saliency of political activity.

As indicated by our earlier discussion, the extension of the franchise has historically been an important political issue in Latin America. By the 1960s, all Latin American states except Paraguay had universal suffrage in principle. Yet numerous and sometimes subtle legal restrictions remain in most Latin American states. For example, in Colombia, where the electoral system retains much vigor, all adults, whether literate or not, may vote. However, a voter must vote in the municipio where his national identity card was issued or where he has taken the trouble to reregister his card. Given the high rate of rural-to-urban migration, reregistration has been an important bureaucratic impediment to voting for many potential voters. In Colombia's case it most likely works against the greater success of Rojas Pinilla and his party. To use another example, Brazil's electorate is reduced in size by a literacy requirement. If age alone were the sole qualification in Brazil, the potential electorate would be twice what it is today.

The liberal reformist advocates of competitive election systems can be expected to continue the effort to eliminate restrictive barriers to mass enfranchisement. Their efforts will be joined by populist political movements for different, yet obvious, reasons. Nevertheless, it is unlikely that technocratic and elitist groups, especially where they are in power, will encourage further liberalization of the legal and bureaucratic qualifications for voting. An exception to this could arise in Peru where the regime may find it convenient to create a popular party similar to the PRI in Mexico and then hold a controlled endorsing election.

While the removal of legal obstacles to voting is necessary for an increase in the size of potential electorates, it will not, by itself, produce an expanded effective electorate for the 1970s. The most critical of all variables affecting voting is the communication of a personally relevant and salient political message. Unless he is motivated, a legally enfranchised potential voter does

---

8. For an excellent discussion of demographic and legal issues affecting the size, composition, and possible behavior of Latin American urban electorates, see Lars Schultz, "Urbanization and Changing Voting Patterns: Colombia 1946–1970," *Political Science Quarterly,* Vol. LXXXVII, No. 1, March 1972.

nothing. And if there is an administrative process required to become a voter, stimulation of some sort is needed to convert the qualified elector into an actual voter.

In brief, the expansion of the electorate has been and will be a continuing phenomenon of Latin American electoral politics. That expansion, however, is conditioned by demographic, legal, and communication factors. The conversion of any expanded potential electorate into an effective political force depends much on the complex methods of communication currently available in Latin American societies.

The Impact of New Communications Technology and Political Parties
It is already a well-worn cliché that Latin America is now transistorized and that television is having a phenomenal impact on public opinion. It is, after all, over a decade since Fidel Castro began conducting government by TV. However, it would be valuable to summarize briefly some of the more important qualities of the modern political communications media, especially as they may affect future electoral situations in Latin America.

The rise of television means that the individual candidate often assumes greater importance than his political party. This has been a marked event in the United States and in Western Europe (where it has undermined the discipline even of the great multiparty systems, as in France). There is no way for a traditional party organization to keep pace with the direct transmission of messages afforded by television. Latin America is an excellent example of this dynamic. General Rojas Pinilla in Colombia, like George Wallace in the United States, can draw votes from persons who unhesitatingly identify themselves as members of a party opposed to him, but are voting "for the man."

Not all aspects of the impact of television are clear, but it clearly affects campaign styles as well as outcomes. Contrast the television message, usually short, pithy, generally issue-oriented, and addressed to a relatively detached audience, with the emotion, length, and historic symbolism of a plaza orator.

Like the role of radio, television's long-range impact may well be one of substance as well as style. Television is a truly mass medium that carries its own message. Its message is that the masses have a role in determining who will run things, even if the expression of that role is a programmed response to a previously selected alternative. To use electronic mass media well requires "market research" into habits, desires, and tastes of the target audiences. And since the audience in question is generally a large heterogeneous urban population, there is a premium on the analysis of an extensive list of sociological, psychological, and economic variables that present themselves in a number of political contexts. Success in winning Latin American elections in the 1970s, no matter which motivations we have described previously predominate, will depend greatly on the level of analytic competence in utilizing the electronic media of mass persuasion.[9]

In spite of the increased importance of electronic media and their attendant processes in Latin America, other forms of communication, from the bayonet to the whispered word of a parish priest to the color of the party flag, will continue to have a major role in influencing election outcomes. Putting aside the role of coercion, which is generally the form of communication used by a political force unable to persuade voters by other means, the longer established structures of communication such as political parties require comment.

The principal function of political parties in elections is to aggregate public opinion and to give it a simple means of expression through a vote for the party candidate or symbolic label that best summarizes whatever the voter stands for or thinks the party stands for. In a sense, political parties save voters much work by having the minority that dominates them do most of the political work and thinking.

In those few Latin American countries where political parties have penetrated through the various strata of society, widespread party allegiance has permitted the luxury of making political decisions without too much threat of direct and volatile popular reaction. In this way political parties operate as social control mechanisms, allowing other institutions of the liberal political system, such as legislatures, to function relatively well. Examples of states with penetrating party systems include Chile, Colombia, and Uruguay.

However, the same party system which may shield the elite from excessive popular demands can, under certain circumstances, promote fanatical loyalty to party symbols which will not admit defeat in any election contest. In Colombia such fanatical party feeling has contributed to widespread political violence. In Chile, it contributed decisively to the partisan polarization that marked the latter stages of the Allende regime.

The role of political parties in Latin American elections in the 1970s will vary according to the type of election. In Mexico, for example, the PRI will continue to provide the institutional process in which future presidents are selected prior to endorsement by popular vote. In another of its roles, it will

---

9. Relatively little is available on the use of modern campaign techniques in Latin America, even though it is clear that a new generation of technically proficient political managers is emerging in party organizations. The authors are particularly aware of this in Chile, Colombia, and Venezuela. See also H. Goldhamer, ed., *The Social Effects of Communication Technology,* R-486-RSF, The Rand Corporation, Santa Monica, California, May 1970, for a more general discussion.

contribute both organizationally and symbolically so that Mexican voters will continue to "vote for the flag." Wherever endorsing elections are or become the rule, a political party of the regime might well take on some of the properties of the much studied Mexican PRI.

Elsewhere, however, the importance of political parties for the selection of candidates and for the disciplined organization of voting blocs should diminish. Wherever access to news and advertising media is relatively free, elections should witness more candidacies and campaigns in which the personality of the candidate and his capacity for direct communication with voters through the media will be more important than the vote gathering of party activists or the psychological hold of the party label on political allegiances.

Nevertheless, it would be wrong to forecast the total eclipse of political parties as electoral agents in those states that already have parties with formal structure and popular followings. Not everyone who wishes to participate in politics can be a charismatic television star; political party activities, especially where there is a tradition of bureaucratic organization, provide means for many to have or think they have some political role. Furthermore, party bureaucracies in states with frequent competitive elections have been in the forefront of adapting the modern media of political communication to the local situation. As we pointed out earlier, fruitful use of these media requires sophistication and an analytical approach. While the personality of the candidate may be the most critical variable in stimulating voters, a party organization may be essential for providing the technical expertise and the finances to utilize mass media effectively. Where parties still have mass followings, traditional vote gathering techniques continue to be of value. There is no conflict in objective between the prophet on television and the missionary or boss in the ward.

Finally, traditional party allegiances can be expected to continue through the decade. To be a Liberal or a Radical or a Copeyano, to judge from the public opinion and voting behavior studies on hand, appears to be an ingrained part of the personal identity of large numbers of citizens in the Latin American states where party life has flourished. These allegiances, in spite of the siren of extra-party charismatic politicians, should persist in the 1970s as other politicians seek to capitalize on their existence.

Conclusion

Elections play too important a part in Latin American political life for them to fade away. In most countries, elections have historic roots in political and social life. Even authoritarian regimes need elections as escape valves for the pressures of popular discontent and, in the long run, for themselves. The impact of growing electorates and new communications technology has nonetheless raised the level of uncertainty facing political leaders seeking to organize public support.

When elections are held in Latin America during this decade, sophisticated use of mass media to deal with expanded electorates will be increasingly in evidence, no matter the relative degree of freedom of choice in the given electoral contest.

Elections in the 1970s may therefore conform less than ever to the competitive liberal democratic model in which parties dispute power on the basis of programs. Nevertheless, elections to endorse or select national leaders during the 1970s seem likely everywhere but in Cuba, where the basic concept of popular sovereignty as expressed through elections survives only in the organizational life of certain mass organizations.

III. INSTITUTIONS

Chapter Six

THE CHANGING CATHOLIC CHURCH [1]

*Luigi R. Einaudi, Michael Fleet, Richard L. Maullin,
and Alfred C. Stepan*

Summary

The Roman Catholic Church in Latin America is today in great ferment centering on attempts to change its multi-faceted temporal presence in such a way as to encourage modern social development without losing its own institutional integrity.

In the late 1950s, the revolution of rising aspirations and the possibility that anti-Christian forces would champion these aspirations posed a challenge to the moral relevance and institutional survival of Catholicism. The initial responses, endorsed and to some extent prompted by Rome, emphasized the external shoring up of the Latin American Catholic churches through the importation of money and religious personnel and the adoption of European anti-Communist political strategies.

By the late 1960s, however, the evolution of Catholic social doctrines, including Vatican Council II's condemnation of underdevelopment and imperialism, the relaxation of systematic anti-Communism, and controversy over the proper role of bishops contributed to diverse and even radical responses among Catholic clergy and laity. Increasingly, Catholics in each country have been constructing their own strategies of survival and change.

Central to these new strategies of survival and change is an organizationally and religiously based posture of political independence from the state. Most bishops now give broad moral endorsement to social and economic change, emphasizing social justice as a central Christian goal. Independence of the Church from the state enables Catholic leaders to avoid partisan identification with the status quo and to exercise a "prophetic mission" by criticizing living conditions and government programs that do not meet moral criteria of social

1. This chapter is a condensed version of *Latin American Institutional Development: The Changing Catholic Church*, RM-6136-DOS, The Rand Corporation, Santa Monica, California, October 1969, to which readers are referred for documentation and for specific case materials on Brazil, Chile, Colombia, and Peru.

justice. Coupled with rising nationalism and the commitment to change, this has meant that recognized religious leaders have occasionally contributed to criticism of Latin America's relations with the United States, and particularly to support for initiatives designed to decrease dependence on the United States.

Because of the institutional complexity of the Church, and particularly as a result of the social and economic diversity of its lay members, Catholics are active in virtually every major social movement to be found in any particular country, from radicals of left and right to moderates and conservatives. In Brazil in 1963–1964, for example, the Catholic right mobilized mass movements against Catholic left activists.

While there are unquestionably more Catholics interested in basic social change now than in the past, the Church's fear that internal diversity could increase to the point of fragmentation; the caution engendered by organizational complexity, extended physical resources, and financial dependence on the state; and the decreasing likelihood of successful violent revolution will all tend to temper the practical endorsement of revolutionary change by the Church as an institution.

Viewed historically, however, a major contributor to conservatism in Latin America is undoubtedly experiencing change. Latin America itself is thus more open to all kinds of change than in the past. By assuming the prophetic role of independent moral critic, some Church leaders are attempting to encourage political leaders to channel that change in the direction of greater social justice and political participation for all.

The Changing Place of the Church

The early Catholic Church in Latin America, as an arm of Spanish and Portuguese royal authority, placed primary emphasis on the role of religion as legitimating existing political authorities. The sword and the cross borne by the crown's two representatives, the *conquistador* and his accompanying *padre,* were the joint symbols of conquest. Despite this unity, strikingly expressed in the *patronato real,* which gave the King formal control over many Church activities, the colonial period was not free of tensions over the place of the Church. Father Bartolomé de las Casas was but the first of several persistent, partially successful defenders of Indian populations against Spanish landholders. The expulsion of the Jesuits from the New World in the eighteenth century seriously weakened the Church, elements of which had always had differences with royal authority. All in all, however, European colonial authority in Latin America was simultaneously royal and ecclesiastical.

Enough legal and social vestiges of this early intimacy of religion and power remain today to support the impression that colonial relations between Church and state have often survived largely unchallenged into the present. Where Catholicism is recognized as the official state religion, for example, the government is constitutionally obligated to support teaching and practice in conformance with Church doctrine. In virtually every country the Church plays a major role in education. Everywhere, Catholic institutions are also active in public health and charity. Finally, on many matters, such as divorce or birth control, religio-cultural attitudes may in practice determine the fate of government programs.

But there is nothing preordained or automatic about these varied roles of the Church. Conflict over the proper place of the Church has been a touchstone of Latin American political life since the nineteenth-century struggles for independence. The extent of Church prerogatives and the different levels to which Catholic doctrines permeate state institutions today are thus in some cases attributable to struggles of a hundred years ago. Many of these early arrangements, however, have recurringly been called into question. New issues have arisen. Church-state relations have accordingly been a continuing problem whose current status is an important though varying feature of the national politics of each country.

Peru and Colombia exemplify the legally sanctioned interdependence of Church and state in which the Church receives subsidies and protection from the state in return for educational services and implicit religious acceptance of political institutions. The Peruvian Constitution of 1933 and the Colombian Constitution of 1886 make Roman Catholicism the state religion. Legislation in both countries requires that religious observance and instruction in public schools be under supervision of the Catholic hierarchy. Church buildings and personnel are partially supported out of the national budgets. Some Church activities are regulated under public law, and clergymen may not hold public office in either Colombia or Peru.

Some Catholic leaders in both Peru and Colombia have questioned the wisdom of continuing legal dependence on the state. In Peru interdependence of Church and state has been relatively harmonious. In Colombia, however, government sanction of clerical prerogatives has contributed to bitter civil conflicts as recently as the 1950s. From these and similar experiences, it could be argued that close legal identification of Church and state could, under some circumstances, weaken both parties.

The vigor and operational strength of the Church does not, it is clear, necessarily depend on state support. In modern Mexico, for example, there is no state religion, and many religious activities are illegal. The Constitution of 1917 confines religious practices entirely to places of worship operated under state control, forbids religious ownership of property, and even forbids the wearing of religious garb outside Church premises. Mexico's revolutionary constitution stands as a permanent warning of the constraints that could be placed on the Church should it be considered an important political enemy. Today, however, as Mexico's post-revolutionary governments concentrate more on other social and economic matters, observance of anticlerical restrictions, including the ban on teaching by members of the clergy, has softened. Catholic institutions, even schools, have regained much of their vigor despite the constitutional bans. More new priests—211—were ordained in 1967 in Mexico than in any other Latin American country, more than the total for all of Mexico in 1935, when priests were banned in fifteen states.

Chile provides additional evidence for the proposition that legal protection is not necessary for Church strength. The Chilean Constitution of 1925 ultimately resolved conflict over the legal status of the Church by completely separating Church and state, without prejudice to the Church's social and cultural activities. The Chilean Constitution thus effectively freed the Church of political constraints, and set the stage (largely unexpectedly) for its revitalization into what is today one of Latin America's most progressive churches.

Brazil represents an intermediate case, both as regards legal status and the relationship of legal status to operational vigor. The Republican Constitution of 1891 in Brazil formally separated Church and state. After 1931, however, Cardinal Leme, the Archbishop of Rio de Janeiro, informally renegotiated many prerogatives in return for implicit support for the revolutionary government of President Getúlio Vargas, who had come to power in 1930. This reestablishment was later explicitly recognized in the 1934 and 1946 constitutions. Today, public funds support secondary education, nearly half of which is controlled by the Church. Brazilian law grants full political rights to the clergy, several of whom have served in state and federal legislatures and as state governors.

These different and continuously changing solutions to the relations between Church and state have been subjected to new pressures deriving from the emergence of new social and political environments. Catholic teachings and moral and political influence have traditionally stood arrayed against such innovations as divorce, secular education, or contraception. Under the impact of uneven economic development, expanding networks of modern communications, and changes in the international environment, however, the direction of some Church activities has changed in recent years to favor programs of agrarian reform, enforced minimum wages, and mass education, as well as more general demands for greater political participation and democracy.

Institutional and Social Complexity

What are the organizational and human resources of the Church as they come into contact with different Latin American societies? This is, in part, a definitional question: What is the Church and how is it organized to carry out its several roles? Many Latin American constitutions, in their attempt to define Church-state relations, refer to the legal qualities of a national Church. At no level, however, does the Roman Catholic Church, despite the unifying religious symbolism of the Papacy, exist in fact as a single, united entity.

Competing theological conceptions of "the Church" have come into prominence in recent years as one result of often conflicting attempts to adapt Catholicism to changing social and economic environments. Some of these conceptions, as for instance that of the "Pilgrim People of God," have considerable potential political significance, particularly when compared to the more traditional Catholic notions of the Church as a sacramental mediator between man and God. While the more widely accepted views emphasize the Church as an institution, the concept of the "People of God" escapes institutional structures, and stresses the Church as independent movement and as a life style embodying Christian values.

At a more operational level, the structural complexity of Catholicism is instantly apparent. The basic organizational chain of the Church from Vatican to diocese to parish makes no explicit provision for the modern nation-state. Each diocese is headed by a residential bishop with independent authority under Canon Law. In accepted theory and to a large extent in practice, for example, Cardinal Jaime of Rio de Janeiro, who happens to be generally conservative, has no institutional authority over Dom Helder Câmara, Bishop of Recife e Olinda, who is an outspoken critic of certain Church traditions and of social injustice in Latin America, even though both men are institutionally within "the Brazilian Church." The inherent potential of such a structure for political and even religious diversity has led to considerable theological and political controversy over the selection of bishops and the definition of their relations to each other and to the Bishop of Rome, who is the Pope.

The rise of modern nation-states with effective power over significant territories and groups of faithful made it essential for the Pope to be represented at their councils. The apostolic nuncios, as these emissaries are called, are usually titular bishops empowered to "treat of matters even political, and of daily business." Nuncios, however, have no independent *de jure* authority over the bishops whose dioceses fall within the boundaries of the state to which the nuncios are accredited. When conflicts arise, both bishops, the titular bishop serving as nuncio, and the residential bishop with diocesan authority, may appeal directly to the Pope through the Roman Curia, or papal bureaucracy, in Vatican City. The nuncio's greater personal experience and contacts with the Curia often, though not always, give him an advantage over local bishops in such appeals. The fact that all roads lead to Rome has presumably strengthened the reputation of that city as well as the image of papal power; it also reveals a structure with a seemingly endless and often frustrating capacity to absorb conflicts and resolve them symbolically.

Largely since World War II, a process of "nationalization" of the Latin American Catholic Churches has begun, principally through the medium of national bishops' conferences. Increased ties among members of the hierarchy have strengthened national organizations and even facilitated some communication at a regional Latin American level. Nevertheless, the basic diocesan structure creates within the nation-state a series of largely unrelated centers of authority under individual bishops.

The fragmentation of practical authority implicit in the organizational complexity of the Roman Catholic Church is compounded by the presence within each diocese of several types of religious personnel. In particular, there are two structurally and sometimes functionally unrelated major categories of priests: secular priests assigned to the diocese, and religious (or order) priests, who operate within the geographical confines of a given diocese but without necessarily being under the immediate authority of the bishop. In Brazil alone there are more than four hundred separate religious orders, each with an autonomous authority structure, whose headquarters are in most cases outside Brazil. In any given diocese, the secular bishop may manage to coordinate the activities of these religious orders, but they are not subject to him in any direct chain of command beyond the original permission to enter the diocese and preach and hear confession.

Human diversity combines with this structural complexity to produce an institution that is highly differentiated internally. In a continent about half of whose population is under sixteen, the average age of Latin America's thirteen cardinals in mid-1968 was over 73. Despite Pope Paul VI's suggestion in 1966 that bishops retire at 75, the continuing absence of mandatory retirement exacerbates within Church structures more than in most organizations the perennial problem of the renewal of leadership and creates an inherent "generation gap." The divisions between generations over questions of social change that have long characterized Latin American life have recently made their appearance in the clergy. In Colombia, for example, whose government is often looked upon as a supporter of the Church, younger clergy have begun to emerge as critics of the government and of the older clergy who support it.

Within any given diocese, in addition, priests are set apart from each other by their diverse social backgrounds and even nationalities, as well as by their ages and secular or religious statuses. The social perspectives of the lower clergy often reflect the provincial isolation of the predominatly small-town, middle-class and lower-middle-class origins of its members. But even were this characterization accurate for the native Latin American clergy as a whole (and in many cases there are significant upper-class elements), it would overlook the cosmopolitan factor introduced by extensive periods of training abroad and by the presence of a large number of foreign priests. Indeed, one of every three priests in Latin America is a foreigner, often a Spaniard or a German, but Americans, Canadians, and other nationalities are represented as well.

The presence of thousands of foreign priests is one of the paradoxes of Latin American Catholicism: By the year 2000, Latin America may contain approximately half the world's Catholics, yet there are proprotionately far fewer priests (including foreigners) there than in Europe or in the United States. In comparison to other Catholic countries, even to Poland with a Communist government, or to France with a strong anti-clerical tradition, Latin America is hardly "priest-ridden." This is true no matter whether the yardstick used for comparison is the number of baptized Catholics, or the total population. So great is the disparity, in fact, that the United States, where Catholicism is a minority religion, has more Catholic priests per person—Catholics, Protestants, Jews, and nonbelievers—than does Latin America, nearly 90 percent of whose population are believed to be actually baptized Catholics.

Any analogies drawn from the Irish tradition of the Church being able to communicate its social messages on a "face-to-face, pulpit-to-parishioner" basis are therefore extremely misleading for Latin America, where the Church simply does not have the manpower necessary for this type of continuous socialization. In fact, though but 15 to 20 percent of baptized Catholics are generally thought to practice their religion, the clergy often feel hard pressed to minister to the religious needs of even that minority. In Brazil, for example, some 500 of nearly 5,000 parishes have no permanently assigned priests. Recruitment for the priesthood, furthermore, varies widely by country, but in all cases seems to be restricted to rather small numbers. To maintain even the relatively low current levels will require continued large-scale infusions of foreign priests. These difficulties are somewhat offset by the use of lay catechists, but the ability of the Church to transmit its doctrines directly to its faithful is still severely limited.

Within Latin American societies, furthermore, the capacities and influence of the Church may be as unevenly distributed as are the benefits of national economic growth in dualistic societies. In all Latin American countries, Catholic education of those who continue beyond primary schools encompasses significant portions of those who in adulthood constitute the middle and upper classes of Latin American society. Still, the degree of contact through education with potential elites varies considerably by country and no clear association appears between higher percentages of students in Catholic schools and measures of relative economic development.

The Church may not, in addition, be as strong as is often assumed in the more rural countries (and, by implication, in the rural sectors of the more developed Latin American countries). Some social science concepts associate "modernity" (for instance, growing urbanization and declining labor-intensive agriculture) with the weakening of "traditional" institutions (for instance, the Church). The relative weakness of the Church in rural areas could force modification of the simpler formulations of the conditions and effects of development to allow for either the possibility that the Church is declining in some areas while growing in others, or that it is not sound to consider the Church as simply a "traditional" force.

From the viewpoint of conservatives, the apparent shortage of personnel in contact with rural society may be offset by rural attitudes that are generally supportive of Church influence on local customs. But for Catholics anxious to develop a new consciousness on social and religious issues among rural populations, the lack of active Catholic advocates may pose great problems. Church-related activities are often operationally unrelated to each other. Most priests are occupationally immobile, whether they are engaged in conventional parish work, secondary-school or university teaching, intellectual, literary, and scientific endeavors, or community organization. And these activities may even be mutually contradictory. In many rural areas, for example, parish priests are pillars of nondemocratic tradition, indistinguishable from local elites in their support of the status quo. In other rural areas, however, members of the clergy, infused with notions of popular participation, may be found organizing peasant leagues or acting as agents of change for reformist government technocrats. In either case, so long as their activities have the support (for whatever reason) of the local bishop or the superior of the order, they may proceed on their contradictory courses.

Any attempt to reorient Church activities in a politically consistent direction must overcome the diversity of present commitments and attitudes of a very heterogeneous clergy as well as the bureaucratic inertia of a fragmented organizational structure. In fact, when these institutional and social complexities are combined with political conflicts within the clergy and with exceedingly diverse local conditions and national histories, it becomes evident that there can be no single "Catholic position" on the practical problems of social and economic development in Latin America.

Responses to Social Change

The Catholic Church in Latin America is probably today in as great ferment as at any time in its history. In part, this ferment reflects events that have brought traditional religious roles into question among Catholic clergy and laity throughout the world. But it also reflects the particular circumstances of Latin America.

The trauma of independence, which had found them (with certain notable individual exceptions) closely associated with royal colonialism, weakened most Latin American Catholic churches and left them isolated from both the largely anticlerical republican elites and the generally illiterate popular majorities. Though the patterns of Church-state relations which emerged from the turmoil of the nineteenth century were, as we have seen, quite diverse, they had in common the relative isolation of the Church from the "social question." This is particularly evident by comparison to Europe, where the crisis brought on by the emergence (and generally the loss for Catholicism) of the industrial working classes led ultimately to the first social encyclicals, especially the *Rerum novarum* (1891) of Pope Leo XIII.

Particularly since World War II, Catholic leaders in Latin America have been under increasing pressure to make the Church more relevant to the promises of material well-being and individual fulfillment for the common man implicit in modern society. Initially, much of the pressure came from outside Latin America, brought by Catholics returning from Europe and the United States, and supplemented by the efforts of the Vatican and Pope Pius XII to prevent the spread of Communism.

By the late 1950s the stage had been set for a remarkable moral reawakening from within. The wave of authoritarian regimes, which had compounded the frustrated democratic aspirations engendered by World War II, was receding. Renewed political instability, inadequate economic performance, and pressures on existing social structures by exploding populations challenged the moral relevance and institutional survival of the Church itself. The views of men like the Chilean Alberto Hurtado, S.J., who had argued that Catholicism, because of its isolation from the lower classes, was essentially a minority religion, had previously gone largely unheeded. Now the arguments of Hurtado's disciples, among them his fellow countryman, Manuel Larraín, Bishop of Talca, that revolution would come with or without the Church, and that if it came without the Church it would necessarily be against the Church, convinced many that Latin American Catholicism was threatened by impending social revolution. By 1959–60 this practical argument was buttressed (and was often caused) by the contention that subhuman conditions of physical misery denied man his spiritual being. For important groups, the egalitarian implications of Christian notions of the infinite worth of the individual therefore provided a religious foundation for a humanist and even a revolutionary consciousness.

The Cuban revolution was seen by many as underscoring the practical and moral imperatives for change. The lack of native priests and the consequent inability to minister to the entire national community that had characterized prerevolutionary Cuba were taken to demonstrate the general weakness of the Church in the face of mounting social change. This pessimistic view was intensified by criticism of the hierarchies' historical ties to conservatism, of the restriction of much religious education to the children of the wealthy, and of Church administration of charity as a political palliative.

The keynote of the predominant initial response as it emerged in the early 1960s was internal revitalization of the Church combined with active support for social reform and political anti-Communism. International Catholic structures like the Latin American Bishops' Conference (CELAM, founded in 1955) and the Papal Commission for Latin America (founded in 1958) became, under the guidance of the Vatican and in coordination with individual nuncios and international lay Catholic movements, instruments of pressure on the Latin American hierarchies.

Rome's tactics were to shore up Church structures in Latin America by an infusion of foreign priests to offset the vocational gap, and to strengthen lay Catholic institutions through assistance from their American and European counterparts. According to some plans, in ten years, by 1970, ten percent of the U.S. clergy were to have served as missioners in Latin America. Promising Latin American priests were to be sent abroad, particularly to Louvain (Belgium) for training in socially useful disciplines like sociology. European sources of money, such as Misereor and Adveniat, the German Bishops'

Funds, and of personnel, such as the Belgian Father Roger Vekemans, S.J., were used to assist the development of Christian Democratic parties and Catholic trade unions.

In addition to these general approaches, renewed prominence was given to numerous movements and proposals, such as the worker-priest experiments and specialized Catholic Action (such as women's and university organizations), which had earlier developed in Europe but had not received much attention among Latin American Catholics. The effectiveness of the traditional parish structure was questioned and sometimes bypassed in favor of Catholic Action organized not on a geographic or parochial basis but along specialized functional lines enabling lay Catholics with similar professional or class interests to band together. Specialized worker, student, and youth movements, peasant leagues, and other action-oriented lay organizations sprang up in many countries under progressive religious and lay sponsorship. Finally, leadership training and research institutes began to develop the staff and knowledge required by these many activities.

Attempts to mobilize the laity profoundly influenced the number and activities of Catholic social organizations. The membership and particularly the leadership of these many different organizations still reflect better penetration of the middle and upper classes, but though reliable estimates are particularly difficult to obtain for private voluntary associations, the numbers themselves are sometimes impressive. To take but one example, by the late 1960s the four major branches of Catholic Action in Mexico claimed nearly 400,000 members. Also in Mexico, the largely middle-class Christian Family Movement grew to include 18,000 families by the end of the decade, while the more frankly elitist Cursillos de Cristiandad had had some 50,000 participants, and the Movement for a Better World more than 25,000.

At a more directly political level, Chile and Venezuela soon emerged as national centers of political inspiration and organization, in large part because they already had what appeared to be reasonably well-developed, European-style Christian Democratic parties. In Chile in 1964 the Christian Democratic Party successfully challenged Marxist opponents on the left, and a traditional Catholic Conservative Party on the right, to elect Eduardo Frei as Latin America's first Christian Democratic President. In Venezuela, where the Social Christian Party COPEI provided the political base, reformist Catholic activists shared power with local social democrats before winning the presidency in 1968. Both countries, in turn, became organizational headquarters for attempts to spread these political formulas throughout Latin America.

The "European Christian Democratic experience" was, however, something of an illusion as a united strategic solution, in that it was itself highly differentiated, including many national situations, each with a different lay-clerical balance. Thus, while many Catholics accepted the Vatican's endorsement of a Christian Democratic model along Italian lines, others felt it to be inappropriate, or simply dragged their feet. Still others, particularly more radical lay Catholics with prior political commitments, resisted anything that smacked of clerical participation in secular matters, often turning for external inspiration to secular French precedents.

In any event, barely had the reformist, anti-Communist strategy begun to take effect in Latin America when there was a new change in the international environment, and specifically in the content of policies emanating from Rome. In an attempt to bring the Church more up to date, Pope John XXIII shifted away from a defensive approach to the outside world, seeking to modify institutional rigidity and anachronistic liturgy. In *Mater et Magistra* (1961) and *Pacem in Terris* (1963), Pope John gave new weight to social issues, including standards of living, educational opportunity, and political equality, as having value both in themselves and as prerequisites for spiritual development. In more practical terms, Pope John's emphasis on the social uses of private property and on the legitimacy of some forms of public ownership (e.g., *Mater et Magistra*, Sections 23 and 24), moved Rome toward a middle position in the ideological cold war between capitalist individualism and socialist collectivism. In the search for peace and for a more just temporal order, indeed, Pope John seemed to regard non-Catholics, and even traditional secular enemies like Socialists and Communists, as potential allies (*Pacem in Terris*, Section 61).

Latin American Catholics found themselves responding to this infusion of often contradictory pressures in a number of different ways. At first, the internal diversity of the Church itself encouraged adaptation by simply absorbing these varying and sometimes conflicting impulses without reconciling them. To a certain extent, this was facilitated by the lack of precision in Catholic social doctrine as well as by the difficulties inherent in the application of moral principles to social issues. In addition, the complexity, for example, of the structural relationship between the diocese and the religious orders, and between both of these and the lay community allows for the expression of differences within, not to mention outside, the institutional Church.

One of the many interesting phenomena set off by increased Catholic participation in social problems was renewed pressure on the Latin American Churches to change their structures. The mobilization of the laity encouraged by Pope John inevitably tended to increase the relative weight of lay groups within the Church. The young lay activists, mobilized initially to defend the

Church, often returned from foreign training or simply from contact with the poor filled with generous enthusiasms and plans to reform the Church to increase its relevance to the many problems they were uncovering. Student and youth Catholic Action groups became major vehicles for the importation of radical intellectual and social doctrines, often including forms of Christian existentialism that implied new limits on Church roles in a highly secular environment.

The initial attempt to adapt Church activities by developing a corps of priests trained in secular disciplines, such as sociology, economics, psychology, and similar bodies of profane knowledge, also created the basis for further internal differentiation within Church structures between "staff" and "line" activities. The differences in outlook between young priest-statisticians designing expensive programs of social reform while sitting in urban university research institutes and aging bishops with degrees in medieval philosophy presiding over isolated and impoverished dioceses in the provinces could hardly be greater—and both were objects of scorn in the eyes of priest-workers seeking participatory identity with the poor.

By 1962, when Vatican II convened, religious and political ferment among Latin American Catholics had already reached unprecedented heights. The Council in many respects intensified this situation. It provided a certain legitimacy for persons and groups who had previously dissented from anti-Communist political orthodoxy, and in many cases also opened Church structures to increased internal democratization. In the face of growing diversity and nationalist resentment of foreign influences, for example, Vatican Council II reemphasized the independent role of the bishops, weakening the Papacy somewhat in relation to national episcopal councils, and opening these to the possibility of increased collegial influence of the clergy. Although in part undertaken at Vatican initiative, these conciliar measures were nonetheless a reversal for the international influence of the Church of Rome. They had the practical effect of forcing local bishops whose dioceses fell within the same nation-state to relate to each other and to their societies in unprecedented fashion. It also undermined much of the remaining coherence of the attempt to impose European and American formulas on the very different Latin American environment.

Vatican II thus laid the basis for important changes in the internal structure of the Church and its relations to the world. Recognition that the internal structure of the Church was not sacrosanct contributed in turn to a more general crisis of authority. De facto fragmentation of authority became commonplace, raising questions of the proper extent of a bishop's authority and of the proper role of a priest both within the Church and in society and threatening the reliability of traditional chains of command. Dare a bishop act in certain areas without consulting his priests? What is the place of lay deacons in the Church? What is the Church?

Politically, Vatican Council II continued the Church's own version of the opening to the left, as seen in the establishment of a Vatican Commission led by the late Cardinal Bea on the delicate issue of Marxist-Christian dialogue. From Rome, this was mainly an adjustment to deal with Eastern Europe. In Western Europe, nonetheless, those Catholics and Communists who remembered their successful wartime cooperation in the anti-Fascist resistance were implicitly encouraged to consider the terms on which cooperation might take place again. In Latin America, as elsewhere in the less industrialized world, this form of political ecumenism weakened the religious legitimacy of those who would continue Cold War politics, and opened the way to possible alliances between progressive Catholics and Communists.

These processes culminated in the adoption of the *Decree on the Church in the Modern World,* one of the principal documents approved by Vatican II. On the heels of Pope John's encyclicals, and as ratified by Pope Paul VI's *Populorum Progressio* (1967), the *Decree* does much to break down the ideological isolation and conservatism of Catholic doctrine toward Latin America. Colonialism and underdevelopment are now condemned, and although Rome's primary audiences were probably meant to be in Africa and Asia, Latin American radicals took immediate notice. In *Populorum Progressio,* furthermore, Latin America is identified as part of the Third World rather than the Western World, thereby implicitly recognizing the need for revolutionary change and criticizing those who would defend the status quo in the name of Western civilization and Christianity. Capitalism, and, more indirectly, imperialism were criticized for their inhumanity. Despite later qualifications by Pope Paul himself, these positions seemed to reaccept within the faith all political currents, including the most radical.

CELAM: The "Prophetic Mission"
The shifts in Rome's views of Latin America during the early and mid-1960s generally strengthened the position of Catholic progressives. Statements issued by national conferences of bishops, of which the two most important are probably those of Chile and Brazil, and by a regional grouping, the Latin American Bishops' Conference (CELAM), provide an interesting documentary review of the evolution. Once the reader has become accustomed to looking beyond the rather emotive denunciations of imperialism and injustice with which these documents are liberally sprinkled, it is possible to find evidence of shifting religious concerns and often sharply differing political attitudes

within the generally progressive tone of the papers produced at the CELAM conferences.

The first general assembly of CELAM, in Rio de Janeiro in 1955, was largely devoted to consideration of the operational weakness created by the scarcity of priests. An ordinary session in 1959 attacked Communism in Latin America. In 1960 and 1961, CELAM meetings began to scrutinize the Church itself in its relations to its environment and to wonder whether both needed changing. At the 1966 ordinary session in Mar del Plata, Argentina, the central theme was "The Active Presence of the Church in the Development and Integration of Latin America." The CELAM conclusions of Mar del Plata reflected technocratic optimism and enthusiasm, at least partly inspired by the triumph of Christian Democracy in Chile.

By the time of the second general assembly of CELAM in Medellín, Colombia, in 1968, the atmosphere was considerably less propitious for controlled social change according to European and American models. The first six months of 1968 had witnessed an explosion of activity which provided ample testimony of the dimensions of the moral reawakening taking place within the Latin American Churches. Ad hoc groups of priests in Peru, Bolivia, Nicaragua, and Uruguay issued proclamations on the struggle for social justice. In May, meeting in Rio, and perhaps influenced by the escalating Church-state controversy in Brazil, the Latin American provincials of the Society of Jesus discussed the recasting of Jesuit-controlled education to serve better the needs of the community and of social change. The alleged participation of Maryknoll missioners in Guatemalan guerrilla activity also contributed to incessant discussion of the moral limits and justifications of violence in processes of social and political change.

The depth of feeling in these matters was revealed at Medellín, when the assembled bishops of Latin America, on the heels of Pope Paul's statement in Bogotá that "Violence is neither Christian nor evangelical," asserted that Latin America nonetheless found itself

in a situation of injustice which could be termed one of institutionalized violence, because current structures violate fundamental rights, creating a situation which demands global, bold, urgent, and profoundly renovating transformation.

Conference working papers and resolutions provided additional evidence of fresh political attitudes. Conservatives were criticized as usual for having "little or no social conscience." But this time "developmentalists" and technocrats were also criticized for "placing more emphasis on economic progress than on the social well-being of the people" and for failing to support increased popular participation in government. In an obvious appeal to the politically dissatisfied and the young, CELAM found a new hero: the *revolutionary* "found most frequently among intellectuals, researchers, and students." According to CELAM, unlike a technocrat, a true revolutionary understands that social injustice must be cured through radical change, with the common man as participant rather than as object.

The new emphasis on *participation* and the frequent use of phrases like "revolution," "revolutionary," "violence," "internal colonialism," and "liberation" (this last being included as a religious objective) combine to give the impression that CELAM attained in Medellín a new level of radicalization and political involvement. Three factors suggest that such a conclusion should be viewed with caution: first, the operational context within which joint statements of this type are adopted; second, confusions over definitions, particularly that of "revolution"; and third, the practical political program suggested by CELAM which seeks to dissociate the Church from the state to enable the Church to preserve its tutorial moral posture while remaining above the partisan political battle. Let us consider each of these factors in turn.

The emphasis on change should not be allowed to obscure the fact that the Latin American Church, like all large and complex institutions, continues to include persons opposed to change and still others completely unaware of the issues at stake. While some Catholics believe that contemporary Latin American life, with its gulf between rich and poor, is neither Christian nor democratic and hence is in need of drastic change, others feel that changes threaten their own way of life, which they consider to be already Christian and democratic. Acceptance of the modernizing and often egalitarian language of secular protest may therefore conceal traditional hierarchical values. The ideas of corporatism, perhaps the original and peculiarly Catholic attempt to marry traditional authority with social revolution, have retained currency, particularly when combined with a technocratic style, "revolutionary" language notwithstanding.

Even among advocates of social and economic change there is a fundamental difference between those who speak of "being in" a revolution, and those who speak of "making" a revolution. For some Catholics, growing self-consciousness among rural and urban poorer classes and a much higher level of popular aspiration for better material circumstances constitute a revolution already in progress. The mission of the revolutionary, this view argues, is to recognize and direct these pressures into appropriate constitutional, democratic, and nonviolent channels. For others within the Church, however, revolution requires a drastic restructuring of the ongoing socioeconomic system in order to eradicate human exploitation.

If a revolution is conceived as already underway, or as a natural out-growth of prevailing trends, the principal political problem becomes less that of defining what a revolution is or should be and more that of how to react to and channel it. This explains, at least in part, why the Chilean and Venezuelan Christian Democratic parties emphasize parliamentary, libertarian, and non-sectarian procedural norms. Those who conceive of revolution in these reactive terms are essentially attempting to reform ongoing political and economic structures, and tend to emphasize bread-and-butter issues promising short-run achievement of material benefits.

For those in the Church who believe that revolutions must be created rather than simply reacted to, the belief persists that unless the process of transformation is properly conceived and promoted, no true and lasting revolution will ensue. Revolutionary activity is thus not a response to existing pressures, although these may contain high revolutionary potential, but rather the conscious, relatively explicit realization of an ideal. The holders of this view, although they may speak of revolution as a historical inevitability, do not believe the revolution will come spontaneously or automatically. And even among those who agree on the need for structured social and political changes to redeem man from his marginal status, both the means and the timetable provide ample basis for further disagreement. *Why* is man so often faced with injustice? *What* should be done about it?

The CELAM conclusions suggest that a major interest of the bishops was to find a formula that would offer some hope of reconciling these conflicting views of revolution and social change with each other and with the institu-tional survival of the Church. The essence of this formula as it emerged at Medellín seems to be independence from partisan politics. Since any govern-ment is inevitably open to criticism for failing to meet the existential needs of the poor, the Church should not be identified with governments. This call for at least the *de facto* separation of Church and state is given the following form in the "Pastoral Recommendations" adopted from Commission 5 at Medellín under the rubric of relations with "political authorities":

1. Contacts and dialogue must be sought between the Church and consti-tuted authorities over the requirements of social morality, including, whenever necessary, the energetic and prudent denunciation of injus-tices and abuses of power.
2. The pastoral action of the Church shall stimulate all categories of citizens to collaborate with the constructive programs of governments, and to contribute also to the attainment of the common good by criticism based on responsible opposition.
3. The Church must always maintain its independence with regard to constituted authority and the governments which emanate from it,

renouncing, if necessary, even those legitimate forms of presence which, because of the social context, make the Church suspect of alliance with constituted authority and represent by that very fact a pastoral contradiction.

4. The Church, nonetheless, must cooperate in the political education of elites through religious movements and educational institutions.

With the exception of a union between Church and state, many different practical political positions can be reconciled with these formulas. The endorsement of political independence, however, appears to counsel a retreat from partisan political participation, as, for example, explicit support for Christian Democratic governments. Independence does not, however, constitute indifference to the actions of government.

The belief that a central role of the Church is to say what a just and good society should be and to argue for the attainment of this society, may be called "prophetic," to emphasize its claim to religious, that is, divine, as opposed to worldly, inspiration. The Medellín formula of combining independence from the state with an emphasis on the prophetic mission to denounce impartially all injustices should thus be understood as an attempt to transcend political controversy among Catholic activists by retreating to something all Catholics presumably have in common: their religious values. The attractiveness of the prophetic mission is precisely that it enables Catholics to surmount the divisive impact of partisan political participation, while linking Catholic religious values to the general need for progressive social change.

Catholicism, Nationalism, and the United States

The identification of Roman Catholicism with national cultures, often looked upon with despair by religious purists, is a sign of the potential strength of the Catholic Church in Latin America. It also means the Church will inevitably reflect the growth of stronger assertions of nationalism in Latin America. In popular political discourse, economic problems are frequently blamed on outside powers, most notably the "capitalist" United States, and the internal ruling elites, commonly labeled "the oligarchy." These perceptions are often welded together in a nationalist synthesis linking the outside power with the internal oligarchy in a vast anti-national, imperialist conspiracy based on greed.

Much Latin American opposition to the United States, including criticism of arrogant uses of American power, has historically found a receptive echo and even origin in certain Catholic doctrines. Two traditional Catholic views are particularly worth noting in this connection: the criticism of capitalism as an economic system, and the attack on liberal democracy as a political system. Capitalism is not generally criticized by Catholics on the economic grounds employed by Marxists, but rather for reasons of morality: the obsession with profit is equated with selfishness. This moral criticism is often extended beyond primitive forms of capitalism to condemn any system based on profit. Similarly, liberalism is seen as a political system which, in addition to originating much anti-clericalism in its nineteenth-century European form, also overemphasizes individualism at the expense of the common good.

The sense of national failure and fear of impending revolution that dominated political life during much of the past decade in Latin America seems to be giving way to new attitudes in which disillusionment with the Alliance for Progress and with extensive cooperation with the United States increases receptivity for Catholic anti-liberal and anti-capitalist attitudes. At the same time, Latin American Catholics are influenced by their countries' political and economic conflicts with the United States. In addition, two issues seem to be particularly relevant to Catholic attitudes. These are a sense of foreignness, which particularly affects relations with the U.S. Church, and disagreements on population policy.

Latin American Catholic leaders are sensitive to the presence of large numbers of foreign priests, often not subject to control by Latin Americans. A Chilean bishop commented recently:

> The Chilean Church at present depends on foreign money, foreign clergy, foreign ideas. The reconstruction of the Church will begin when it has to depend on itself.

In Brazil, 65 of the 243 bishops are foreigners, and although the foreign bishops are not the most politically active, there is nonetheless increasing criticism of the conditions, often unconscious, attached to foreign assistance. Throughout Latin America, as we have noted, about one priest in three is a foreigner. Among these foreign priests, those of U.S. origin tend generally to be "doers," working in rural and slum areas. European priests, on the other hand, tend to be more intellectually oriented and to become more involved in both national and Church politics.

The largely post-Castro upsurge in American Catholic interest in Latin America was greeted in some quarters as an indication that the U.S. Church acted as an unwitting agent of U.S. imperialism, operating on the heels of the Peace Corps, the Defense Department's Project Camelot, and the C.I.A., and helping to implant an American brand of Catholicism. These suspicions are fed by the militant anti-Communism of which American churchmen remain prominent exponents. Important groups and personalities in the Latin American Church have moved away from monolithic anti-Communism, even while retaining anti-Communist organizational interests.

The issue of birth control brings out an additional difference in perspective between the industrialized northern centers of the world and less developed Latin America. The encyclical *Humanae vitae* (1968), in which Pope Paul VI reiterated the most conservative opposition to artificial birth control measures, was greeted by one melodramatic commentator as definitely aligning the universal Church with underpopulated Latin America's liberation struggle against the "contraceptive imperialists of the North."

These criticisms should not be interpreted to mean that Latin American Catholics are on the verge of an outburst of xenophobic nationalism which would leave them sharing relatively little with their foreign coreligionists. It is certainly possible that nationalism, to the extent that it continues to grow, will contribute to a greater radicalization of Latin American Catholicism as well as of Latin American political life more generally. But to suggest, for example, that American and Latin American Catholics share no common ground is to exaggerate national and intellectual differences and to overlook the political diversity of Catholicism, both north and south of the Rio Grande. The religious symbolism of universal Catholicism remains a powerful popular myth, capable of reconciling international as well as national political differences. That Latin Americans of the most diverse political views were receptive to John Fitzgerald Kennedy on the simple basis that he was a Catholic illustrates the potential for Catholicism as a link between North and South America.

Conclusion: The Signs of the Times

Ferment among Latin American Catholics continued, if anything, to increase immediately after the CELAM meeting at Medellín. But there were also some notable hints of caution. Although they appeared to have been given considerable provocation in the course of their persistent conflicts with the military government, the Brazilian bishops, for example, carefully refrained from a direct confrontation, even as the Church remained a major forum for the expression of opposition sentiment.

This ambiguity should no longer surprise the reader. Seen in historical perspective, numerous complex factors of "institutional drag" slow the process of change. These include the historical conservatism of the Church, its institutional interests, the question of financial and other relations with the state, and finally, the impossibility of translating moral abstractions into concrete political action without creating strains that might undermine Catholic survival as a united Church.

The very fact that the Church is a religious institution lessens the potential political effectiveness of religious radicals in a further, somewhat unexpected, fashion. Debates over internal Church organization and liturgy consume energies which might otherwise be spent in more direct political action. Internal debate also weakens the already somewhat uncertain organizational unity of the Church. Particularly since Vatican Council II, Rome seems much less able to impose any given solution, at least in the short run. The priest who leaves the Church weakens the forces within the Church favorable to change. But the radicalized priest who chooses to remain a priest runs the risk of becoming but one of many conflicting tendencies within the diversity of the Church.

Relations with the state, particularly when they involve state financing and support for Church institutions, constitute a practical limit on the autonomy of Church leaders more important than the tradition of the *patronato,* and more complicated than implied by most concepts of separation of Church and state. Economically and culturally, and therefore politically, the interests of Church and state, although they can be separated in specific situations, are inextricably intertwined in the long run, and can therefore be expected to reflect different national accommodations. The one certain outcome is that Catholic authorities will no longer automatically confer religious legitimacy on state authorities or on the politics of the status quo.

In the face of the difficulties of bringing about a revolution by direct action, and during the search for new solutions to old problems within Latin America itself, most Catholic leaders have come to consider the basic role of the Church to be one of attempting to orient the values of the new society, rather than to lead the process of social and political change. A recent study of the Chilean episcopate, for instance, has indicated that the younger bishops were more interested in the pastoral task of internally revitalizing the Church than were the older bishops, who, in leading the battle for social relevance, had allowed themselves to become entangled in partisan politics. As currently defined, of course, the phrase "pastoral activity" may be interpreted to include sermons denouncing unjust land distribution. But as political revolutionaries and even reformers know full well (and as the conservatives within the Church also appreciate), the existential denunciation of injustice does not specify corrective action.

The increased moral awareness of social issues and the humanist emphasis on immediate social justice give an element of radicalism to the creation of

consciousness that may under certain circumstances create political confrontations. The Brazilian military regime, which is committed to limiting current
consumption and curbing inefficient producers for the sake of planned
economic growth (and, in their eyes, long-term economic justice), has come
under direct attack by members of the clergy who believe they are fulfilling
the prophetic mission by systematically denouncing present economic injustices. Thus, what is a duty to many in the Church can be seen as subversion
by others.

The ultimate outcome of these attempts at reform will be in large part
determined by the laity. The new emphasis on the creation of consciousness
underscores not merely the limits of direct political action, but also the
importance of the lay response. The impact of the changing values of the
Catholic Church will in the long run be seen not in the behavior of clergy or
even of Catholics, but of Latin Americans, rich and poor, military and
civilian.

We have made an effort to understand the design of God in the "Signs of
the Times." The aspirations and demands of Latin America are the signs
which reveal the divine plan.

Thus, in accordance with the *Decree on the Church in the Modern World,*
Latin America's bishops, assembled in Medellín, emphasized that they had
sought to respond to the "signs of the times." In doing so, they served notice
that the changing attitudes of the Catholic Church were themselves one of the
leading "signs of the times." The Church remains a participant, with all the
uncertainties that implies, in the process of Latin American development. Its
assumption of the prophetic role of independent moral critic places the
predominant weight of Catholicism on the side of social change and political
freedom.

Chapter Seven

CHANGING MILITARY PERSPECTIVES
IN PERU AND BRAZIL*

Luigi R. Einaudi and Alfred C. Stepan

Summary

Since the mid-1960s the military forces of Peru and Brazil have radically transformed their political styles. Before then, military interventions did not normally lead to direct military rule. When they did, military regimes were generally "caretaker" in style, "moderating" between competing political groups and favoring essentially conservative policies.

In 1964 in Brazil, and in 1968 in Peru, political-economic crises led to the ousting of civilian presidents by military commanders acting with strong institutional support. In both countries, the military have insisted on being labeled "revolutionary," and appear intent on retaining control of government for the indefinite future, in accordance with national security doctrines that justify more extensive military rule than their societies have previously known.

These national security doctrines were developed by military intellectuals in the national war colleges in the late 1950s and early 1960s. In both Peru and Brazil, the military studied all aspects of the "crisis of development" because they saw internal security as inextricably tied to national development. Two categories of enemies to the internal security of their countries were identified: persons seeking to impose violent change, and, somewhat secondarily, those seeking to block peaceful change. Military professionals, in other words, came to consider political change necessary to bar subversion and to bring about economic development.

The military governments that have since emerged in Peru and Brazil

---

*This chapter presents the summary and an excerpt from the conclusion of *Latin American Institutional Development: Changing Military Perspectives in Peru and Brazil,* R-586-DOS, The Rand Corporation, Santa Monica, California, April, 1971. David Ronfeldt's essay on patterns of civil-military rule places these questions in broader perspective and provides references to additional research.

97

resemble each other in being politically authoritarian and favoring the structures of a corporate-style mixed economy as the best means to rapid growth. But contrasting perceptions of internal threats, based on differing national societies, economies, and political histories, suggest that, despite the common characteristic of increased military institutional capacity, the policies of military governments will continue to vary from country to country.

The Brazilian government was led initially by officers deeply sympathetic to the United States and began by placing primary emphasis on the need to contain "Communist" subversion. Peruvian leaders, in contrast, were initially suspicious of U.S. intentions, and saw traditional landowning and capital-exporting groups, both Peruvian and foreign, as their primary antagonists.

In Brazil, government policies have tended to be politically conservative and economically favorable to private enterprise. Particularly during the mid-1960s, the working classes bore the brunt of stabilization policies. In any assessment of the military's role, the substantial economic growth of the past three years must also be balanced against the tendency to repress dissent.

In Peru, extensive legislation pertaining to agrarian reform, industrial communities, and government organization has revealed the military's generally statist approach to social and economic change. The government's attempts to "rewrite the rules" for foreign and domestic private enterprise, and its 1968 seizure of the International Petroleum Company, have earned Peru greater international attention than it has had in many years, but have somewhat slowed private economic activity. Perhaps because of its more "progressive" aura, the Peruvian military government has thus far successfully avoided the use of repression.

In the future we may expect the military in both countries to continue to reflect national tensions and, with increased governing experience, to adjust their policies in shifting alliances with civilian elements. Internationally, the Peruvian and Brazilian militaries will retain and perhaps increase their interests in regional security and power relationships. The military and civilian leaders of Brazil, in particular, see their eventual successors as having the potential for a major world role. For both, however, their own domestic development, not foreign affairs, will be the critical determinant of policy.

Brazil and Peru: What Do They Demonstrate?

In both Peru and Brazil, the key to changed military perspectives and expanded military participation in politics was similar: The military institutions came to see existing social and economic structures as security threats because these structures were either so inefficient or so unjust that they created the conditions for, and gave legitimacy to, revolutionary protest. In both countries, the officer corps believed that these conditions were ultimately a threat to the military institution itself. In their leading war colleges—the Escola Superior de Guerra (ESG) in Brazil and the Centro de Altos Estudios Militares (CAEM) in Peru—military men increasingly turned to a wide range of social problems, such as land reform, tax structure, foreign policy, and insurgency, as well as to the formulation of policies and reforms that the military thought necessary to ensure stability. The result was that military policy became much more closely linked to political policy than it had been in the past. For in both military establishments the conviction was spreading that the existing political institutions were incapable of implementing the social and economic policies which the officer corps now thought necessary to military security.

At the same time that their concern for development was growing, the military in Peru and Brazil, as in the United States, reacted to the fear of revolution by significantly increasing the level of military expertise in counterinsurgency tactics and doctrine. By this standard, the military rapidly became more "professional." A working hypothesis in much academic literature and a rationale sometimes used for certain U.S. military assistance programs is that "professionalism" contributes to lessened political involvement on the military's part, and to their concentration on exclusively military affairs. Logic, however, suggests that to the extent that military expertise, or professionalism, is increased in the areas of counterinsurgency, nation-building, and multisector development planning, the military would tend to become *more* rather than *less* involved in politics. This is certainly what happened in Brazil and Peru.[1]

Changes in military political roles were closely related in both countries to expanded military education, which in the eyes of the military increased their relative capability (and hence legitimacy) when compared to civilian leader-

---

1. A thorough and brilliant analysis of some psychological and political implications of the military ideology of total counterrevolutionary warfare (especially in the context of a weak political system) is Raoul Girardet's discussion of the French army; see his "Problèmes Idéologiques et Moraux," and "Essai d'Interpretation" in Raoul Girardet (ed.), *La Crise Militaire Française, 1945–1962: Aspects Sociologiques et Idéologiques,* Librairie Armand Colin, Paris, 1964, pp. 151–229.

In the early 1960s, the Indonesian army's Staff and Command School also formulated a development and security doctrine, much of which was implemented when the military assumed power in 1965. For the doctrine and a penetrating analysis, see Guy J. Pauker, *The Indonesian Doctrine of Territorial Warfare and Territorial Management,* RM-3312-PR, The Rand Corporation, Santa Monica, California, November 1963.

ship elements. New generations of officers, with training and life experiences different from those of their predecessors, and, occasionally, representing new institutional interests, served as a means of internal renewal. Characteristically, the changes emerged first among officers and civilians assigned to staff schools and to intelligence functions, and only later affected the military's participation in politics. In both Peru and Brazil, changes in military perspectives may thus be said to have originated from within the military institutions themselves, and to have then been confirmed by the latter's interaction with society.

Our analyses of Peru and Brazil also suggest that the military tend to become increasingly involved in politics in periods of social stress that accompany pressures for rapid economic growth at what might be called the middle levels of development. It is precisely in those countries that have broken the cycle of tradition and are actively seeking still higher levels of development that the military's perceptions of suitable paths to development are likely to diverge most sharply from those of many civilians. The indispensable social function of force is particularly evident during the crises over legitimacy which frequently accompany the break from tradition, when coercion is often seen to be necessary to preserve order in the face of the conflicting and often violent claims of opposing groups. Military force is thus presented as an alternative to chaos, whether to defend a ruling group or to replace it with another. In addition, heightened military activism may also correspond to a desire to limit popular consumption so as to increase investment and to silence political opposition to the accompanying austerity.

Some of the most significant elements that contributed to the shift from the "moderator" or "arbiter" patterns of civil-military relations to direct military rule in Brazil and Peru during the 1960s are in one degree or another in existence, or coming into existence, in other Latin American countries. These include, though frequently in varying combinations, substantial growth in popular political demands; the apparent ineffectiveness of parliamentary and other liberal democratic forms of government when faced with the need to industrialize increasingly modernized societies;[2] the growth of the military's concern about internal security threats, frequently identified as the result of an inefficient, corrupt, and unjust middle-class and upper-class parliamentary and social system; the belief that traditional military roles centering on the preservation of order do not contribute to the solution of

---

2. For a perceptive discussion of the difference between modernization and industrialization, see David Apter, *The Politics of Modernization,* The University of Chicago Press, Chicago, Ill., 1965, pp. 43-80.

the problems of development; and the growth of confidence among the military that their superior war colleges and advanced nonmilitary training have, for the first time, produced a cadre of specialists in support of development programs superior to those of bankrupt, and therefore no longer legitimate, professional politicians.

Although the Brazilian and Peruvian militaries to date have had only mixed success in their new roles, the mode of military involvement in Latin American politics generally may be shifting increasingly from that of "systems maintenance" to that of "systems transformation."[3] The current effort at structural change led by the Peruvian military, for example, is clearly more systematic and thorough than previous military reform attempts. To what extent can it be said that the Brazilian and Peruvian experience is relevant to other Latin American countries? Will similar patterns of civil-military relations emerge elsewhere? Despite the very real differences among the countries of Latin America, the area as a whole has undergone certain common political experiences: the unifying dictators of the mid-nineteenth century, the authoritarian reformist regimes of the 1930s, and the military governments of the early 1950s. Are basic similarities in social and economic structures, world trade, and political atmosphere likely to contribute to what one might call a Latin American "demonstration effect," and lead to a general continental resurgence of military nationalism and support for structural reform?

In speculating about the future course of other Latin American countries, it seems that Peru provides a more politically sympathetic model than Brazil. The initial pro-United States internationalism of the Brazilian regime will probably not be imitated elsewhere. A key source of pro-Americanism among the Brazilian military—the World War II experience of the Brazilian Expeditionary Force (FEB) that fought in Italy side by side with American troops—is not shared by any other country in Latin America. The Peruvian path, in contrast, has been explicitly acknowledged as a model by factional leaders in other countries, including Argentina as well as Bolivia. Even in Brazil, the Peruvian experience is so much in the air that, although in 1969 a leader of

---

3. Morris Janowitz, in correspondence with Stepan in November 1969, commented that he had not included Latin America in his book *The Military in the Political Development of New Nations: An Essay in Comparative Analysis,* The University of Chicago Press, Phoenix Books, Chicago, Ill., 1964, not so much because the Latin American countries were not new nations, but because Latin American military establishments were much less concerned with efforts at system change and modernization than were those of the new nations. He observed that the system-level changes we had described in Brazil made it a "new nation" in this sense, even though Brazil was an "old" nation in independent status and even "developed" in parts of its modern industrial sector.

the authoritarian nationalist wing of the military, General Alfonso Albuquerque Lima, felt it necessary to deny publicly that he had sent a personal emissary to observe the Peruvian military, by 1971 the Brazilian military seemed intent on carving out its own brand of nationalism, including the defense of a claim to a 200-mile jurisdiction over territorial waters similar to those previously advanced by Peru. Given the declining state of the Alliance for Progress, could Peru become for the decade of the 1970s something akin to what Cuba was for the 1960s—that is, a nationalist model for other countries, with military radicalism, rather than Communism, the keynote?

This discussion of possible demonstration or "domino" effect of military radicalism has thus far overlooked differences between Peru and Brazil that are sufficiently great to raise doubt as to whether we are in fact dealing with a single model. The national security doctrines developed in the higher war colleges of Brazil and Peru both stress the nexus of development and security, but the absence of an immediate security threat when the military actually assumed power in Peru in 1968 has contributed to the Peruvian emphasis on development, whereas the Brazilian military have emphasized security issues, and have often countered terror with terror, even while seeking development. In Peru, on the other hand, the brief and effective military campaign of 1965–66 against rural guerrilla forces assumes historical significance largely because of the impetus it gave to the military's interest in changing a political system which they associated with guerrilla violence and with the failure of development programs.

In domestic politics, inflation and attempts to unionize sergeants contributed an anti-labor bias to the Brazilian revolution of 1964. Their antipathy to the "populist demagogy" of Vargas gives the Brazilian military a reactively austere and almost aristocratic style. In Peru, in contrast, the dominant military leaders consider the upper-class landowners, the urban middle-class politicians, and their foreign allies as the greatest obstructions to long-term development and security, and are not above engaging in almost Vargas-like populist rhetoric to enlist popular support. The Peruvian land reform was aimed as much at eliminating upper-class political and economic power as it was at modernizing the agrarian sector.

In the international policy sphere, the Brazilian military experience of World War II in the FEB, the intense anti-Communism after 1963, the fear that the labor unions would infiltrate the noncommissioned officer corps, and the soaring inflation all contributed to a pro-American, pro-private capital (foreign and domestic), anti-labor bias in the first government by the Brazilian military. Peru experienced many similar tensions, but the circumstances in which they occurred were very different and have led to striking disparities between the two regimes. The refusal by the United States to sell supersonic military aircraft to the Peruvian Air Force in 1965–67, and the small allocation of funds from the Alliance for Progress, became sources of anti-Americanism among Peruvian officers, who came to share suspicions of the United States that previously had been confined primarily to civilian intellectual circles. This sense of "breach of alliance" united many Peruvian officers and civilians in bitterness at what they considered virtual betrayal by the United States, which broke off diplomatic relations after the 1962 coup, and maintained an initially cool attitude toward the 1968 revolution. In Brazil, in contrast, President Lyndon Johnson's public endorsement of the 1964 revolution while it was still in progress has associated the United States with many of the successes—and excesses—of the Brazilian military government.[4]

These contrasts between Peru and Brazil suggest that the fact of military dominance in two countries does not necessarily imply common policies. As our analysis of Brazil, which has had three different military presidents since 1964, reveals, military dominance need not even imply stability of policy in one country. As a natural consequence of the fact of military power, civilian politicians have for the most part historically joined in competing for military favor. One result is that today, despite greater emphasis on military roles and power, there are still built into the military institutions themselves a whole series of potential coalitions in formation with different civilian elements. Should the activities resulting from these political alliances take on an overly partisan cast, or should military policies be unsuccessful, they would be subject to change lest institutional unity be threatened. But the fact that the military institutions can "field more than one team" of senior officers to manage the affairs of state implies some capacity for change and adaptation to new circumstances, even while maintaining basic concerns.

Indeed, if one were to speculate about potential policies in those Latin American countries where the military will come to power in the 1970s, it would appear that many different positions could emerge on economic issues. The military is an institutional rather than a class elite, in the sense that the power and prestige of officers derives from membership in the military institution rather than from inherited position or other social relations. It would therefore be possible for the military to restrict the privileges of the middle and upper classes if they felt that these classes contributed to internal disruption or impeded development. Peruvian military support for agrarian

---

4. A sensitive recent essay by Thomas G. Sanders attempts to place Brazil in contemporary Latin American perspective: *Institutionalizing Brazil's Conservative Revolution,* American University Field Staff Reports, East Coast South American series, Vol. 15, No. 5, December 1970.

and industrial reforms, when compared with more orthodox Brazilian policies, suggests that a wide range of possible positions on economic issues is
available to a military regime.

Much the same diversity may be expected in political rhetoric, although
there will probably be less variation among military regimes on matters of
political organization. With regard to participation, for instance, the desire of
military radicals for control, and their suspicion of professional politicians,
tend to conflict with democratic electoral campaigns, and would be more
congruent with a plebiscitary style of politics. As regards mobilization, the
preference of military radicals for order and unity would probably make
them resistant to the proliferation of autonomous, lower-class mass-action
groups, but favorably disposed toward disciplined mass parades. A natural
military style in Catholic Latin America might therefore be a populist variant
of nationalist socialism, "corporativism," or, to use Kalman Silvert's phrase
"Mediterranean authoritarianism." In our recurrent dialogues, our colleague
Richard Maullin has insistently underscored the general importance for Latin
America of political movements, often associated with military leaders, which
manipulate the symbols of social grievance and of nationality and culture in
an essentially populist manner.

It is illusory, however, to attempt to label Latin American phenomena,
military or political, with phrases imported from the experience of other
lands or eras, just as it is too early to estimate how successful military
attempts at system transformation will be. Compared with most of Africa and
Asia, Latin America has achieved a much greater degree of urbanization and
industrialization, and must reckon with much more powerful social groups
such as labor, intellectuals, industrialists, and other representatives of middle-
class interests. Hence, the control and transformation of Latin American
social systems by the military will prove a politically more complicated task
than military rule of less-developed social structures.

Brazil's large and relatively modern public and private economic sectors,
for example, virtually require that military leaders maintain effective working
relations with civilian professionals and industrialists to supplement even the
expanded skills of the military themselves. From this viewpoint, there is
today considerable agreement among military and civilian elites in Brazil that
industrialization is important as a prelude to the emergence of Brazil as a
highly developed world power. But this consensus could shatter over methods. Certainly in Peru military goals of social justice and rapid development
are not shared with as much conviction by many civilian leaders. Peru, with
its smaller modern economic sector, seems a more likely candidate for

successful military rule than Brazil although this may be counterbalanced by Peruvian officers' relative lack of experience in economic matters.

The experiences of Peru and Brazil reveal a tendency toward increased military involvement in politics in periods of social stress and troubled economic growth. They also suggest that the scope of national security doctrines is greatest in a country characterized by a dualistic economy—partly modern industrial and partly prescientific agricultural—and by wide differences in the cultural styles of urban and rural populations. In the past decade, national security doctrines (and, to a lesser extent, practice) in both countries have made the lessening of these internal differences an important goal of security policies. Each advocates its own solution, but the concern is common, and is likely to spread to other countries and military forces in years to come.

Chapter Eight

PATTERNS OF CIVIL-MILITARY RULE

David F. Ronfeldt

This essay analyzes trends in civil-military relations in Latin America, and arrives at the following major conclusions. The common rigid distinction between "military regimes" and "civilian regimes" seems to be analytically misleading. Rather, virtually all Latin American governments are ruled by fused civil-military coalitions and "civil-military regimes." These come in varied forms, some more civilianized and some more militarized, depending upon the nature of the elite coalitions, their policies, and their institutional bases in the particular country. Though there may be long-run trends in favor of eventual civilian dominance, political participation by the Latin American militaries has been a natural process sustained by both civilian and military elites, and can be expected to continue significantly during the 1970s. In general, the leading countries of Latin America may now be developing toward new civil-military-clerical coalitions of nationalist elites recruited from, or aligned with, sectors within the new middle classes. As in the past, tendencies toward political corporatism will be strong, but each country model will remain unique.

A Conceptual Distinction with Policy Ramifications

In both academic and policy literature, the concepts of "military regimes" and "civilian regimes" are commonly used in discussing Latin American governments. Accordingly, Argentina, Brazil, Ecuador, and Peru are said (in 1972) to be governed by military regimes—while Mexico, Chile, Colombia, Costa Rica, the Dominican Republic, and Venezuela are governed by civilian regimes. Other Latin American regimes—Bolivia comes instantly to mind—might be classified as "mixed civil-military regimes"; yet most are still perceived as pertaining to one polar type or another. One striking consequence of this perspective has been to view recent Latin American political history as a cyclical succession of alternations between the two types of regimes, each considered to be quite different in nature. The hallmarks of civilian regimes are said to be rule by an elected civilian executive, by an active legislature and judiciary, and by a functioning party system. The defining characteristics of military regimes are understood to be forceful, extralegal rule by military officers, and the abrogation of the constitutional rights of civilian participatory institutions (such as legislatures and political parties).

Contrasting stances about the merits and demerits of civilian and military regimes in national development have clearly influenced controversies about U.S. recognition and aid policies toward Latin American countries. In 1969, the Rockefeller report implicitly advocated close relations between the United States government and military regimes in Latin America; and other spokesmen have argued that military takeovers may provide the best protection for U.S. interests threatened by radical nationalism. From a contrary perspective, the Kennedy Administration had earlier brought the ascendance of officials and analysts who believed that diplomatic recognition and foreign aid should be withheld from undemocratic military regimes. Indeed, the debate about whether and how the United States government might discourage militarism through its aid and recognition policies remains very much alive in legislative and executive circles.

Thus we see that an important range of policy consequences is related to the original conceptual distinction between civilian and military regimes. Of course, policy formulation depends upon a variety of factors and distinctions besides the one discussed here. Yet, almost as a matter of course, by establishing such contrasting types the civilian-military distinction facilitates polarization between those who favor siding with one type of regime or the other—to the detriment of what might be a middle course, one perhaps more dependent upon the policies or political style of a given regime than upon its source of recruitment.

Civil-Military Coalitions in Latin America

The chief executive offices of a country may be occupied by civilians or military officers. That usually is the criterion by which regimes are typed as being military or civilian. However, governments consist of much more than just the formal top executive officials. The formal rulers rarely determine the nature of rule by themselves. And it is when we move from asking the question, "Who occupies the chief executive offices?" to asking instead,

"What kinds of persons and groups rule the government?" that we find that the military-civilian dichotomy becomes artificial.

Take a look at what many consider to be examples of military regimes. Upon inspection most are seen to remain highly dependent upon civilian allies, particularly in economic matters. Indeed, without the cooperation of some civilian elements and power elites, most so-called military regimes would probably soon collapse. Military leaders typically require some civilian allies in order to remain in power, almost more so than the ruling officers need the full support of all military sectors, as has often been the case in Argentina and Bolivia. In some cases (such as Brazil and Peru), the role of civilians in military-dominated regimes is exemplified by the technocrats who side with military officers in order to gain power and position. In other, mostly historical, cases old civilian oligarchs have sought to use military executives in order to protect their holdings and privileges. Moreover, in almost all cases civilians occupy many if not most of the cabinet posts, and still staff the federal and state bureaucracies.

Even the most militarized regime in Latin America, that of Peru, has important civilian components. No other Latin American nation has undergone such a rejection of civilian leadership by military officers, no other country has an executive cabinet entirely monopolized by military officers, and in no other country is the military as an institution so completely in charge of the national government. Radical and reformist military nationalists have resolutely seized the reins of power from the old civilian political and economic establishment. Yet in fact, the military rulers need some civilian allies within their coalition in order to sustain the nationalist regime and implement its policies. Civilian technocrats in particular have been invited to participate. The military officers remain the constant in the ruling group, but it is becoming increasingly clear that the varieties of civil-military coalitions that form on different issues help keep the military in power and determine the policy responses to those issues. Indeed, Peru's recent "super-militarization" is not only very rare for Latin America, but may have inherent instabilities which will over time cause the government to resemble less and less a "pure" military regime, and more and more a military-dominated civil-military regime. For the present, however, civilian participation and influence in the regime remain concentrated in the middle levels of the executive bureaucracies and in outside economic pressure groups. Similar coalition analyses can be made of Ecuador, Bolivia, and Brazil, where the roles of various civilian groups are currently much more significant than in Peru.

Let us now look at many so-called civilian governments. Sometimes military officers occupy other cabinet posts than just the Ministry of Defense. Quite frequently military officers are heavily involved in the operation and direction of state enterprises, administrations, and government bureaucracies, as in Argentina under Illia and Brazil under Kubitschek. Not uncommonly, military officers may serve as brokers for particular civilian political groups (such as among peasants) who wish to obtain some concession from the government but are not well represented in the party structure. This is still the case in Mexico. Furthermore, the stability of most civilian rulers in Latin America has depended critically upon the active partisan support and approval of at least some military sectors. Thus, on closer inspection many so-called civilian regimes appear to be unexpectedly dependent upon some military participation in politics.

Even in cases which appear to be highly civilianized, research leads one to doubt the real extent of demilitarization. To take a leading example, Mexico is reputed to have one of the best tamed and most apolitical militaries in Latin America. Yet in fact the viability of party-government rule by the post-revolutionary civilian elites has depended critically upon partisan military support. In particular, military policing and internal security measures have provided a shield for the decades of electoral victories by the government's official party. Military officers continue to occupy some legislative and middle-level bureaucratic posts in the party and the government. At the state level, military zone commanders, as presidential appointees, are second in potential power only to the state governors, and can assume political importance in case of conflicts between the president and the governor. Moreover, the zone commanders and other military officers in the field sometimes serve as alternative routes of political articulation for discontented peasants who feel that they are being mistreated by the state's civilian officials. As a result of internal security problems, it would not be surprising if the army's residual political roles were to assume greater significance. The elucidation of these considerations is not to deny that Mexico has a highly civilianized political system by Latin American standards, but to point out that—especially in contrast to U.S. professional standards—the Mexican military continues to be engaged in a number of partisan political activities, especially at the middle level of the regime, and that the army's conduct of these roles and responsibilities has been very important for the stability and viability of the established institutions.

Indeed, the more research one does on Latin American regimes, the more it becomes apparent that, from a common-sense definitional perspective, neither of the two ideal polar types—pure military or civilian rule—is or has been particularly common in Latin America. The empirically common fact in Latin America is rule by civil-military coalitions, regardless of who formally occupies the chief executive offices. That, then, is what should be conceptualized—as itself, the "civil-military regime," and not as some mixture or the middle of some continuum based upon the civil-versus-military dichotomy.

A civil-military regime is not simply the compromise blend of a civilian regime and a military regime. Nor is it some stopping-off place between the two. Rather, the civil-military regime is a sensible type of its own—just as an authoritarian system is distinct from, and not the mixture of, a democratic and a totalitarian system.[1] Indeed, it appears that rule by civil-military coalitions through some form of civil-military regime may be the archetype for Latin America (and even other areas) under certain conditions.

This is not to deny that civil-military regimes come in many varieties. They do, usually varying according to two major processes. (1) General civilian influence typically declines as military influence increases (and vice versa). (2) Less noticed, but just as frequently however, the influence of certain civilian sectors and that of certain military sectors may rise or fall together, whether because of ideology, class, opportunity, or some other alliance factor. Both of these two general processes are defining characteristics of civil-military coalitions and regimes; and it is particularly the second common phenomenon that prevents the complete exclusion of either civilian or military elements from active political participation. Any simple civil-versus-military approach obscures the latter, with detrimental effects for the analysis of Latin American politics.

Whether government regimes appear more or less civilian, or more or less military, in nature depends upon a variety of complex questions that detail military participation in politics, possibly including:

- Do military officers occupy formal political posts?
- Do they act as policy makers rather than policy instruments?
- Do their political activities occur at higher rather than lower levels of government?
- Are military officers concerned with other than strictly military institutional issues?
- Do they control "nondecision" policy issues, with which civilians are not supposed to tamper according to the rules of the game?

---

1. This latter point is effectively treated by Juan Linz, "An Authoritarian Regime: Spain," a chapter in Erik Allardt and Yrjö Littunen, *Cleavages, Ideologies and Party Systems,* Translations of the Westermarck Society, Helsinki: The Academic Bookstore, 1964.

- Do civilian politicians treat the military as a significant political constituency affecting government stability?
- Are policy implementation and enforcement accomplished through military or paramilitary coercion?
- Is political conduct expected to conform to standards of military discipline?

The answers would tend to be generally affirmative for militarized regimes, whereas civilianized regimes would be characterized by a relative absence of these characteristics. Of course, this is a very tentative and frequently interrelated listing of possible dimensions. Nevertheless, the list illustrates the complexities of measuring military participation in politics, and of describing regime types.

This is not necessarily to argue that the terms "civilian regime" and "military regime" should be abandoned as pure imagery, for they may be too ingrained for that to happen. At least, however, they should be understood in a different light than before: as they apply to Latin America, both types are typically dependent upon civil-military coalitions and alliances, neither type occurs in a pure form, and in many cases the term "civil-military regime" may provide a more accurate intermediate image. In that sense, there has been as much continuity as change in Latin American political development over the decades. Analyses that have emphasized the cycling between civilian and military regimes tend to be overdrawn—even though there may be a long-run historical thrust in favor of thorough civilian control and military depoliticization.

Contemporary Trends in Military Participation in Politics[2]

What makes military participation in politics, and therefore civil-military coalitions, so normal? Basically, the complex answers lie both in:

(a) conditions that are internal to the militaries, and comprise a "push" toward political participation; and

---

2. This entire section draws extensively on earlier Rand work on the changing roles of the Latin American militaries in national development, including the study on Peru and Brazil excerpted in the preceding essay. Readers can also consult Luigi R. Einaudi, "U.S. Relations with the Peruvian Military," in Daniel A. Sharp, ed., *U.S. Foreign Policy and Peru,* The University of Texas Press, Austin, 1972; Alfred Stepan, *The Military in*

(b) external characteristics of the civilian political context that comprise a "pull" for political participation by the militaries.

Some of the factors that need to be taken into account are politicizing trends in (1) constitutional realities, (2) institutional developments, (3) elite orientations, and (4) critical public policy issues—for their effects on both internal military conditions and on the external political contexts.

Constitutional Realities

In the first place, strictly civilian standards of legitimacy and authority are neither constitutionally established nor widely accepted. Political actions by the militaries are constitutionally sanctioned in a majority of Latin American countries in times of assessed legitimacy crises or domestic disturbances. These well-established constitutional prerogatives contribute to both the internal and external bases for military political roles, and will certainly continue into the 1970s—and indeed until such time as legitimacy attaches only to civilian rule.

Institutional Developments

Secondly, and perhaps above all else, military participation in politics follows from weaknesses in the civilian political institutions, which often lack relative power and effectiveness.[3] As gross generalizations, the major civilian political institutions are the national parties and the federal bureaucracies. The weaknesses of so many party systems, and therefore of most legislatures, have frequently allowed institutional power (that is, political power deriving from organizational, as distinguished from personal or factional, bases) to concentrate in the federal bureaucracies. Further weaknesses in the civilian bureaucracies have enabled some institutional power to disperse into the military branch. Though of course conditions vary from country to country, marked improvements in the institutionalization and stability of political party systems do not appear to be generally likely during the 1970s, especially where

Politics, Changing Patterns in Brasil, Princeton University Press, Princeton, N.J., 1971; Richard L. Maullin, *Soldiers, Guerrillas, and Politics in Colombia, op. cit.,* and Caesar D. Sereseres, *The Impact of Military Aid to Guatemala,* Ph.D. thesis, University of California, Riverside, July 1971. Elizabeth H. Hyman, "Soldiers in Politics: New Insights on Latin American Armed Forces," *Political Science Quarterly,* Vol. LXXXVII, No. 3, September 1972, pp. 401–18, reviews recent research.

3. An illuminating analysis of the complicated concept of institutionalization is found in Samuel P. Huntington, *Political Order in Changing Societies,* Yale University Press, 1968—though he underplays the roles of the national bureaucracies in favor of political parties.

populist pressures arise. Consequently, the institutional bases of political power will generally continue to center in the federal bureaucracies, including the military branch.

The power and effectiveness of the civilian bureaucracies are likely to increase in many leading countries, as increasingly competent, technically professional, nationalist elites rise to control the middle and upper bureaucratic echelons. This will have varying institutional consequences for military participation in politics, in some cases increasing the roles, while elsewhere delimiting them, depending upon coalitions and other factors, as discussed further below. Eventual professional institutionalization of the party and bureaucratic systems would greatly reduce the "pull" on the militaries as political actors; but the struggle for institutionalization in the hands of a new generation of elites may transitionally expand the militaries' participation in both political leadership and public administration.

In addition to such external conditions, the internal dynamics of many military institutions, and especially the processes of military development, will continue to have independent politicizing effects on the officer corps. In a number of countries increasing military professionalism, centralization of staff and command functions, concern for corporate autonomy from civilian interference in military affairs, and improved military education systems are fostering elite integration and military power as well as facilitating active developmentalist orientations among the officer corps. This has been most marked in Brazil and Peru. As a result, the potential for institutional political participation has increased at the expense of factional or personal caudillistic political tendencies—particularly where military institutional capacities have strengthened more rapidly than have the civilian party and bureaucratic institutions.

Elite Orientations

Thirdly, among both civilian and military sectors changing elite orientations and coalition opportunities will continue to favor military participation in politics. At present, socioeconomic modernization, with the accompanying emergence of new urban generations and middle classes, is leading less toward a "civilianization" of politics than to a reorientation of the military toward modernizing roles in national development.

In the nineteenth century, ruling coalitions frequently consisted of civilian, military, and clerical elites associated primarily with a few landed upper-class families; and in various forms regimes based on civil-military coalitions became the established norm, with the historic rivalry between Liberals and Conservatives. In recent decades, the emergence of new elites associated with new class, generational, and institutional backgrounds has complicated coalition and institutional processes in ways that have sustained political participation by military officers. During the 1970s an uneasy balance between traditional and new elites will still probably prevail in many Caribbean, Central American, and smaller South American nations. The most viable governments will probably continue to be based on coalitions that cut across generational and class lines, and that include civilian as well as military leaders—whether the regime resembles a dictatorship or a democracy.

In the few larger and more developed Latin American nations, the 1970s will be increasingly characterized by the institutional predominance of the newer political and economic elites, especially those that favor rapid socio-economic and technological growth. Many of them also favor radical reforms. Nevertheless, the emerging reformist ascendancy will probably not be accompanied soon by a general rejection of military participation in politics.

What are some of the reasons for this? Among civilian sectors, the newer elites are competing not only with their institutional, generational, and class predecessors, but also with each other. In the ensuing struggle for power, some factions will continue to seek and use political allies among military elites; and indeed nationalistic civilian technocrats in the bureaucracies may prefer like-minded "efficient" military officers over "incompetent" party leaders as political allies in the drive for rapid national development and reform.

Within the military institutions, the newer officer groups appear to be just as politicized as their predecessors. They frequently seem to retain historic military dispositions toward anti-Communism and anti-populism, though individual officers have become notorious populists during their political careers. Moreover, though it is difficult to generalize whether younger officers are more or less anti-oligarchic, pro-democracy, pro-U.S., or pro-Marxist than their predecessors, in general the newer officers tend to favor institutional over caudillistic or factional standards of political participation, to have relatively high expectations regarding civilian performance in the parties and bureaucracies, to increasingly rely on technical criteria in the evaluation of government policies, and to advocate rapid national economic development. The overall result is not to decrease the political interests of the military elites, but rather to reorient them in the political direction of active military support for national development and reform.

National Development Problems

Finally, certain public policy problems foster a politicization of military roles in national development. Three problems that had this consequence during the 1960s are: internal security, civic action, and public administration.

Internal security and civic action missions have induced concern among officers for national development, and have facilitated the formulation of security doctrines that encourage radical or reformist political roles for the military as an institution. Likewise, domestic violence has increased the political dependence of ruling civilian elites on military allies, especially in cases where the violence was partly rooted in inter-elite competition. Moreover, government efforts to establish central control over unruly rural regions, as spearheaded by military civic action teams, often oblige civilian elites to draw military officers into the political and economic processes in those regions, partly because the military may initially be the strongest national institution there.

In public administration, the quest by reformist civilian sectors for professional and technical competence within the bureaucracies charged with resolving critical development problems may facilitate political as well as administrative reliance on military participation in countries where the military education system produces skilled officers. Likewise, nationalist military officers who perceive that the civilian bureaucratic agencies are inefficient at resolving critical development problems may resort to political activities in order to rectify the policy-making process and further national development.

These three problem areas—internal security, civic action, and public administration—will probably continue to sustain military participation in politics in a number of countries during the 1970s. However, they may be countered to some degree by newer trends, such as a subsidence in the seriousness of internal security threats; a military reorientation toward conventional external defense missions; and the gradual enlargement within the bureaucracies of competent, technically trained, civilian cadres.

Political Strategies
Because of the foregoing factors, then, it becomes natural for civilian elites (or at least significant elements of them) to include military institutions and officers in their political strategies. From a power perspective, civilian elites tend to need military officers as political allies in order to establish durable governments and exercise legitimate political force. Indeed, even elites who would prefer to exclude the military from politics may also need to attract military allies in order to counter military support for a rival civilian (or civil-military) faction, or even to prevent a military coup. Such general conditions can be expected to prevail in most of Latin America during the coming decade, thereby making it politically unrealistic to expect civilian sectors to foster the general exclusion of the military from political participation. Politicizing pressures on the military will ease when the major civilian political institutions (the parties in particular) acquire a stability and effec-

tiveness such that civilian needs and competition for military allies begin to assume lowered political significance—a development that does not seem likely during the 1970s on a hemisphere-wide basis.

Meanwhile, internal military dynamics—and especially the processes of military development as a component of national development—will also continue to foster varying political roles for the officers and the institution during the 1970s. Even any eventual revulsion among officers against military institutional domination of the political system in such countries as Argentina, Brazil, and Peru will not eliminate (though it would reduce) the internal pressures for some political participation. At least some segments of the officer corps will retain political interests, and important residual military political roles will continue, as in Mexico.

Collectively, these trends lead to two conclusions: (1) that military participation in politics is becoming increasingly institutional, as opposed to personal or factional, in nature; and (2) that, in the interests of national development, military participation in politics is increasingly oriented to modernizing "system-transformation" roles as well as historic "system-maintenance" roles. These emerging developments contrast strikingly with traditional military roles that were based on personalistic caudillismo and oriented to the preservation of the traditional status quo.

Trends in Civil-Military Coalitions

Varying civil-military coalitions and regimes will thus continue to predominate in Latin American politics during the 1970s. Narrowly civilian or highly militarized ruling coalitions will prove to be inherently unstable, and thus will either be supplanted in power or become transformed into more balanced civil-military coalitions. For example, while the Peruvian military has sought to attract civilian allies, Allende's Chilean government needed military allies, and fell when it lost them.

What general forms may civil-military relations be expected to assume during the 1970s? The four regime patterns that are identified here are: (1) the disorganized regimes; (2) the "liberal democratic" regimes; (3) the institutionalized military regimes; and (4) the "incorporative" regimes. These four patterns are distinguished primarily according to the balance or imbalance between civilian and military members of the ruling coalition (that is, an elite dimension); and according to whether the ruling coalition derives its institutional power mainly from the bureaucracy, the party system, the military, or all three institutions together (that is, an institutional dimension).

In general, the "liberal democracy" and the institutionalized military regime conform most closely to the original concepts of civilian versus military regimes, whereas the disorganized and corporate versions do not necessarily correspond to either polar type. All are essentially authoritarian in nature, though the Latin American version of "liberal democracy" is usually the least authoritarian.[4]

Disorganized Regimes

Bolivia and Guatemala currently exemplify what is here termed the disorganized civil-military regime. Moreover, since the mid-1960s the unstable Argentine governments have also resembled disorganized civil-military regimes. In such cases, elites within both the party systems and the military are highly factionalized, and neither the parties nor the militaries alone provide strong institutional bases for political rule. The result is a highly unstable political system, with considerable political power centering in personalistic oligarchies within the government bureaucracies, and with political rule subjected to fluid civil-military alliances. The needs of civilian and military factions for mutual alliance are aggravated by the fact that both elite types lack stable institutional bases of power and support. Competition for allies becomes highly active in this situation, perhaps contributing to demagogic and nationalistic political orientations. Since institutional growth is an arduous and time-consuming process, one can expect unstable politics to continue in these countries, though some stabilization of the party system is appearing in Guatemala, and military institutionalization is moderately high in Argentina. Of course, as in the comparable European example of the French Fourth Republic, government instability is reflected mainly in frequent personnel changes at the top, while general institutional conditions really remain quite unchanged and therefore stable.

"Liberal Democratic" Regimes

"Liberal democratic" regimes have recently governed in Chile, Colombia, Costa Rica, Uruguay, and Venezuela (and were earlier dominant in Peru and

---

4. These patterns represent four general ways of viewing and grouping the varieties of civil-military relations that continue to occur in practice in Latin America. They are not ideal types. Moreover, they allow for considerable fluidity in practice, since particular countries are so often characterized by different kinds of regimes at different times in their history. Furthermore, it should be noted that the rough typology is based mostly on the structure of civil-military relations, and indicates or includes very little about actual government policy orientations. Policies may and indeed do vary widely among

other countries). Though liberal democracies are highly civilianized, in Latin America they have also tended to be a type of civil-military regime. The ruling civilian (often including retired or inactive military) elites have fairly strong institutional bases in competing parties and the bureaucracy, but not necessarily in the military. Moreover, at first the military may be institutionally rather weak as a power contender (the case in Costa Rica and Uruguay) or rather weakly institutionalized as a military organization (initially the case in Colombia and Venezuela). Attempts are usually made to separate military officers from open political participation and to relegate the military institution to residual political roles. As in Colombia, attempts may also be made to exclude some civilian contenders from gaining power through the electoral process. At the same time, the civilian leaders depend upon some political support among military leaders, as a guarantee of government stability, or as a prevention against coups. With the exception of Costa Rica, in very recent years such highly civilianized regimes have not proven their stability. In several countries both the parties and the bureaucracies are having trouble coping adequately with socioeconomic development problems and with populist political pressures. This is most clearly recognized by nationalist technocrats in the bureaucracies, by skilled political leaders (including retired army officers) who see the potential for organizing populist movements, and by developmentalist military officers. Moreover, in Colombia and Venezuela mass opinion remains relatively receptive to renewed military rule; and while bureaucratic performance and party viability have faltered somewhat, military institutionalization has progressed—perhaps increasing the pressures and opportunities for an expansion of the military's roles. This has been particularly evident in Colombia, where the military has assumed a greater developmental as well as coercive role in coping with left-wing insurgency in the 1960s. Thus the liberal democratic regimes are apparently not yet offering stable long-term solutions to Latin America's problems, even though trends may favor eventual civilian dominance. This does not necessarily mean that military coups are likely in such countries. Yet it does mean at least that even liberal democratic regime forms in Latin America remain dependent upon civil-military coalitions, and that there may be limits to the extent of civilianization that is practicable without endangering regime stability.

---

the cases which pertain to each pattern, a point (discussed below) that further dilutes the utility of civilian-military dichotomies as a basis for policy. Finally, the typology emerges mainly from a consideration of politics in the leading countries in recent decades. Yet it has roots in earlier history and is also relevant for considering conditions in the smaller, less developed Latin American countries.

Institutionalized Military Regimes

Institutionalized military rule, as in Peru and Brazil (and to some extent Argentina before the return of Perón), provides a contrasting form of civil-military regime. Military elites predominate in the ruling coalition, in alliance with civilian bureaucratic elites. Indeed, the military institution is the strongest and best integrated in the political system, sharing political power with the federal bureaucracies. The political party system is disorganized as an institutional basis for effective rule—and indeed its prior disorganization, and the ineffectiveness of party elites, provided preconditions for the institutional coup.

In Brazil and Peru national development processes gave rise to advanced military institutionalization, and created both politicized military officers interested in rapid national development and civilian technocratic allies who rejected the party in favor of administrative and military politics as the rapid path to national development. In both the Brazilian and the Peruvian cases the new ruling coalition deliberately dismantled the old party system and spurned the old party elites. However, in both cases the military officers are acutely aware of their need for civilian allies.

In Brazil, civilian technocrats are included in the military's high quality educational and training programs, and moreover halting efforts are being made to reinstitutionalize civilian political participation in a new—and for now very subordinate—party system. If the military rulers and their civilian allies are eventually successful, the Brazilian regime will acquire a strong integration between new civilian and military elites, and strong party as well as bureaucratic and military institutional bases, the most favorable context for prolonged political stability, whether under continued military or subsequent civilian leadership.

In contrast, the Peruvian officers have so far paid much less attention to the development of new civilian elites. The integration of military and supportive civilian elites is much weaker. And very little is being done to restore party bases for future civilian political participation, which currently is left to focus on the bureaucracies. Any civilian-dominated successor regime might be unstable, and highly dependent upon military allies, if popular participation problems are not resolved.

According to this analysis of both the Brazilian and Peruvian cases, the institutional military regime is likely to be but a temporary approach to Latin America's development problems—yet it is an approach that may be tried in other countries when their elite and institutional conditions resemble those described here.

Incorporative Regimes

The fourth, and in many ways the most stable form of civil-military regime in Latin America may, for want of a clearer term, be called the "incorporative" regime. Alternative terms for this phenomenon include the "organic" or "integral" state. Virtually the obverse of the disorganized regime, this pattern is characterized by relatively strong elite integration among civilian and military leaders; by rather equally strong institutional bases for the ruling coalition's power in the executive bureaucracy, the party system, and the military together; and by an interlocking or corporative relationship among these three basic institutions, such that the military institution is an integral though not necessarily dominant partner of government rule. Many single-party or government-party systems best exhibit these characteristics.

Perhaps the clearest historical examples from the 1940s and 1950s are Argentina under Juan Perón. Brazil under Getúlio Vargas (despite the late addition of the party system), and Mexico since Lázaro Cárdenas. An example from a small Caribbean country is the Dominican Republic under Trujillo. The current Brazilian leadership, presiding over an institutionalized military regime that has destroyed the old liberal democratic structure, appears interested in moving toward an incorporative style of civil-military regime, by reorganizing the party system.

The nature of the corporate pattern of civil-military relations may be clarified by contrasting it to the other three patterns. Whereas disorganized civil-military regimes lack institutional bases, incorporative regimes typically have relatively strong institutional bases. Whereas liberal democratic regimes involve the military's separation from and subordination to civilian elites and institutions, incorporative regimes normally entail considerable integration between civilian and military elites, as well as extensive institutional inter-locking among the executive bureaucracy, the military, and the party system. Whereas institutional military regimes are ordinarily headed by military officers who dismantle the party system and concentrate decision making within the military, incorporative regimes often depend upon civilian or military executives who concentrate decision making in national bureau-cracies and also organize government-favored parties for mass support.

Incorporative regimes have tended to appear when the ruling coalition became dominated by a new generation of elites, often as a result of revolution or a radical succession. Once such regimes are established, further strengthening of the party system and the bureaucracy as instruments of control and development may enable the military's roles to become residual (though still important) in nature, as in Mexico. However, if civil-military elite integration diminishes, if the party base of institutional support for the ruling elites erodes, or if the bureaucracy proves incapable of managing development problems, the pressures and opportunities may increase for renewed military participation through a challenging civil-military coalition. Thus over the short run many specific incorporative regimes have become unstable and fallen, giving way to other regime patterns.

The similarity between the jargonistic term "incorporative regime" and the more traditional concept of "corporatism" is intentional. The former term is used in this paper to refer only to the relationship of the military as a functional grouping or institution to the other elites and institutions that control the government. The latter concept of corporatism, however, refers to a general approach to organizing a political system and the relations between society and government. Corporatism denotes an authoritarian, hierarchical system of political integration through functional representation: functional organizations are established to mediate between the individual and his government. As such, corporatism is commonly contrasted with social-ism/communism (in which class is the organizing principle) and liberalism (in which the individual is the organizing principle).

The historic and continuing appeal of the incorporative pattern of civil-military relations is linked to the fact that corporatism has been and will probably continue to be a strong tendency in Latin America, perhaps stronger than either liberalism or socialism.[5] Indeed, most of the examples cited above were also governments based on general principles of corporatism.

It should also be noted that socialist/communist regimes in Latin America take on some incorporative features, if only in reference to military participation in politics. This is indicated by Fidel Castro's emphasis on the revolutionary army in Cuba, and by Allende's (ultimately unsuccessful) efforts to attract military allies in Chile.

---

5. While socialist potentialities have received extensive attention in recent years, scholars and analysts have only begun to study corporative tendencies in Latin America. The best analysis to date is Howard J. Wiarda, "Toward a Framework for the Study of Political Change in the Iberic-Latin Tradition: The Corporative Model," *World Politics,* Vol. XXV, No. 2, January 1973, pp. 206–35. He writes: "The 'corporative framework' thus refers to a system in which the political culture and institutions reflect an historic hierarchical, authoritarian, and organic view of man, society, and polity. In the corpora-tive system the government controls and directs all associations and corporate bodies holding the power not only to grant or withhold juridical recognition (the *sine qua non* for the group's existence) but also access to official funds and favors without which any sector is unlikely to succeed or survive. Group 'rights,' or *fueros,* hence take precedence over individual rights; similarly, it is the 'general will' and the power of the state that prevail over particular interests. The government not only regulates all associations and corporate bodies, but also seeks to tie those that have earned their place in the existing

Toward New Civil-Military-Clerical "Oligarchies"?

Oligarchy and corporatism have constituted two main tendencies of political organization in Latin America, appearing in both more democratic and more dictatorial versions.[6] Moreover, as a related theme, it appears that the most stable civil-military regimes have involved elite coalitions that enjoyed relatively strong support in the three basic political institutions, the executive bureaucracy, the military, and the party system, plus the Catholic Church; and elite recruitment patterns that were generationally and socioeconomically similar in all institutional sectors. These tended to be features of the classic civil-military-clerical oligarchies, where they existed, and of both the old-style conservative dictatorships and the more modernizing corporativist govern-

---

system into a collaborative effort for integral national development. Obviously, the system works best where the number of interests is small and within a context of shared values, but it is not necessarily incompatible with a growing pluralism of ideologies and social forces."

Some historical roots in Spanish liberalism are also traced in Frederick B. Pike, "Making the Hispanic World Safe from Democracy: Spanish Liberals and *Hispanismo,*" *The Review of Politics,* Vol. 33, No. 3, July 1971, pp. 307–22. Additional early writings that focus more directly on contemporary and future corporatist tendencies (though other terms than corporatism may be used, such as statism, centralism, falangism, and "Mediterranean authoritarianism") include Kalman H. Silvert, "Leadership Formation and Modernization in Latin America," *Journal of International Affairs,* Columbia University, Vol. XX, No. 2, 1966, pp. 318–31; Silvert, "The Cost of Anti-Nationalism: Argentina," in Silvert, ed., *Expectant Peoples, Nationalism and Development,* Random House, New York, 1963; and Claudio Véliz, "Centralism and Nationalism in Latin America," *Foreign Affairs,* Vol. 47, No. 1, October 1968, pp. 68–83. Various Catholic and Christian Democratic writers have also expressed corporative ideals. Furthermore, continuing studies of paternalism, personalism, patronage politics, and general authority patterns may demonstrate that Latin American political culture is quite suited to corporative government.

6. Whether the so-called classic oligarchy ever ruled is disputed by Abraham F. Lowenthal, *The Dominican Republic: The Politics of Chaos,* The Brookings Institution, Washington, D.C., 1969; by James L. Payne, "The Oligarchy Muddle," *World Politics,* Vol. XX, No. 3, April 1968, pp. 439–53; and by Robert L. Gilmore, *Caudillism and Militarism in Venezuela, 1810–1910,* Ohio University Press, Athens, Ohio, 1964.

Taking into account their criticisms, the concept "oligarchy" continues to have some utility for describing Latin American political processes. As used here, the word refers broadly to relatively small, closed sets of elites who can and do concentrate political and economic power in their hands for private use, through authoritarian measures, even though they may fight among themselves. In a similar sense, the classic academic work by V.O. Key, *Southern Politics,* Alfred A. Knopf, Inc., New York, 1949, also occasionally uses the term oligarchy to describe certain historical features of U.S. state-level politics in the South.

Indeed, in general Key's analyses of various state administrations and party systems indicate that the Latin American characteristics of the disorganized, liberal democratic, and incorporativist civil-military regimes may sometimes also be strikingly present in local U.S. experiences.

ments that have appeared in more recent decades. The classic oligarchies are now relics of the past, and few countries in Latin America still can sustain old-style dictatorships.

In the years ahead we can expect the continuing formation and rise of a new generation of nationalist and technically skilled elites; this is especially attested by the recent and spreading influence of technocratic planning, research, and educational/training institutes and agencies that are found within or appended to the national bureaucracies (including the militaries), and which operate at the middle and upper-middle levels of government. As such elites gain influence in the major institutional sectors and as they seek mutually beneficial alliances, new civil-military-clerical "oligarchies" may acquire political power and adopt regime forms that will continue the trends toward corporatism. At least it is tempting to forecast this as a real possibility, one that is already reflected in some recent nationalist and Catholic writings. Such new civil-military-clerical coalitions of nationalist and technocratic elites, many of them probably drawn from recently developing middle-class sectors, would provide a modern historical counterpoint to cases of the classic oligarchies based upon traditional upper-class elites. It is too soon to tell, however, whether future corporate regimes will lean in more democratic or more authoritarian directions.

The Uniqueness of each Country's "Model"

Because conditions vary so greatly from country to country, one cannot expect uniform models of civil-military coalitions and regimes in practice. Rather, they will assume diverse, country-specific forms, though some institutional forms and general policies may be widely adaptable. Certainly, neither the historic revolutionary Mexican or Cuban models, nor the Christian-Democratic Chilean model of the 1960s have been copied elsewhere, though each was widely regarded as the hemispheric trend-setting standard of its time. Likewise, neither the recent Marxist socialist Chilean, the radical nationalist Peruvian, nor the conservative nationalist Brazilian regimes will prove to be repeatable models. National conditions are too diverse.

Compare the contrasting styles of the Peruvian and Brazilian cases, both institutionalized military regimes. From those cases, it appears that (1) the relative size and economic strength of the middle sectors, and (2) the entanglement of civil-military relations, both have a profound effect on the ruling coalitions and their policies. In Peru the middle sectors are relatively small and weak, partly because of the small industrial and manufacturing base; and moreover, the military officers have maintained a strong isolation or apartness from the civilian political elites. These conditions have facilitated the radicalism of the military government's policies—for it can proceed relatively unrestrained by moderating civilian peers.

In contrast, in Brazil manufacturing and industrial growth has produced some large and influential middle-class sectors and pressure groups (allied with new and older upper-class sectors); moreover civil-military relations have historically been quite entangled. These conditions have helped to channel government economic policies in conservative directions—though the rejection of the old civilian governing elites has resembled the radical severity of the Peruvian case.

What other countries in Latin America have civilian middle-sector conditions and civil-military entanglements—to take just those two variables—that resemble the case of either Brazil or Peru? Very few. If an institutional military coup were to take place in Colombia, for example, its characteristics would be just as unique as the others. The Colombian military has its own traditions, both internally and internationally. In addition, the Colombian export economy is less diversified and more dependent upon U.S. markets than is the Peruvian, for example. Both these conditions would probably inhibit the emulation of policies adopted elsewhere. In Ecuador or Guatemala, traditional upper-class elites remain so powerful within and without the military that more than a decade may pass before a radical nationalist military regime becomes practicable with much possibility of stability. In Bolivia, the military is so factionalized and uninstitutionalized that disorganized civil-military regimes seem inescapable. Moreover, sectors within the Argentine military that favor a "Peruvian solution" lack institutional strength and have to contend with such complex civilian economic sectors that again only an Argentina-responsive, not a Peru-emulating, regime has much probability of holding power during the 1970s.

Returning to the Brazilian case and just the two influential variables of middle-sector development and civil-military entanglement, we can see again that comparable conditions do not clearly exist in other countries, although there are some similarities in Argentina and even Mexico. Yet the differences between country conditions and regime politics are legion. In particular, in Argentina the general social structure is very different from Brazil's, labor unions exercise greater influence over economic policies, the capitalist entrepreneurial interests are weaker, and factional politics tend to take greater precedence over institutional unity within the military. Consequently, a civil-military coalition that may try to emulate the Brazilian technocratic model will encounter great resistance, and will probably not succeed in other than partial ways. Thus, once again, the complexity and diversity of national conditions and circumstances obfuscate the relevance of foreign models.

Similar comparative analyses might be made regarding the relevance of civilian regime models, such as examples of Mexico since 1940, Colombia under the National Front, and Chile under Frei and Allende. The findings would undoubtedly support the conclusion that, even though particular institutional practices and policies might be adaptable in other countries, attempts at thorough transference of one country's political model to another country will produce a quite different end result.

Concluding Observation

In essence, the foregoing discussion suggests that neither military regimes nor civilian regimes may be the wave of the future, and that the customary conceptual distinction between the two types of regimes may not provide an accurate standard for policy analysis. Instead, different kinds of civil-military coalitions and civil-military regimes will continue to be the wave of the future, as they have been in the past. In the short run, Latin American nations may appear to oscillate between more civilianized and more militarized regimes. By the late 1970s, it would not be surprising to see a return to civilian executives in those countries that now appear to be setting the current trend for military executives. Over the longer run, however, civil-military coalitions will continue to be a central feature of Latin America's institutional development.

IV. ECONOMICS

Chapter Nine

INDUSTRIALIZATION AND GROWTH [1]

Daniel M. Schydlowsky

The Basic Policy Conundrum

In the last decade, the fastest growing sector in the Latin American economies has been the industrial sector. This preeminence is likely to continue. Thus it is appropriate to think of Latin American growth as being led by industry. At the same time, Latin American industry operates to various extents with imported inputs and almost always has some imported component in its output. Thus it is appropriate to speak of industry as foreign exchange using. On the other hand, the foreign exchange producing sectors, mainly agriculture, fishing, and mining, have grown at relatively slower rates.[2] As a result, the growth of industry has been constrained by the rate of growth of the primary activities traditionally producing foreign exchange.

The disparity in the rates of growth of foreign exchange using and foreign exchange supplying sectors was sustainable for a time while industry proceeded to substitute existing imports with domestic production, thus freeing foreign exchange for the purchase of components and raw materials. Now, however, the import substitution cycle has been played out in all of the large economies of Latin America and is well on its way to being played out even in the smaller ones. As a result, the basic conundrum of growth squarely facing policy makers is this: *Either industry begins to generate its own foreign exchange earnings in order to support its high rate of growth, or the rate of growth of industry and thereby of the economy as a whole must slow down to the rate of increase permitted by the availability of foreign exchange, i.e., roughly to the rate of growth of primary production.*

Foreign aid is not a solution, for it merely postpones the problem. The greater availability of foreign exchange it provides allows a temporary increase in the rate of growth of industry, but upon repayment requires a reduction in the level of activity sufficient to permit a saving of foreign

1. Research support from the Development Advisory Service, Harvard University, for part of the underlying research is gratefully acknowledged.

2. The Peruvian fishing industry is the main exception. However, its processing component is classified as "industry" in the National Accounts.

exchange expenditure on imported inputs large enough to repay the foreign loans. Foreign private investment is of no greater help unless it is specifically in export industries. If, as has increasingly occurred, foreign investment is directed toward the new industrial sectors, it provides a very temporary relief and then immediately adds to the problem by creating new demands for various kinds of service and capital payments. Only if the inflow of foreign aid and foreign private investment grew exponentially and forever, would it be possible to regard these sources as providing a solution to the basic inconsistency of growth based on a foreign exchange using industrial sector.

It should be noticed, however, that there is no inherent reason why industry should be foreign exchange using rather than foreign exchange producing. We must therefore turn to a brief investigation of the factors which make industry foreign exchange using rather than foreign exchange producing in Latin America.

Origin of the Conundrum: Postwar Development Policy

Latin American economic development since World War II has been overshadowed by balance of payments crises. These have produced a strong import substitution drive that responded both to the desire to save foreign exchange expenditure per unit of output and thus relieve the obvious import scarcity, and to the desire to industrialize Latin American countries at the fastest possible rate in order to bring about modernity, higher employment, and a better income distribution.

In order to accomplish import substitution and industrialization, measures were adopted to restrict imports. These consisted at various places and at various times of tariffs, quotas, pre-import deposits, and foreign exchange auctions or outright allocations.

The combined effect of all these measures has been to create an exchange rate system of a particular kind, the structure of which is fairly similar throughout most of the Latin American countries. Although it is customary to think of the exchange rate as referring to the price paid for the transfer of financial assets, from an analytical standpoint it is more useful to think of an exchange rate *system,* consisting of the financial rate and of commodity exchange rates, the latter being defined as the number of units of local currency paid in the internal market for a dollar's worth at international prices of each commodity. Thus the commodity exchange rates include tariffs and other costs that are incurred by the importers when introducing imports into the country's economy, as well as export taxes or rebates paid or received by exporters.

The typical exchange rate system structure of Latin America may be illustrated by that of Argentina in 1966 which consisted essentially of seven categories of rates as follows:[3]

Rate	*Composition*	*Pesos per $*
Agricultural Export	Financial less 10% tax	200
Financial	Financial	220
Nontraditional Export	Financial + 18% tax rebate	260
Raw Material Import	Financial + 50% duties	330
Semimanufactured Import	Financial + 120% duty	460
Component Import	Financial + 175% duty	600
Finished Product Import	Financial + 220% duty	700

Cursory analysis of this rate structure points to the likelihood of some very specific consequences:

(a) Substitution of imports is likely to be very profitable because of the escalating levels of the exchange rates affecting imports of successively more complex goods. Thus the producer of finished commodities for the Argentine market would be protected since a dollar's worth of his product competes with imports that pay an exchange rate of 700, while his raw materials and inputs would cost him somewhere between 330 and 600 pesos. It might appear that this relationship holds only if imported inputs are used, but domestic suppliers are unlikely to charge prices much below the price of the imported competing goods since they, also, wish to make use of the protection available to them. Finally, wage rates also incorporate the protection given to industry and reflect an exchange rate of say 550–600 per dollar's worth of marginal product.

(b) The export of industrial goods tends to be highly unprofitable since the producer who has to pay between 330 and 600 pesos per dollar's worth of inputs only receives 260 pesos per dollar's worth of exports.

(c) An inefficiency illusion of industrial production appears in which industrialist and policy maker alike believe that domestic industry is much more high cost than in fact is the case. This illusion results from converting costs of production into dollars through division by the financial exchange

---

3. Taken from "Proyecto de Modificación de la Estructura Arancelario-Cambiaria," Cámara Argentina de Radio, Televisión, Telecomunicaciones y Afines (CARTTA), September 1966.

rate and comparison with the c.i.f. price of competing imports. Since domestic costs are based on the commodity exchange rates and these are usually considerably above the financial rate, it is not surprising that the domestic costs appear so much higher than international prices. A large part of this apparent high cost, however, is merely the result of converting local costs of production into dollars by use of an exchange rate not applicable to those costs. When domestic costs are converted by a more appropriate rate, i.e., one that is related to commodity rates, Latin American industrial costs turn out to be substantially closer to international levels than is generally believed. An indication of the size of the inefficiency illusion can be derived from the data for Brazil shown in Table 1 where for simplicity the same average industrial cost rate is used for conversion of costs in all sectors.

The exchange rate system structure and the inefficiency illusion act in a reinforcing manner. Industrialists are unable to export because of the implicit export tax in the exchange rate system. Policy makers conclude that industry is inefficient and therefore ought not be supported, certainly not for the export market. As a result, no policy is adopted to offset the implicit export tax. In consequence, industrialists continue to be unable to export, and policy makers find their conviction that industry is inefficient reinforced by the fact that industry is not exporting. At the same time, to maintain the rate of industrial growth, it becomes necessary to increase import substitution by ever high tariffs. These raise the input cost exchange rates and increase both the implicit export tax on industrial exports and the inefficiency illusion. As a result, industry is ever farther away from being able to export and policy makers, ever more convinced that industry is hopelessly inefficient, become ever more likely to refrain from adopting a suitable export promotion policy!

The Conundrum's Long Shadow:
Current Policy Problems in Its Perspective

With the structure of the basic conundrum of Latin American growth policy in mind, it is useful to examine some of the major policy concerns of Latin American governments and the policy responses that have traditionally been mooted and adopted.

(a) *Raising the growth rate:* This of course has the policy conundrum at its heart. Unless the conundrum is recognized and the industrial sector is made into a foreign exchange earning sector, it is very unlikely that the rate of growth can be substantially raised and maintained at a higher level. Current policy discussions appear to emphasize foreign private investment and foreign aid as solutions. As mentioned above, however, foreign private investment

Table 1

THE "INDUSTRIAL INEFFICIENCY ILLUSION" IN BRAZIL

Excess of Domestic Price (=cost) over International Price

Sector	At Financial Exchange Rate	At Industrial Cost Exchange Rate* and **
Nonmetallic Minerals	40%	− 5%
Metallurgy	34	−10
Machinery	34	−10
Electrical Equipment	57	6
Transport Equipment	57	6
Wood Products	23	−17
Furniture	68	13
Paper and Products	48	0
Rubber Products	78	20
Leather Products	66	12
Chemicals	34	−10
Pharmaceuticals	37	− 7
Perfumes and Soaps	94	31
Plastics	48	0
Textiles	81	22
Clothing	103	37
Food Products	27	−14
Beverages	83	24
Tobacco	78	20
Printing and Publishing	59	7

SOURCE: Joel Bergsman and Pedro Malan, "The Structure of Protection in Brazil," in Balassa and Associates, *The Structure of Protection in Developing Countries,* Johns Hopkins Press, 1971, ch. 6, Table 6.6 and 6.8.

*Derived as follows: rate for intermediate products	1.49
rate for wages	1.48
	1.48

**A negative sign indicates domestic price is below international price.

and aid will both help only if they are used to raise the level of exports. If foreign private investment is in the industrial sector and foreign exchange using as well, then it merely aggravates the problem. Indeed, to the extent that such investment produces "new" goods which shift the demand pattern of domestic consumption and investment towards more import intensive goods, the effect will be even more harmful.[4]

Foreign aid used for infrastructure (i.e., local currency expenditure) will produce a temporary cushion; upon presentation of the bill for repayment, however, severe balance of payments problems may ensue and either the rate of growth of the economy has to be reduced, a recession has to be induced, or the debt has to be rolled over. In no case has a permanent solution been achieved.

(b) *Employment:* Three possible routes to raising the level of employment exist:

(1) Increasing the growth of capital stock with a constant capital labor ratio.

This alternative runs into the same problem as raising the growth rate since that is precisely all that it involves.

(2) Better use of existing capital formation through investment in more labor intensive industries, i.e., change in the capital labor ratio.

This alternative holds more promise of not being totally inhibited by the basic policy conundrum, but it should be noted that it is not at all certain that labor intensive technologies are also import saving. Indeed, it may well be that the opposite occurs (e.g., higher raw material wastage) in which case greater labor intensity would mean an aggravation of the growth problem.

(3) More intensive use of the capital stock.

While the underutilization of labor has been recognized in Latin America for a long time, evidence is only gradually accumulating on the underutilization of capital. Not only do many of the Latin American economies periodically use installed productive capacity at levels below their own customary norm, but the norm itself is based on utilization of capital at less than 24 hours a day, 365 days a year, less maintenance. While detailed information on the amount of shift work is unavailable, it appears that multiple shifting takes place primarily in the process-centered industries in which 24-hour operation is required for technical reasons. In Colombia, available data show that capital is used at about 50 percent of 24-hour capacity on the average. Available data from Argentina show deviations from the usual norm of utilization to have fluctuated between 55 percent and 67 percent of this norm on average. The details for each sector of data are shown in Table 2.

---

4. The contribution of shifts in consumption patterns to the aggravation of the conundrum is discussed in David Felix, "The Dilemma of Import Substitution—Argentina," in G. F. Papanak, ed., *Development Policy: Theory and Practice,* Harvard University Press, Cambridge, Mass., 1968.

Table 2

ARGENTINA: UTILIZATION OF INSTALLED CAPACITY

Sector	Percentage of Actual Output with Respect to Maximum Output			
	1961	1963	1964	1965
Food and Beverages	48.8	53.2	48.9	51.5
Tobacco	82.7	81.9	88.6	91.2
Textiles	83.2	59.2	68.9	77.1
Clothing	88.3	64.2	72.5	78.4
Wood	72.7	48.6	55.2	70.4
Paper and Cardboard	55.1	48.3	52.7	62.4
Printing and Publishing	73.3	58.3	62.4	70.8
Chemicals	73.4	59.9	68.1	73.8
Petroleum Derivatives	87.9	78.2	84.7	83.6
Rubber	80.5	54.0	66.2	77.6
Leather	84.2	66.8	77.8	79.9
Stones, Glass, and Ceramics	70.2	59.0	68.7	71.8
Metals, excluding Machinery	59.4	40.8	50.3	66.6
Vehicles and Machinery (excluding Electrical Equipment)	78.6	44.6	56.5	65.6
Electrical Machines and Equipment	59.2	43.5	47.6	61.0
Weighted Average	67.2	54.6	59.5	66.1

SOURCE: CONADE, Results of the Survey on Production and Investment Expectations of Industrial Enterprises (Buenos Aires: CONADE, March 1965), Table 3.

Whereas it is plausible to believe that private decision makers maximize profit when they design the size of their factories in such a way as to leave capital idle a large proportion of the day, it is difficult to believe that such a situation is optimal from society's point of view. Indeed, systematic distortions in the price of capital goods as well as in the wage rate, in the allocation of credit, and in the tax system, make it plausible to believe that decisions which, when calculated at private prices, lead to profit maximization through numerous plants operating at one shift, would lead, if calculated at shadow prices, to multiple shifting with fewer plants.[5]

Tackling this problem, however, requires coming to grips with the basic conundrum itself. Expanding utilization of capacity implies expanding the level of industrial output which in turn means larger imports of industrial inputs. Thus a higher level of employment through improved utilization of capacity is possible only if the availability of foreign exchange increases. The most plausible source of such an increase would be the export of some of the product arising from the increased utilization of capacity. Making industry foreign exchange generating, however, would require solving the basic policy conundrum! We are back where we started.

(c) *Price stabilization:* Whatever their origin, Latin American inflations, once under way, are sustained by a mix of demand pull and cost push factors. Budget deficits are usually considered the main demand pull factor, whereas wage increases are usually pointed to as the primary cost push factor. A third equally important factor is usually not mentioned. This is the cost push arising from changes in the exchange rate which has as pervasive an effect as a wage increase.[6] With government expenditure linked to some extent to the price level through the purchase of services, and government revenue linked in many cases very closely to the balance of payments, it is not surprising that there should be very complex interactions between the three major elements maintaining inflation at high rates.

Stabilization will thus be successful only if action can be taken concurrently on fiscal deficit, wage increases, and balance of payments. If only the first two are controlled, the balance of payments problem will eventually cause the failure of the stabilization program. Such a situation is almost certain to arise as long as industry continues to be primarily foreign exchange using. Under such circumstances, the balance of payments adjustment process relies almost exclusively on the income effect, with relative price changes between traded and untraded goods having minor influences. As a result, any unexpected short fall of foreign exchange availabilities has to be dealt with through a rundown of reserves and/or a reduction in the level of economic activity. Should a short fall of foreign exchange earnings coincide with the stabilization effort, the strain of a domestic recession is likely to tear apart

5. For a more complete discussion, cf. D. M. Schydlowsky, "Fiscal Policy for Full Capacity Industrial Growth in Latin America," presented at the 21st Annual Latin American Conference, University of Florida, February 1971, Center for International Affairs, Economic Development Report No. 201, Harvard University, 1971.

6. Cf. M. Diamand, "Seis Falsos Dilemas en el Debate Económico Nacional," pp. 22–26.

the coalition keeping wages and prices to the lower rates of increase, and thereby undo the stabilization effort. On the other hand, the carrot of higher levels of activity, if only unions and employers will cooperate in keeping the wage-price line, is also hindered in its effectiveness by the basic policy conundrum, since higher levels of utilization are constrained by the foreign exchange situation. If the rate of growth is pushed to a point where devaluation becomes necessary, the higher exchange rate will by itself cause price repercussions which will undo the stabilization effort. It thus appears that the peculiarly rigid balance of payments adjustment mechanisms of the Latin American economies are one of the significant impediments to successful price stabilization.

(d) *Distribution:* Changes in the regional, personal, and public versus private distribution of income are an increasingly important policy goal for Latin American governments. In addition to the greater difficulty of achieving such readjustments under the conditions of relatively slow growth forced upon the economy by the continuation of the basic conundrum, there are some direct connections between the sources and uses of foreign exchange and the possibility of executing a successful redistribution policy. One major connection runs from the exchange rate of export prices to the income of exporters as compared to urban laborers. This is most obviously the case if wage goods are also the country's primary export products. If the exchange rate goes up, agricultural producers get higher incomes and the cost of living rises. If agriculture is in the hands of large landowners, this will mean a negative redistribution of income, although it may at the same time be a necessary adjustment in the incentives to provide foreign exchange. Thus distributional policy clashes directly with balance of payments policy. If industrial exports existed, balance of payments policy could accommodate a lower increase in prices for farmers by generating foreign exchange from industry instead of agriculture.

On the other hand, a reorganization of land tenure, or the institutionalization of worker participation in management of mines or indeed of government participation in mining or in the merchandising of export products may lead for a time at least to some disorganization, lower productivity, and lower value of exports, thus causing contraction in the rest of the economy and producing reductions in everybody's income rather than redistributions. Were industry foreign exchange producing rather than foreign exchange using, adjustments of an organizational nature in the primary sectors would be much more bearable since the economy would be able to compensate a short fall of earnings from these sectors through an increased amount of industrial exporting.

Solving the Conundrum:
Some Policy Alternatives

The solution to the conundrum lies, as might by now be expected, in the conversion of the industrial sectors of Latin America from foreign exchange users to foreign exchange generators. Such a conversion would require at the very least the elimination of the anti-export bias in the exchange rate system.

The most obvious remedy that comes to mind is devaluation. It should be noted, however, that a simple devaluation will not be effective in removing the anti-export bias. There are several reasons. The first is that upon a modification of the financial exchange rate, the whole exchange rate system will change proportionately, since the commodity rates are usually linked to the financial rate through the system of trade taxation. Secondly, given the size of the anti-export bias, the overt devaluation necessary to make at least some industrial products price competitive would be of such a magnitude (50 percent or more) as to make it very unlikely that substantial cost and wage push reactions would fail to appear. Thus, a very major part of the devaluation would be purely nominal, with the real devaluation being a fraction of the change in the financial exchange rate, perhaps less than a third.[7] In turn, however, such an erosion of the effect of devaluation implies that the initial devaluation should be even higher in order to take the erosion into account. The repercussions of a higher devaluation are likely to be even more considerable and thus the initial devaluation would have to be higher still. The process may well be convergent at some point but surely at a rate of devaluation and concomitant inflation that would be politically unacceptable, without in any case being very effective in generating industrial exports.

A much more appropriate remedy is the use of a compensated devaluation in which simultaneous and offsetting adjustments are undertaken in the financial exchange rate and in the trade restrictions such that all the commodity exchange rates for imports and traditional exports stay unchanged, the only net change taking place in the financial rate and in the nontraditional export rate. The result is the equivalent of a subsidy for nontraditional exports.[8] An example can be given using the Argentine exchange rate system cited earlier:[9]

---

7. For an attempt to quantify the domestic cost repercussions of a devaluation, cf. B. Cohen, "Measuring the Short Run Impact of a Country's Import Restrictions on its Exports," *Quarterly Journal of Economics*, Vol. 80, August 1966.

8. For a more complete discussion, cf. D. M. Schydlowsky, "From Import-Substitution to Export Promotion for Semi-Grown-Up Industries: A Policy Proposal," *Journal of Development Studies*, July 1967.

9. Taken from CARTTA, *op. cit.*

Pre-Compensated Devaluation				Post-Compensated Devaluation		
Total	Tax/Subsidy	Basic	Rate	Basic	Tax/Subsidy	Total
200	−10%	220	Agricultural Exports	330	−40%	200
220	0	220	Financial	330	0	330
260	+18%	220	Non-Traditional Exports	330	+18%	390
330	+50%	220	Raw Material Imports	330	0	330
460	+120%	220	Semi-Manufactured Imports	330	+47%	460
600	+175%	220	Component Imports	330	+80%	600
700	+220%	220	Finished Product Imports	330	+115%	700

Inspection will show that with this compensated devaluation, the exchange rate for nontraditional exports has had a real increase of 50 percent in comparison with the remainder of the rates. It is now much closer to the industrial cost rates, and indeed exceeds the raw material import rate. Under conditions of increasing returns to scale and marginal cost pricing for exports, the structure emerging after a compensated devaluation of the kind given in the example may be sufficient to make a number of industries competitive. At the same time, it is worth noting that the cost push effects of this kind of devaluation are minimal since the prices of most import competing goods will have stayed unchanged.

A second alternative with similar effects is the institution of tax rebates on export sales. Such a measure, which might take the form of a percentage on the f.o.b. value of exports, directly affects the commodity exchange rate for nontraditional exports and thereby eliminates the preexisting bias. Whereas the administrative simplicity of such tax refund schemes generally is regarded as a recommendation, it is also widely believed that they are very costly for the exchequer. Such an objection is not necessarily valid, however. A tax rebate on exports, once enacted, will only generate fiscal expenditure if exports in fact take place under its provisions. Such exports would at the same time, however, imply additional economic activity which in itself and through the foreign trade multiplier would generate a substantial increase in the tax base. This increase in the base would in turn generate additional revenue for the exchequer. The new revenue would serve to cover in whole or in part the rebate necessary to generate the exports in the first place. Thus through a combined foreign trade and fiscal multiplier, the export rebate generates its own (partial or total) financing. Under prevailing Latin American conditions in which the import propensities are rather low, foreign trade tax multipliers tend to be high and as a result fairly large export rebates can be supported by the revenue generated in this form, particularly if they are paid only to new exports.[10] In essence, what is at issue is the use of a full capacity utilization budget to estimate the fiscal impact of export rebates.[11]

In addition to price competitiveness, the existence of marketing channels must be assured for industry to become rapidly foreign exchange generating. Whereas it is probable that the existence of price competitiveness alone will gradually bring about the establishment of marketing channels, it is worth considering briefly what government policy can do to hasten the process. It is useful in this context to divide potential export commodities into two kinds: (a) standardized commodities, and (b) differentiated commodities. Into the first group fall items such as steel and chemicals which are sold on a specification basis and which have a highly competitive international market. In these, the marketing problem is relatively simple. Any preexisting import house can become an export house and sell standardized commodities on the world market simply by having an attractive quotation. Price is everything, as quality is easily determined and there are standard rebates for quality differences. In the marketing of nonstandardized commodities, whose quality is hard to measure, and where brand names or user preferences are important elements, the multinational enterprise offers a unique potential, because of its own substantial internal markets and because of its ability to monitor and guarantee quality and performance worldwide. Thus an important element in government policy to develop export markets must consist of the induce-

---

10. For an estimation model and estimates for Argentina, cf. D. M. Schydlowsky, "Short Run Employment Policy in Semi-Industrialized Economies," *Economic Development and Cultural Change,* April 1971.

11. This full capacity budget is analogous to the full employment budget introduced recently in the United States. However, whereas in the U.S. version the issue is the spending (reduction) of government revenue to generate domestic activity and additional domestic employment which will in turn then finance government expenditure, in Latin America we are faced with a situation in which it is the use of public funds for the creation of exports which generates a higher level of economic activity and in consequence an increase in revenue.

ment, by carrot and/or stick, for multinational enterprises to become active users of Latin American industrial goods in the rest of their multinational enterprise system.

The Solution of the Conundrum: Will It Occur?

Before policies to solve the conundrum can be adopted, the conundrum itself must first be recognized. Such recognition, in turn, implies the abandonment of the partial truths on which most economic policy has been based in the postwar period.[12]

Continent-wide, the omens are good. The prestigious Raúl Prebisch has issued a manifesto pointing to export promotion as a new road towards success, superseding import substitution. Several nations have adopted a crawling peg to prevent periodic overvaluation of their currencies; a few (Brazil and to a lesser extent Colombia) have been vigorously promoting their exports and have met with considerable success.

At the same time, old and deeply held convictions still hold sway in most policy makers' minds. The notion that Latin American industry is inefficient, bolstered by the simple and erroneous calculation underlying the inefficiency illusion, is so widely held that the adoption of a strong industrial export promotion policy is frequently regarded as a subsidization of inefficient and undesirable industry rather than as the elimination of a discriminatory tax which produces biases in the industrial development pattern, underutilization of industrial capacity and lower rates of income, employment, and growth.

The prevalence of outmoded dogma notwithstanding, the prospects for adoption of a more outward-looking policy which is likely to include the promotion of industrial exports is, on the whole, good. Brazil already uses strong tax incentives as well as direct bargaining with potential exporters, especially multinational enterprises. Argentina's next technically conducted stabilization is likely to include a strong export plank. Such a modification in Argentine policy is likely because this is precisely where the Krieger effort failed, and because of the increasing strength of that part of the technical opinion inside the country which has recognized the conundrum and is pushing for its solution. Chile cannot fail to follow the same road after the 1971 experience in which six months of high-level industrial activity was

---

12. For a very interesting discussion of the process involved, cf. M. Diamand, "Seis Falsos Dilemas. . . ." pp. 50–63.

sufficient to totally exhaust the country's reserves. Whatever tendency predominates in the conduct of economic affairs in Chile, the need to find new sources of foreign exchange will be an overwhelming and inescapable reality. Among the Andean Group countries as a whole, pressure for harmonization and the push to heavy and capital intensive industrialization will make it increasingly necessary to look to the industrial export market for both adequate scaling of plant and for providing the foreign exchange to pay for the imported inputs needed to run the new plants.[13] In addition, Colombia's membership in the Group will eventually force the other members to adopt an export policy including features similar to those incorporated in Colombia's promotion of nontraditional exports. Venezuela and Central America are likely to lag behind this development since considerable import substitution still seems to be feasible in these countries. Mexico, for its part, is likely to continue basing its growth on a pragmatic mix of capital imports, increased tourism, and increased exports. It is likely that the Mexicans will achieve an increase in the foreign exchange generating potential of industry in the same way as they have begun the process of conversion, namely through a process of negotiation on a case by case basis without an overt modification of the exchange rate system.

If the Latin American countries do indeed pursue an active export promotion policy in an attempt to solve their basic policy conundrum, access to the markets of the industrialized countries will become of crucial importance to them. The slogan "trade not aid" may thus be increasingly brandished by Latin Americans as a key to their foreign economic relations and development prospects.

Conclusion

The basic conundrum of Latin American economic growth arises out of the foreign exchange using nature of its industry. Unless the industrial sector becomes foreign exchange producing, it can no longer function as the leading sector and act as the engine of growth for the whole economy.

The foreign exchange using nature of industry is largely the result of policy. Prevailing exchange rate systems are structured in such a way as to implicitly tax industrial exports, thereby creating at the same time an illusion of industrial inefficiency which further inhibits exports.

---

13. The increase in Ecuador's oil revenue may prove a delaying factor, and the same may occur if Peru's recent finds are of as significant size as they now appear to be.

The conundrum drastically limits the possibility of success in attaining the major policy targets: increased growth, increased employment, greater price stability, and more equitable distribution.

Whereas conventional devaluation is inappropriate to deal with the conundrum, either a compensated devaluation or export rebates are likely to be effective.

Policy makers are likely to increasingly recognize the conundrum and adopt export promoting policies. Such a change in policy will bring the trade restrictions of the industrialized countries into the center of the stage, and make trade, not aid, the fulcrum of international economic debate.

Chapter Ten

EVALUATING DIRECT FOREIGN INVESTMENT IN LATIN AMERICA

Shane J. Hunt

Social and political attitudes toward foreign participation in Latin American economies are changing fast. Since these attitudes are the foundation from which government policy is made, policies are also changing, although with a lag. This essay addresses the challenge that faces every Latin American country in reassessing its policies regarding direct foreign investment. The first part reviews techniques for assessing the costs and benefits of foreign investments, discussing both arguments that are customarily given, and arguments that ought to be given. It begins with evaluation techniques that take a narrowly economic focus, and continues by broadening out to cover externalities and psychic costs not easily handled with the economist's tools. The final section of the essay hazards some judgments as to how evaluations will be made by the Latin American countries in coming years.

Economic Evaluation of Foreign Investment

The simplest view of foreign investment comes from traditional neoclassical analysis, which treats of only two factors of production—labor and capital—and views foreign investment as an addition to the capital stock in the domestic economic system. If we assume the conditions dearest to the heart of the economic theorist, that markets are competitive and changes are marginal, then an increment to foreign-owned capital causes gross domestic product to increase, but that increase is the marginal product of newly introduced foreign investment and is paid to the foreign owners of the investment. Therefore, factor payments to nationals—GNP—remain what they had been previously.[1]

---

1. This conclusion is overturned if the increment to foreign capital is so large that payments to capital are driven down and payments to labor raised throughout the economy. If some portion of the preexisting capital stock was foreign-owned, then

145

The assumptions necessary for arriving at this negative conclusion regarding the contributions of foreign investment are obviously highly restrictive, so much so that the result cannot be considered to represent a real world situation. Nevertheless, this approach performs the only function that should be expected of models of perfect competition: to make us rethink assumptions and not take conventional wisdom for granted. In the case of foreign investment, conventional wisdom suggests that it is a Good Thing, because foreign investment brings jobs and progress. It is perhaps more valid to start from the conventional wisdom of perfect competition, which says that foreign investment will take away from a country as much as it contributes to domestic output.

The conventional wisdom of perfect competition should also remind us that foreign investment is more favorable to the recipient country if capital can be obtained at rental rates below the marginal product of capital in the domestic economy, e.g., through bond financing or bank borrowing at fixed interest rates, or through levying taxes on the foreign company's profits in a situation where the tax cannot be shifted. Also, the gain to the domestic economy is all the greater if wage payments by foreign firms are above the domestic opportunity cost of labor.

The Focus on Balance of Payments

In recent years the purely economic evaluation of foreign investment has been conducted not by comparing increments to output with payments to foreigners, but rather by focusing exclusively on balance of payments effects. The thrust of the argument is by now well known. It has appeared in a variety of published articles and speeches, including the statement made by Chile's Minister of Foreign Affairs, Gabriel Valdez, upon presenting the Consensus of Viña del Mar to President Nixon.[2] It generally focuses on three items in the

---

payments to local labor are raised partly at the expense of preexisting foreign capital, and GNP rises. GNP also rises by a "welfare triangle" equal to one-half the change in marginal product of capital times the increment of foreign capital. These points are elaborated in G. D. A. McDougall, "The Benefits and Costs of Private Investment," in American Economic Association, *Readings in International Economics*, Irwin, Homewood, Ill., 1968, pp. 172–94. A similar analysis has been applied to emigration of labor—the brain drain. See R. Albert Berry and Ronald Soligo, "Some Welfare Aspects of International Migration," *Journal of Political Economy*, September/October 1969.

2. "Private investments have meant, and mean today for Latin America, that the amounts that leave our continent are many times higher than those that are invested in it. Our potential capital is diminishing while the profits of the invested capital grow and

balance of payments: long-term capital inflow, long-term capital outflow through amortization and repayment of indebtedness, and outflow of profits and interest payments from Latin America to the rest of the world. For nearly any time period chosen, the result is the same: outflows exceed inflows. The mild criticism of this situation holds that foreign investment has contributed nothing to the Latin American economies. The more severe interpretation states that foreign investment has "decapitalized" those same economies.

This statistical argument is, however, almost devoid of interpretative significance. Any given investment, by the time it is fully amortized, will return an outflow greater than its original inflow even if it pays the foreign investor only one percent annually on invested capital, and yet such a return could hardly be considered excessive. In fact, a net inflow favorable to the Latin American balance of payments would create its own problems, as it would indicate increasing foreign influence and greater Latin American economic dependence.

This approach to balance of payments analysis contains a glaring omission in its failure to consider foreign investment effects on the merchandise account. Foreign investment earns dollars by producing exports and saves dollars by producing import substitutes, so its net balance of payments effect must include these contributions as well. The case of import substitutes presents severe measurement difficulties, however, both because domestically produced goods are never perfect substitutes for similar imports, and because the quantity of imported intermediate product required to sustain domestic production can be estimated only through the statistical imperfections of an input-output table. Different assumptions on these matters lead to drastically different results.[3] The most recent study of this nature, done by Herbert May

multiply at an enormous rate, not in our countries but abroad." Partially quoted in *The New York Times*, June 12, 1969, p. 1. Other references to this argument include Teotonio dos Santos, "Foreign Investment and the Large Enterprise in Latin America: The Brazilian Case," in James Petras and Maurice Zeitlin, eds., *Latin America: Reform or Revolution?*, Fawcett Publications, Greenwich, Conn., 1968, pp. 441–42; Keith B. Griffin, *Underdevelopment in Spanish America*, Allen and Unwin, Ltd., London, 1969, pp. 145–47.

3. A U. S. Treasury Department study analyzed the consequences of two assumptions: (1) domestic production generated by new foreign investment replaces an equal amount of imports, and (2) that same production replaces a purely local source of supply. In the first case, the net balance of payments effects are strongly positive, in the second strongly negative. See G. C. Hufbauer and F. M. Adler, *Overseas Manufacturing Investment and the Balance of Payments*, Washington, 1968, pp. 6, 60, 62, 64. For summary and discussion of the Hufbauer-Adler results, see Raymond Vernon, *Sovereignty at Bay. The Multinational Spread of U.S. Enterprises*, Basic Books, Inc., New York, 1971, pp. 163–78. Theoretical issues are touched on in the literature on domestic

under the sponsorship of the Council of the Americas, assumed replacement of an equal physical amount of imports, but also assumed the c.i.f. value of replaced imports to be only two-thirds of domestic manufacturers' sales.[4] These assumptions lead to the conclusion that the most important balance of payments effects are accomplished through the merchandise account, and that direct foreign investment makes a strongly positive contribution to the Latin American balance of payments.

This exclusive focus on the balance of payments could lead us to the unsettling conclusion that a dollar's worth of exports, for which domestic factors of production must be used, is as valuable in a country as a dollar's worth of capital inflow or a dollar received as a gift. But the curious truth of the matter is that hardly anybody is interested in pure balance of payments effects anyway. When Latin American critics of direct foreign investment complain that foreigners have invested X over a given time period and taken out 2X, their fundamental concern, I think, has been with the rate of profit earned by foreign investment, a concern that such profit is in some sense excessive. Not having access to profit statistics, they have couched their arguments in terms of the balance of payments, and poorly at that, doing a disservice to themselves as well as to their readers.[5] Herbert May and the Council of the Americas have picked up the argument and hoisted Latin American critics on their own petard. It would, however, be equally fallacious to argue that favorable balance of payments effects produced by direct foreign investment imply that such investment has been beneficial and desirable. May's report should help put a permanent stop to arguments couched in terms of the balance of payments, and oblige us to turn directly to the overriding concern: excess profits.[6]

---

resource cost of foreign exchange earnings. See, for example, Bela Balassa and Daniel Schydlowsky, "Effective Tariffs, Domestic Cost of Foreign Exchange, and the Equilibrium Exchange Rate," *Journal of Political Economy*, May–June 1968, pp. 348–60.

4. Herbert K. May, "The Effects of United States and Other Foreign Investment in Latin America," Council of the Americas, New York, January 1970, esp. pp. 12–13.

5. "Foreign capital retains control over the most dynamic sectors of the economy and repatriates a high volume of profit; consequently, capital accounts are highly unfavorable to dependent countries." Teotonio dos Santos, "The Structure of Dependence," *American Economic Review*, May 1970, p. 233. In some cases, however, balance of payments effects are so lopsided as to give good indication of excess profits. For example, repatriated profits of foreign nitrate companies are said to have reached fully 7 percent of Chile's gross domestic product during 1880–1930, yet the foreign capital inflow induced by the nitrate boom was insignificantly small, the major foreign entrepreneurs having borrowed Chilean funds through local banks. See Markos Mamalakis, "The Role of Government in the Resource Transfer and Resource Allocation Process: The Chilean Nitrate Sector, 1880–1930," in Gustav Ranis, ed., *Government and Economic Development*, Yale University Press, New Haven, 1971, esp. p. 195.

6. May, *op. cit.*, p. 20.

The Concern Over Excess Profits

Critics of direct foreign investment have stayed away from the study of profit rates because reported profit rates are low and seem reasonable. For example, the battery of numbers reprinted in Magdoff's *Age of Imperialism* draws heavily on data of the U.S. Department of Commerce, yet not once does it make reference to Commerce data on profit rates.[7] Nevertheless, Commerce data are the standard source, virtually the only source, for this crucial statistic. They show U.S. earnings in manufacturing in Latin America to have averaged 10.7 percent of capital invested during 1960–1970.[8] This figure is higher than the 8.8 percent earned by investments in Canada during the same period, but lower than the 12.8 percent earned in Europe. All these figures are very similar, however, and not different from the average return of 11.0 percent reported on domestic operations in the United States.[9] From the viewpoint of Latin America, a region accustomed to high interest rates even when inflation is not proceeding apace, these rates must appear low and reasonable, certainly not a source of exploitation.

In the last few years, however, we have come to realize how totally unreliable these Commerce Department figures are. Not because the reporting companies lie; it is fairly well accepted that multiple sets of books are too confusing and dangerous for a large company to maintain. To be sure, suspicions have existed for some time that profits have been transferred out of Latin American countries by arbitrary overpricing of technical services and royalties sold by the U.S. parent to its Latin American subsidiary. But in the absence of solid data the magnitude of such transfers has remained unknown, and *faute de mieux* Commerce data have retained their respectability.

This respectability has been jolted by revelations in Colombia, where the government put the following problem to its economic planners: Why did American companies operating in Colombia report such low profits, the Colombian government asked, when at the same time they seemed so intent upon expanding their Colombian operations? The problem devolved upon Constantine Vaitsos, who undertook a massive task of data collection that obliged him to examine a large sample of economic transactions between

---

7. Harry Magdoff, *The Age of Imperialism: The Economics of U.S. Foreign Policy*, Monthly Review Press, New York, 1969.

8. U.S. Department of Commerce, *Survey of Current Business*, various issues, esp. 1971, pp. 28–29.

9. U.S. Federal Trade Commission and Securities and Exchange Commission, *Quarterly Financial Report for Manufacturing Corporations*, various issues. Figure shown is profits after Federal taxes expressed as percent of shareholders' equity. Corresponding figure before taxes for 1960–1970 is 19.0 percent.

foreign parent companies and their Colombian subsidiaries. This included not only royalty payments and technical assistance consultations, but also valuations of raw materials and semi-finished products purchased from the parent and imported into Colombia for final processing.[10] For each such purchased input, Vaitsos compared the transfer price charged by parent to subsidiary with world market prices for precisely the same commodity. The table below shows the results.[11]

Profit Rates of Foreign Companies in Colombia (1968)

Industry	Average Rate of Overpricing	Declared Profits	Effective Profits
Pharmaceutical	155.0%	6.7%	79.1%
Rubber	40.0%	16.0%	43.0%
Chemical	25.5%	n.a.	n.a.
Electronics	16 to 66%	n.a.	n.a.

In the pharmaceutical industry, for example, a chemical input selling for $100 on the world market was, on the average, sold by parent to Colombian subsidiary for $255. Systematic overpricing of this sort served as a convenient means for removing undeclared profits from Colombia. In the most extreme case, foreign firms in the pharmaceutical industry declared annual profits of 6.7 percent on the value of invested capital, but their total effective return turned out in fact to be 79.1 percent per year. Some 80 percent of the extra profits accrued through ˈoverpriced inputs. Royalties and consultant fees turned out to be substantially less important.

Vaitsos's results are a dramatic consequence of an increasingly widespread phenomenon: A large portion of world trade today is conducted between various branches of the same multinational corporation, and pricing assigned to such trade is totally arbitrary, serving merely to shift profits about and permit them to be realized in any country of the corporation's choosing.

---

10. Constantine Vaitsos, "Transfer of Resources and Preservation of Monopoly Rents," Economic Development Report No. 168, Development Advisory Service, Harvard University, 1970 (mimeo), Appendix No. 2.

11. *Ibid.*, pp. 34, 59–62, as corrected by personal communication. Figures for electronics give the range of overpricing discovered. Weighted average could not be calculated due to absence of data on import volumes. Effective profits expressed as percent of net worth, with capital valued in constant dollars. Two electronics subsidiaries that declared profits of minus 18 percent and plus 11.4 percent were estimated to have earned effective profits of 7 percent and 50–80 percent respectively.

Generally profits shifted out of one country reduce tax liabilities there only to increase liabilities in some other country; thus tax gains from such transfers should be negligible.[12] However, high profits may be shifted out of Latin American countries to evade regulations concerning profits remissions as well as to avoid the political embarrassment of showing that certain foreign companies are making a killing.

It is difficult and dangerous to generalize from the Vaitsos results alone. The pharmaceutical industry is notorious in the United States as well as in other countries for its high profits and deceptive competitive practices. Nevertheless, there are other pieces of evidence available, each one amounting to little more than casual empiricism, but accumulated they substantiate the impression of high profit rates. For example, regarding payback periods required by investors in Latin America, I have heard the following figures quoted, mostly by businessmen: for automobile factories, two and one-half years; for a major durable goods producer, three years; for American clients of a major U.S. bank, three and one-half years. These payback periods imply that required annual gross profits, including depreciation, are 40 percent, 33.3 percent, and 28.6 percent of invested capital respectively. If we assume that the length of life for invested fixed capital averages 20 years, then annual depreciation would amount to 5 percent of the original investment, and the gross profit estimates should be reduced by five percentage points to arrive at estimates of net profit rates. Another similar estimate comes from a Rand Corporation study of Colombia, which estimates the profit rate on investment in the modern manufacturing sector, including both Colombian and foreign companies, to be at least 30 percent and probably as much as 40 percent per year.[13]

Other pieces of evidence suggest substantially lower profit rates, however. A survey of 41 locally owned firms in five Latin American countries concluded that after-tax net profits averaged 12.4 percent during 1958–1962, with Argentina producing the highest return (18.3 percent), Chile the lowest (8.7 percent), and Colombia a modest 10.5 percent.[14] Another questionnaire survey of 90 U.S. firms found that their expected return on Latin American

---

12. If the parent company has managed complete avoidance of tax liability through depletion allowances or other means, such shifts could result in substantially reduced tax payments.

13. Richard Nelson, T. Paul Schultz, and Robert Slighton, *Structural Change in a Developing Economy*, Princeton University Press, Princeton, N.J., 1971, p. 82 n.

14. Frank Brandenburg, *The Development of Latin American Private Enterprise*, National Planning Association Pamphlet, No. 121, Washington, May 1964, pp. 36–38.

investment averaged about 19 percent.[15] These expected returns undoubtedly fail to include parent company profits obtained through transfer pricing,
but on this point as well we should generalize from the Colombian results
only with great caution. To be sure, similar overpricing phenomena are being
revealed in other parts of the Andean Group, including Chile, Peru, and
Ecuador.[16] However, studies of Australia and New Zealand found great
variation between transfer prices and world market prices, but no systematic
tendency for transfer prices to be higher.[17] Moreover, in the case of mineral
petroleum sales by subsidiaries to parent, the tendency seems to go in the
opposite direction, with transfer prices raised above world market prices, thus
shifting profits *toward* the less developed country. Thus companies may
register higher depletion allowances against tax liabilities in the United
States.[18]

In the age of the multinational corporation, the calculation of country
specific profit rates presents difficulties for the corporation itself. It also
presents a statistical challenge that the U.S. Department of Commerce has
failed to meet, at least up to the present. Furthermore, it presents a statistical
and a policy challenge that Latin American countries have only recently
confronted. The rough profit estimates we have presented range from 8 to 80
percent. Such gross divergence no doubt derives in part from error in
measurement and from calculations being based on different definitions. But
much of the divergence is undoubtedly a correct reflection of different
realities, and should remind us of the dangers of generalization across heterogeneous groupings. Some, but not all, foreign investment in Latin America
earns very high rates of profit. One suspects that high-yielding investment is
concentrated particularly in manufacturing, where a cascading of tariffs,
quantitative restrictions, and exchange controls generally bestow solid monopoly positions to producers of import substitutes.

---

15. Guy B. Meeker, "Fade-out Joint Venture: Can it Work for Latin America?"
Inter-American Economic Affairs, Spring 1971, p. 37. (Not clear if figures are before or
after taxes.)

16. Constantine Vaitsos, personal communication.

17. Studies by Brash and Deane cited in Kindleberger, *op. cit.,* p. 139.

18. Vernon, *op. cit.,* p. 138. An earlier countervailing tendency to set export prices
low and collect profits tax-free by reexporting through tax havens like Panama was
eliminated by provisions in the 1962 Revenue Act. Some cases of transfer prices
controversies are discussed in Jack N. Behrman, "Taxation of Extractive Industries in
Latin America and the Impact on Foreign Investors," in Raymond Mikesell, ed., *Foreign
Investment in the Petroleum and Mineral Industries,* published by the Johns Hopkins
Press for Resources for the Future, Washington, 1971, pp. 56–80. On recent Middle East
controversies, see *The New York Times,* January 9, 1972, III, p. 9.

Indeed, if profit rates of say 25 percent per year were not available in Latin America, one would wonder why North American manufacturing companies would be interested in expanding investments there. After all, the U.S. multinational corporations whose investment horizons extend to Latin America are generally high-technology companies with market positions in the United States sufficiently entrenched to give assurance of solid and substantial profits. Doing business in Latin America is more complicated and riskier than in the United States, and corporations should require correspondingly higher profits. It is often suggested that corporations invest abroad for reasons of security and control more than for profits, but with few recent exceptions one has little impression that U.S. corporations are hanging on in Latin America through adverse times. Certainly that was not the impression of the Colombian government when it commissioned the Vaitsos study in the first place.

Cost-Benefit Considerations

While high profit rates earned by foreign companies are naturally a cause for concern, they too are a deceptive guide for evaluating the desirability of foreign investment proposals. Direct foreign investment is merely another type of investment project, and the proper way to evaluate any investment project lies with the tools of benefit cost analysis. A properly executed benefit cost analysis will give particular weight to balance of payments effects through using a shadow price for foreign exchange. Domestic resource costs would also be considered, however, each resource valued at its social opportunity cost. If benefits exceed costs when both are evaluated with correct shadow prices, discount rates, and distributional adjustments, then the project should be undertaken. And it is quite conceivable that a project providing a 100 percent return to foreign investment will nevertheless produce benefits in excess of costs.

Should the project therefore be accepted and foreign investment given such a bounty? Not necessarily, because there may be less expensive ways of getting the same project done. In the terminology of benefit cost analysis, we have here the case of mutually exclusive projects. If various projects can be undertaken to furnish the same need (e.g., hydro versus thermal power plants for supplying electricity), the project with the highest benefit cost ratio should be undertaken, and other mutually exclusive projects, even those also having benefit cost ratios in excess of one, must be passed up. In the case of direct foreign investment, various institutional arrangements for undertaking the same production facility may be considered separate projects, e.g., 100 percent foreign ownership with existing tariff structure, joint ventures with lower tariffs, domestic enterprise relying on purchased technology, and all other possible combinations of protection, ownership shares, and tax liabilities.

Here we arrive at the policy significance of the high profit rates recorded by Vaitsos and others and the policy insignificance of statistical exercises showing that contributions of foreign investment to Latin American income or balance of payments have been positive.[19] Such high profits strongly suggest that there existed other institutional arrangements that would have induced the same inflow of foreign investment at lower cost to Colombia, or to other Latin American countries. In this special sense profits were probably excessive and Latin America has given away too much for the foreign investment received. Such is the lesson of the transfer pricing revelations.

A Broader Framework of Economic Evaluation

Thus far, our analysis of foreign investment has taken the narrow view, considering capital the only factor thus provided to the host country and ignoring repercussions of foreign investment on households and other firms. Direct foreign investment provides a whole package of inputs, however—capital, technology, organization, and, in the case of some exports, an overseas distribution network. Since the evaluation of foreign investment proposals should oblige a country to identify the institutional arrangements by which a given output may be produced at lowest cost, alternative means for obtaining each of these factors must be assessed. A country should always consider the possibility that these factors will cost less when obtained separately, since when they are obtained together as direct foreign investment the foreigner rather than the national receives opportunities for monopoly profit.

Capital presents the fewest problems. It can be borrowed overseas from banks, bond markets, or international official agencies, and it can be mobilized domestically. For all the emphasis given foreign investment in Latin American development, it should not be forgotten that the bulk of savings funneled into investment in Latin American countries comes from domestic sources.

---

19. E.g., May, *op. cit.;* U.S. Department of Commerce, Office of Business Economics, *U.S. Investments in the Latin American Economy,* Washington, 1957.

Alternative sources of supply for technology and organization are more difficult to come by. Multinational corporations exert much of their bargaining power in Latin America through control of these factors. Nevertheless, technology is also available through licensing arrangements, and organizational capability is available through both management contracts and domestic sources. While great strides have been made in recent years, it still seems fair to say that Latin America is hobbled in its dealings with representatives of direct foreign investment through ignorance of licensing arrangements and lack of capability in evaluating the alternative technologies available for licensing. Additional knowledge in these fields could pay tremendous dividends to them by opening up lower-cost alternatives for given investment projects.

Managerial ability and entrepreneurship may be considered another factor of production. It is developed by experience, through learning by doing, and so the presence of foreign investment has repercussions on the rate of domestic accumulation of this crucial factor. No general statement can be made about the direction of its effect, however. On the one hand, certain projects may be accomplished only through technology and organizational skills available to the foreigner. Then foreigners undertaking such projects would in no way diminish opportunities to domestic entrepreneurs; in fact, opportunities would be increased if the projects generated backward linkages to domestic suppliers. On the other hand, foreign investment would diminish entrepreneurship to the extent that national entrepreneurs are shut out of projects they otherwise would have undertaken.[20] Each particular case must receive its own evaluation. Such evaluations need to be made not only by host countries, but also by scholars in pursuit of better understanding. Up to now, virtually all we have in the way of published material is intensely partisan, either totally favorable to foreign investment as in the case of May and the National Planning Association, or totally opposed to it as in the case of the CIDA studies, and the dependence literature.[21]

---

20. Albert Hirschman argues that this negative effect has acquired increasing significance in Latin America, since national entrepreneurs are increasingly able to undertake projects formerly undertaken by foreigners. Cf. *How to Divest in Latin America, and Why*, Essays in International Finance, No. 76, International Finance Section, Princeton University, 1969, pp. 4–9.

21. May, *op. cit.;* and among studies published by the National Planning Association: Simon Rottenberg, *How United States Business Firms Promote Technological Progress* (Washington, 1957); E. W. Burgess and F. Harbison, *Casa Grace in Peru* (Washington, 1959); Wayne C. Taylor and John Lindeman, *The Creole Petroleum Corporation in Venezuela* (Washington, 1955); Stacy May and Galo Plaza, *The United Fruit Company in Latin America* (Washington, 1958). For the CIDA viewpoint, see Comité Interamericano

Noneconomic Factors in the Evaluation
of Foreign Investment

The impact of foreign investment on domestic entrepreneurship is but one of several types of external effects that must be considered in evaluation, even if prospects for quantifying the effects are dim. Other externalities lead us out of the realm of conventional economic accounting, into what may be called the noneconomic or psychic costs of foreign investment. Costs are no less real if they are merely psychic and nonquantifiable, however. In fact, such costs may represent the most onerous burdens placed upon Latin America by the presence of direct foreign investment.

Consider the case of a foreign investment that not only hampers the creation of new entrepreneurs in the future but also displaces existing entrepreneurs. Those displaced may become employees in the new foreign company, at incomes equal to or greater than what they had been before. But they have lost the decision-making freedom of a self-employed person, and they have also lost the power and prestige that the importance of their previous position had conferred upon them. In this way, foreign investment tends to radicalize a portion of the middle class through the frustration associated with change of status, and thus to polarize the society into which it is introduced.

This process has recently been documented in the case of the large sugar haciendas on Peru's northern coast.[22] As these foreign-owned estates expanded across the coastal valleys, they displaced numbers of medium-sized farms. The foreign concerns generally developed their own purchasing channels; they bypassed the merchants of local cities and brought ruin to many. Income per capita undoubtedly rose in the region, but so did radical politics in the form of the early APRA.

The enlightened policy of hiring nationals for managerial positions only

de Desarrollo Agrícola, *Tenencia de le tierra y desarrollo socioeconómico del sector agrícola: Peru* (Washington, 1966), Chapter 3. In the dependence literature: Osvaldo Sunkel, "Big Business and 'Dependence': A Latin American View," *Foreign Affairs,* April 1972, pp. 519–31; Dos Santos, "Foreign Investment. . . ," *op. cit.,* and "The Structure of Dependence," *op. cit.* For a statement from middle ground, see two papers by Carlos F. Diaz-Alejandro, "Direct Foreign Investment in Latin America," in Charles P. Kindleberger (ed.), *The International Corporation,* The M.I.T. Press, Cambridge, Mass., 1970, pp. 319–44; and "The Future of Direct Foreign Investment in Latin America," Economic Growth Center Discussion Paper No. 131, Yale University, December 1971 (mimeo).

22. Peter Klaren, *La formación de las haciendas azucareras y los orígenes del APRA,* Instituto de Estudios Peruanos, Lima, 1970.

partly alleviates the problem. In the end, the foreigners are still the bosses whose job is to give orders, and in the end this social and political situation may only be described as unstable and intolerable.

Such tensions are by no means confined to the national employees of a foreign company. Indeed, they may be far more severe outside the company, where the foreign boss becomes merely a symbol and not a person. Within the national society outside the company, the very presence of foreigners and direct foreign investment remains a continuing reminder of the meagerness of national economic achievements. The source of friction and of psychic costs lies not in the foreignness of such investment, but in its cultural distinctiveness. Far worse than being merely foreign, it is generally Anglo-Saxon, and thus generates tensions within a Latin culture that feels itself placed on the defensive.[23]

We return to the realm of conventional economic accounting in order to consider one final externality in the demonstration effect of consumption standards brought to Latin American countries by foreign managers and technicians. For Latin America's middle classes, this effect adds yet another inducement to higher consumption and lower savings. Therefore, in two ways, by converting entrepreneurs into bureaucrats and by raising the consumption standards of the middle classes, the presence of foreign investment is damaging to Latin America's savings rate and growth rate.

It bears emphasizing that every North American present in Latin America imposes, by his very presence, a series of psychic and economic costs. Let him ponder his role to make sure that he brings compensating virtues.

Trends in Latin American Evaluation of Foreign Investment

These various externalities and social effects will never be quantified satisfactorily and plugged into a benefit cost ratio. The weights implicitly applied to these factors in the evaluative process will inevitable shift about as new perceptions alter conventional wisdom. Forecasts of future trends in Latin

---

23. For a discussion of the roots of Argentine hostility to British investment, see Carlos F. Diaz-Alejandro, *Essays on the Economic History of the Argentine Republic,* New Haven, 1970, pp. 60 ff. Also Diaz-Alejandro, "Direct Foreign Investment in Latin America," *op. cit.,* p. 329. Also note the opening sentence of the well-known "Latin American consensus of Viña del Mar," a purely *economic* declaration sponsored by the Comité Especial de Coordinación Latinoamericana (CECLA) in 1969; "The CECLA member countries affirm the distinctive personality of Latin America."

America's evaluation of foreign investment therefore proceed on a shaky foundation.

First, it seems likely that Latin American governments will increasingly recognize that they have paid dearly for foreign investment acquired in the past. This recognition is made most dramatic in the Vaitsos study, and will probably be reemphasized as similar studies are produced in other countries. These high profits represent yet another unfortunate result of the uncritical and excessive pattern of tariff protection and quantitative restrictions that Latin American countries have plunged into through firm belief in the virtues of industrialization. The excessive profits obtained by foreign companies are merely one manifestation of generally high profit rates made available to monopolistic industries insulated almost completely from the pressures of world industrialization;[24] they have also exacerbated the already serious problems of unequal income distribution plaguing Latin America. It seems likely that in coming years programs of import liberalization and import substitution in intermediate goods industries will lower effective protection and make astronomic profit rates more difficult to come by.

Direct foreign investment will also prove less attractive as Latin American countries become more able to generate lower cost alternatives. Greater familiarity with licensing arrangements and better knowledge of technologies available for licensing will increase Latin America's bargaining power with multinational corporations, particularly if greater competition arises among sellers of technology through development of Japanese and European technology sources. As Latin American industry acquires greater experience, its own organizational and technological capabilities will also be enhanced.[25]

While these various factors will tend to generate lower cost alternatives to direct foreign investment, on the other hand the perceived psychic costs of foreign investment will increase to the extent that nationalist sentiment gains further strength. One hesitates before the foolhardy task of predicting trends in nationalism, but one can certainly point to a long-run increase in nationalist, anti-foreign-business sentiment that has been running throughout the present century. Moreover, the experience of the 1960s seems to have no exception to this trend.

---

24. It bears emphasizing, in harmony with the arguments of Schydlowsky in this volume, that some but not all Latin American industries bear the mark of hothouse inefficiency.

25. Some of Latin America's new opportunities are discussed in Miguel Wionczek, "The Pacific Market for Capital, Technology and Information and its Possible Opening for Latin America," *Journal of Common Market Studies,* September 1971, pp. 78–95.

On the other hand, some factors make direct foreign investment more attractive. In some sectors the technology gap may be widening. Although Latin American organizational and technological capabilities may be improving, the multinational corporation's capabilities may be improving at a faster rate. In such sectors, Latin American countries will be in a weak bargaining position and must either take foreign investment pretty much on its own terms or give up on production possibilities and import. As the process of import substitution becomes less uncritical during the 1970s, the alternative of importing may be used increasingly.

Another factor favoring direct foreign investment concerns the export of manufactures. Exports of traditional primary products will continue to play their essential role in earning foreign exchange, but new exports, many of them manufactures, must be relied on for an increasing share of dollar earnings. Brazil, Mexico, and Colombia have demonstrated in recent years that appropriate exchange rate policies can do much to encourage manufactured exports, and that foreign companies will be particularly active in this new export trade. The wholly owned subsidiary of the multinational corporation may be a particularly advantageous form for export development. It has the worldwide distribution network of the multinational corporation available to funnel its products to distant markets, and the multinational corporation would have no incentive to discriminate against it in decisions regarding choice of production facility for serving a third country's market. The situation would be different for a joint venture, since the multinational corporation would obtain only a fraction of the profits earned by its exports, whereas it would earn all the profits if the same sales opportunity were served by other plants within the corporation's production network.[26]

The question of export performance is but one of several reservations that may be raised about joint ventures as the institutional solution to Latin America's foreign investment problem. Compared to wholly owned subsidiaries, joint ventures seem generally to make higher payments to the foreign partner for technical services and capitalized technical knowledge, thus adding to the host country's costs.[27] However, they also present distinct advantages, since the partial transfer of control to local partners may be expected to reduce transfer prices for purchased inputs and to diminish psychic costs of a foreign presence.

---

26. For an illuminating discussion of the prospects for joint ventures, see Louis T. Wells, Jr., "Foreign Investment in Joint Ventures: Some Effects of Government Policies in Less Developed Countries," Economic Development Report No. 167, Development Advisory Service, Harvard University, 1970 (mimeo).

27. Wells, *op. cit.*, pp. 21–26.

For these reasons, it seems likely that joint ventures, including the fade-out variety, will be experimented with at an increasing rate. The rather rigid fade-out formula embodied in Decision 24 of the Andean Group seems unlikely to be the final word in the search for new institutional arrangements.[28] In some cases, investments that might be judged socially useful, e.g., labor-intensive assembly plants that reexport back to the United States, may be available only on a 100 percent foreign basis. In other cases, the social purpose of a joint venture may become corrupted by local partners who merely go along for the ride, leaving all decisions to the foreigners and making no effort to perform a watchdog function. Therefore, we may expect the key words of Latin American policy in the next decade to be flexibility and control. Despite the dangers of corrupting traditionally weak bureaucracies by endowing them with discretionary powers, a flexible approach will probably prove imperative as various combinations of joint ventures, production contracts, and special controls over wholly owned subsidiaries prove most suitable in different cases. The constant objective sought by these various institutional arrangements will surely be greater national control over foreign investment.

New institutions and greater control should cut down opportunities for foreign companies to earn excessive profits. At the same time, returns will undoubtedly be cut below minimum levels required by certain foreign companies, and the flow of new investment will be reduced accordingly. This development will hurt growth rates, but it must be accepted as a price to be paid for the rapid social change experienced in some parts of Latin America and desired everywhere in Latin America. Rapid social change may well increase risk to foreign investors and induce them to raise their minimum required profits to levels judged by Latin American governments to be unacceptable.

Although growth targets may suffer, quite possibly social welfare will be increased by stringent controls on foreign investment even at the price of some growth. To state the obvious only because it is occasionally forgotten, the objective of economic policy lies in maximizing social welfare, not GNP.

Finally, we may expect the lively social concern over foreign investment to have effect in statistical reporting and in the explicit setting of social goals. Only ten years ago, for example, the only source available to the Peruvian

---

28. Miguel Wionczek, "Hacia el establecimiento de un trato común para la inversión extranjera en el Mercado Común Andino," *Trimestre Económico,* April–June 1971, pp. 659–702. Also, Meeker, *op. cit.,* and John Lindquist, "The Merits of Forced Divestment: The Experience of the Andean Group," Research Program in Economic Development Discussion Paper No. 31, Woodrow Wilson School, Princeton University, October 1972.

government regarding the extent of foreign investment in Peru was the U.S. Embassy. Ten years hence, we may expect that effective reporting systems on all types of foreign indebtedness, especially direct foreign ownership of capital, will be imperative in Peru and elsewhere. Furthermore, I think we can anticipate the day when regularly produced reports on the stock of foreign-owned capital are given the public attention that reports on GNP receive today, when a decrease in the level of foreign capital is viewed as a measure of social progress in the same way that we now view an increase in the level of GNP.

Chapter Eleven

A NOTE ON INCOME REDISTRIBUTION

Robert L. Slighton

It is perhaps most appropriate for Americans to focus chiefly on those economic problems of Latin America that directly affect the United States. Latin American policies toward direct foreign investment—expropriation policy, profit remittance policy—are by definition such a problem. I trust that it is just as obvious that the problem of increasing nontraditional exports from Latin America is of the same class. How quickly and effectively the Latin American governments will move to deal with domestic disincentives to export will depend in a nontrivial fashion, I expect, on U.S. trade policy.

Yet I think there is some reason for us to consider certain economic policy problems or policy areas that do not create a direct requirement for U.S. policy response. The basic reason for doing so is, of course, that economic policy decisions are highly interrelated. Decisions with respect to the property rights of U.S. investors or bargaining objectives in trade or aid negotiations will reflect a more general policy style that we ought to know something about.

There is no point in my attempting here a survey of trends in the style of economic policy making in Latin America. The subject is too vast. It would also exceed my competence. What I think might well be useful, however, is to discuss what I think will be the most important difference between the styles of Latin American policy making in the seventies and those of the recent past. That difference is an increased emphasis on the objective of redistribution of income. I would like to consider the reasons why I think this change is taking place, the kinds of economic policies likely to be developed as a result of this change in emphasis, and what I think the likely economic consequences of these policies will be.

Why a Change of Policy Focus?

There are several important reasons why we should expect an increased focus on government-directed distribution and redistribution of income. First, the emergence of what is generally perceived to be a serious urban unemployment

163

problem in much of Latin America has shaken the confidence of policy makers that orthodox "developmentalist" policies will yield a satisfactory solution to the distribution problem. Second, there is a fairly widespread pessimism with respect to the rate of economic growth likely to occur in the coming decade. This pessimism is founded both on an estimate of the relative availability of foreign exchange and an estimate of foreseeable reductions in the import requirements of future growth.

It is important to note here that a prediction of a shift of policy focus from growth of income to distribution of income need not depend in any important way on a prediction of a drift of sociopolitical values. I think there is little doubt but that most policy makers feel or will soon come to feel that the "objective facts" of the Latin American growth experience give them no choice in the matter. Any drift in political values or sentiments will only accentuate a trend that is already under way.

The most important of these "objective facts" of the Latin American growth experience that is leading to a shift of policy focus, is a syndrome of changes that I shall call the "urbanization of poverty." The most noticeable features of this syndrome are extremely rapid rates of rural-urban migration, increased urban unemployment and partial unemployment, and a marked wage drift between the technologically modern and the technologically traditional sectors of the economy. The migration phenomenon is a key aspect of this syndrome, for much of what may appear to be an increase of unemployment and a worsening of income distribution is better characterized as a spatial redistribution of poverty and unemployment. The syndrome is most pronounced in those economies that retain a large traditional sector—the Caribbean and Andean countries.

I am using the term "unemployment" very loosely here. I mean it to encompass the phenomena of overt unemployment, partial employment, and depressed average incomes of self-employed workers in technologically traditional activities. As such, I can offer no simple quantitative index of the problem akin to an unemployment rate. The fuzziness of the unemployment concept in a semi-developed economy guarantees ambiguity in empirical demonstrations of propositions about trends in "unemployment" even if consistent time series on unemployment rates are available. And they generally are not. In spite of this, I think there is little reason to argue about whether or not the "unemployment" problem has gotten worse in most Latin American economies, for what is most important is what is believed. And in general I think the problem is believed to be increasing.

In certain respects at least the "unemployment" problem has in fact worsened. In particular, overt employment has increased. This is mainly concentrated heavily among the young and uneducated, and, as such, it is considerably less destabilizing than would be the case if significant numbers of heads of households were involved. But what I suspect may be viewed as even more destabilizing is the rapid growth of that part of the labor force "employed" in nonagricultural but technologically traditional occupations such as artisan-manufacture and certain services and the resultant depression or outright reduction in average earnings in such activities. It is moot whether the urban poor have gotten poorer. But it is obvious that there are more of them. Poverty has become increasingly urbanized.

A second aspect of the income distribution syndrome is easier to document. Wage rates in the technologically modern sectors of the economy have increased rapidly relative to wage rates (or imputed wages) in the traditional sectors. More often than not I suspect they have increased considerably more rapidly than labor productivity. The reasons for this are intimately tied up with those government policies that have promoted import-substituting industrialization (ISI). Monopoly or partial monopoly positions in production arising from tariff protection and import controls create opportunities for labor to exact monopoly rents, and unions have not been backward in exploiting this opportunity. The extent to which this has taken place varies widely, but I know of no country in the midst of the ISI process where important labor monopolies have not developed and where the employees of "modern" firms have not collected substantial monopoly rents.

Whether this represents a redistribution of real income from entrepreneurs to workers or from consumers to workers is hard to say. What is not hard to see is that a working class "elite" has been created, an elite differentiated in part by education and skills but primarily differentiated by possession of a property right—a job. From the narrow point of view of economic policy making, this elite presents something of a problem. It serves as a more or less powerful interest group that acts to make stabilization and export promotion policies more difficult to carry out.

The phenomena embodied in what I have called the urbanization of poverty would probably cause a shift in policy emphasis from growth objectives to distributional objectives even if a relatively favorable growth experience were anticipated. Pessimism with respect to attainable growth rates further increases pressures in this direction. In this respect the style of policy making in those countries that underwent a rapid structural transformation in the fifties and sixties—much of the Andean and Caribbean group in particular—is likely to become more like that in Argentina, Uruguay, and Chile, countries that underwent a similar transformation process at an earlier date and whose growth experience in the past decade has been relatively unfavorable.

A Likely Profile of Policy Change

Thus far I have characterized my predicted change in the style of economic policy making solely in terms of the meta-objectives of growth and distribution. This is fine for a chapter heading, but what does it mean in terms of changes in specific policies? What does it mean in terms of the creation of new policy instruments? A fair question to be sure, but I am afraid that I can give only the sketchiest of answers.

The most predictable change in economic policy is an increased effort to allocate resources by administrative decision. There appears to be both a perennial pessimism in Latin America with respect to the reasonableness of market solutions and a perennial optimism with respect to the ability of the government to remedy market deficiencies by direct controls. The temptation to allocate by decree in the face of the frustrations of stagnation and structural rigidity will thus, I fear, prove irresistible. The greatest push will come in the area of price control over consumer goods. Price controls will be expanded in coverage and more vigorously enforced. An explicit wage or income policy is also likely to be developed. This will aim at reducing wage differentials and establishing limits on wage settlements that are tied in some fashion to a consumer price index.

Income transfers will also be achieved through the fiscal process. In particular, expenditures on labor-intensive public works projects will increase. Social welfare and service expenditures will also rise. Some effort can be expected to fund these expenditures through increased sumptuary taxes, a better enforcement of income taxes, and land taxes, but for the main they will be financed through the banking system. In those governments where the developmentalist tradition is relatively strong, a considerable planning effort will be organized to try to insure that these expenditures are capital creating, that the labor component of expenditure is high, and that a substantial portion of the expenditures is made in rural areas. The impact of this planning effort will be generally disappointing. If it is successful with respect to the investment objective, it is less likely to be successful with respect to the employment objective. The reverse proposition is also likely to hold. If the planning effort is successful with respect to the employment objective, it is less likely to be successful with respect to the investment objective.

An effort will be made to compensate for the monetary effects of the increase in government expenditures through tightened bank reserve requirements and monetary sterilization devices such as advance import deposit requirements. These policies will be periodically relaxed for substantial periods, however, as credit stringency results in industrial and commercial slowdown and a decline in revenue collection. Although fewer countries will maintain a "fixed" exchange rate system than in the sixties, those countries that adopt either a policy of frequent rate adjustments or some form of the "floating peg" system will probably not permit a rate of devaluation that parallels the domestic rate of inflation very closely. A comprehensive system of import controls will be maintained. Controls over profit remittances will be tightened, and the period between approval of remittances and provision of exchange will lengthen, in certain cases to the point of apparent default. An effort to slow down the rate of price increases for items of basic consumption will result in an increased dispersion in the exchange rate structure.

There is nothing very surprising in this predicted policy package. That in itself is, I suppose, a prediction. More radical redistributionist schemes such as the Peruvian profit-sharing experiments will be proposed and in some cases even attempted, but they will not be pursued vigorously. The boundary between the private and public sectors of the economy will probably remain roughly static.

The Consequences of Policy Change

What will be the economic consequences of all this? The answer to a question can be no more precise than the question itself, and since I have given only the most general description of the policy response, I can give only the most general description of the policy consequences. The impact on unemployment will be negligible. The bulk of the changes in the distribution of income will derive from the differential impact of inflation. The rate of inflation will increase. There will be some reduction in the rate of growth of real output.

I think it important to understand from the outset that there is no "solution" to the unemployment-underemployment problem outside the context of more rapid growth of output or less rapid growth of population. Although there are certain features of the policy environment in Latin America that depress the labor-capital ratio and reduce the amount of employment generated by a given expansion of output, the primary reason for increased unemployment-underemployment is simply a supply of savings and a supply of foreign exchange that generate a rate of growth of the demand for labor that would be less than the rate of increase of the labor force even in the absence of market imperfections. The unemployment problem is a special problem—separable from the growth problem—only in a marginal sense. Policies based on the assumption that the problem is structural will have only a marginal impact. Unemployment in Latin America stands out as especially difficult not so much because of the structure of growth or market imperfection but because of demographic facts. I say this not to condemn "structuralist" policies. Many of them are highly desirable. But it should not be expected that they will have a major effect.

The size distribution of income is notoriously more sensitive to the stage of economic development—the occupational structure of the labor force and the distribution of human capital—than it is to most of the policy instruments thought of as redistributive. Barring a Keynesian-like circumstance of deficient aggregate demand, a government is most likely to be able to secure an important change in the size or sector distribution of income by changing the rate of inflation. Yet it is very difficult to predict just what these changes will be. The effect of inflation on income distribution has been widely studied, but there are few conclusions, even of the qualified variety, and no theorems. I suspect that agricultural income will suffer relative to nonagricultural income, that the relative shares of the lowest 50 percent and the top 2 percent of income recipients will remain largely unchanged, and that the share of workers who have property rights in jobs in the modern sector of manufacturing will increase. But I can't defend these propositions very vigorously. The only thing that is reasonably clear is that internal perceptions of the redistributive effects of inflation will be exaggerated relative to the changes themselves. Policy makers will typically begin their endeavors with the objective of redistributing income from the rich to the poor. But they are likely to end up seeking to reassure middle income groups that there has been in fact no redistribution after all.

My statement that the rate of inflation will increase is implied by the prediction that the rate of monetary expansion will increase. Over any but the shortest of time periods this is a trivial conclusion and does not need further discussion here. What is more interesting is what the total effect of the predicted policy package will be on the growth of real output. My conclusion is that there will be some reduction in the pace of economic growth that is attributable to policy change. I do not think the effect will be substantial. It will derive not from monetary "excesses" but from supply dislocations engendered by the enforcement of direct controls over the price of items of common consumption. I am arguing here from the assumption that exchange rate policy during the period of more rapid and variable inflation will not be such as to depress incentives for nontraditional exports, however, and this may be too optimistic. At the existing margin of growth, the dominant constraint on a more rapid rate of economic expansion in Latin America is the availability of foreign exchange. If this remains unchanged, the growth rate is likely to be relatively insensitive to all but the most extreme shifts in economic policy.

An increased emphasis on distributional and redistributional objectives will exact a certain price in terms of reduced growth, but the cost is not likely to be substantial. I cannot share the hopes of some that a focus on redistribution will provide a substitute for import substitution as the major dynamic element in the Latin American economies. But neither can I share the fears of others that a redistributive focus and growth are strongly antithetical. The basic outlook is one of much policy and little change. The public may not feel that much more frustrated, but the policy makers certainly will.

V. INTERNATIONAL RELATIONSHIPS

Chapter Twelve

THE NONHEMISPHERIC POWERS IN LATIN AMERICA

Herbert Goldhamer

The late fifties and the sixties witnessed a sharp growth in the presence of the nonhemispheric powers in Latin America.[1] What the seventies will hold in store for these relations can most readily be assessed by examining the likely fate of those motives, capabilities, and international contexts that during the sixties shaped the behavior of the principal actors in the southern continent and produced the trends that were then established.

The Postwar Period and the Sixties

Developments both external and internal to Latin America shaped the nature of the nonhemispheric presence.

External Developments
The Effect of World War II. World War II and its aftermath had a major effect on the fortunes of the foreign powers in Latin America.

The burdens and sacrifices of war led to the loss by both the European allies and the Axis powers of positions acquired in Latin America during the nineteenth and early twentieth centuries. Both Britain and France as well as Germany suffered sharp setbacks, while Italy and Japan, whose stakes were smaller and who had largely a physical (migrant) presence, suffered less.

The beneficiary of this was the United States, whose presence increased greatly in Latin America after World War II. In 1938 the United States provided only 37 percent of Latin America's imports, but immediately after World War II the U.S. share stood at about 60 percent. In the decade 1950–1959 the United States accounted for about 80 percent of direct

---

1. In this paper the "nonhemispheric powers" should be taken to include Canada. The reader is referred to the author's *The Foreign Powers in Latin America,* Princeton University Press, Princeton, N.J., 1972, for a more comprehensive treatment, which includes the United States.

private investment flow to Latin America. After 1939, U.S. military missions became successors to an earlier important European military presence.

Recuperation. The great upsurge, relative to other powers, in the United States' economic, military, and political presence in Latin America after World War II did not last very long. It was more or less predictable that the nonhemispheric powers, more especially the former enemy nations that had been almost totally cut off from Latin America by the war, would, as their U.S.-assisted recuperation progressed, seek to reestablish themselves in the southern continent.

The United States' 60 percent share in the Latin American market declined steadily after 1948 and did not stabilize until about 1962 at approximately 44 percent. Despite recent favorable U.S. trade balances in Latin America, there are signs of a new, but slower decline in the U.S. share. There is, however, as yet no clear indication that a new long-term trend is being established, especially in manufactured exports where the United States has almost held its own against its nonhemispheric competitors.

During the sixties, Japanese, German, and Italian recuperation had progressed to a point that permitted increasing amounts of capital to be sent to Latin America which was a preferred Third World locus for the investments of these three countries. In 1967, among the fifty largest public and private business enterprises in Argentina, seventeen European corporations outranked thirteen U.S. corporations, the former with 344 billion pesos annually of business and the latter with 260 billion. In Brazil, European and Japanese investment shares rose from about 32 percent in 1956 to 58 percent in 1967. Of course in Latin America as a whole, U.S. investments at the end of the sixties were still larger than those of the nonhemispheric powers.[2]

The Migrant Presence. The return of the foreign powers to Latin America after the war was not only commercial and financial (trade and investments) but also physical in the form of a very substantial postwar wave of emigration to Latin America. Between 1946 and 1960 Argentina, Brazil, Colombia, Uruguay, and Venezuela received about 2 ½ million migrants, who continued to reenforce an already strong Japanese, German, Spanish, Italian, and Portu-

---

2. The predominance of U.S. capital was not the result of a U.S. preference for Latin America as an investment outlet. In 1950, 38 percent (without Cuba, 32 percent) of the book value of U.S. foreign private investment was in Latin America. By 1966, this figure had dropped sharply to 18 percent. From 1960 to 1966 Latin America received only 9 percent of all U.S. net foreign direct investment, or only one-third of such U.S. investments in the less developed countries. By 1968, 38 percent of U.S. direct foreign investment was in Canada as compared with only 17 percent for all the Latin republics together.

guese presence, among others. These migrants, like their forerunners, have facilitated the commercial and financial penetration of the Latin American world by those industrial countries with a substantial migrant presence, that is, Germany, Italy, and Japan.

United States Programs and Diplomacy. The United States economic and military aid programs helped during the early sixties to stabilize the trade decline that had progressed steadily from 1948 to 1962. But the not infrequent tutelary and managerial interventions of both the Administration and Congress counteracted at times the benefits that the United States derived from its efforts to guide political and economic developments in South America. These irritants in United States-Latin American relations were magnified in their effects by the whole history of U.S. interventions in the Caribbean and in Latin America, and by other factors that intensified economic and political tensions while affording increased opportunities for the nonhemispheric powers.

Nonhemispheric Political Offensives. Political offensives on the part of France, the Soviet bloc, and to a lesser extent Italy, encouraged Latin American willingness to risk alienating the United States. That nothing significant came of French and Italian (and for several years of Soviet) gestures did not prevent them from supporting a Latin impetus toward the nonhemispheric powers and away from the United States.

Internal (Latin American) Developments

Diversification. The return of the nonhemispheric powers to Latin America was facilitated by an increasing Latin American interest in commercial, financial, and political diversification. President Frei took well-publicized initiatives in this respect that reflected a general Latin American interest of some duration. This interest was enhanced by U.S. actions and nonhemispheric encouragement on the one hand and by left and left nationalist tendencies with strong anti-U.S. components, on the other hand.

Latin America in the United Nations. Latin American interests in moving on a larger (world) stage and in escaping too great dependence on the United States were further encouraged by the role the Latin states were able to play in the United Nations and by the considerable value of their votes.[3] Unlike the League of Nations, in which participation was passive, hesitant, and only

---

3. At the First Session of the United Nations, 20 Latin American states were 39 percent of the membership. This fell to 24 percent in 1959 and to 19 percent in 1966. African membership is approximately double that of Latin America. Of the 15 Security Council seats, two are reserved for Latin American states.

partial, the U.N. became not only an important world forum for the Latin governments but also a locus where they could experience the political impact of Third World countries.

Politics and Economics. The large role played by most Latin American governments in the economic life of their nations (through the direction of economic policy and through semi-autonomous state enterprises) tended to give international economic relations with Latin America a government-to-government character rather than a private enterprise framework. This seems to have provided some advantages to foreign states with *dirigiste* or centrally managed economies, or with at least counterparts to Latin American semi-autonomous state enterprises or corporations. Thus, when Colombia awarded Renault a contract to build and operate an auto assembly plant, a Colombian official remarked that Renault's status as a government enterprise helped it to win out over nine other bidders. Another firm awarded a contract for an auto assembly plant was also a state enterprise, Mexico's Diesel Nacional. United States bidders—General Motors, Ford, Chrysler, American Motors—thought it "nonsensical" that the successful bidder must agree to buy and market Colombian products equal in value to the automobile components it imported. But for a foreign state enterprise like Renault, there was no apparent problem in buying and marketing (in 1969 and 1970) $3 million worth of Colombian coffee, meat, tobacco, cotton, and rice.

Several of the nonhemispheric countries were able to present themselves as models for the Latin American nations and to imply, but without any convincing results, that relations with them had special value because of national experiences or talents that had Latin American applications.

Marxism, Radical Nationalism, the Soviet Union. The Cuban Revolution, the diplomatic recognition of the Soviet Union throughout almost all of Latin America, the election of Salvador Allende, and various guerrilla outbreaks were only the more conspicuous events in domestic political developments in Latin America that marked the increased influence of nationalist, left nationalist, and Communist tendencies that were hostile to a U.S. presence and that welcomed nonhemispheric relations, especially when it had anti-American overtones. The political right (e.g., the large landowners who found among some Alliance for Progress strategists an enthusiasm for their liquidation) and the political center (businessmen, government officials, and administrators who felt harassed by Alliance for Progress overseers or by the latter's insistence on a tax structure and other reforms that would have touched them too closely) also contributed to this anti-American sentiment. The radicalization and nationalism of the Catholic clergy in Latin America added to anti-American attitudes in a sector formerly attached to the political right.

Relations with the Soviet Union seemed, on the other hand, less dangerous to Latin states that took comfort (after the Cuban missile crisis receded into the background) from the great distance of the Soviet Union from Latin America, just as some of the East European countries find relations with the United States and other Western powers a relief from the disagreeable proximity of the Soviet Union.

The Seventies

As the decade of the seventies opens, there is no clear sign that the rising fortunes in Latin America of the nonhemispheric powers, relative to those of the United States, have stabilized or reached their apogee. Nor is it as yet clear who, among them, will in the long run benefit most from the economic and political competition—an issue important to the United States which may feel less endangered by an erosion of its own influence in Latin America than by the particular parties whose presence may partially replace its own. Nonetheless, if we examine the sources of the increase in the nonhemispheric presence outlined above, and if we assess their future significance, we can make some useful guesses about the later years of this decade. It will, of course, be necessary to take into account new developments that may occur in the seventies, as well as the future fate of those that dominated the sixties.

The effect on trade of nonhemispheric postwar economic recuperation had largely run its course by the mid-sixties. In the seventies any further increase in nonhemispheric shares and a corresponding decline in U.S. trade shares will depend on rather different factors.[4]

The future U.S. trade position will depend in part on the investment policies of Japan, Germany, Italy, Canada, and perhaps several other countries. If U.S. investment in Latin America continues to slow[5] while other

---

4. A decline in U.S. trade shares has not generally meant a decline in the absolute size of U.S. trade with Latin America. Small declines in U.S. trade shares at the turn of the decade were, however, accompanied by absolute declines in Colombia and Peru. U.S. exports to the 22 OAS republics in 1971 increased only one percent over 1970's $6.1 billion. U.S. and parallel Latin American monetary devaluations will probably improve the U.S. position over that of its nonhemispheric competitors, but this may produce only a temporary reversal of present trends.

5. The U.S. Overseas Private Investment Corporation (OPIC) has reported sharp declines in applications for investment insurance. The Department of Commerce anticipated a small decline in 1971 in plant and equipment expenditures by U.S. affiliates in Latin America as compared with accelerating expenditures in all other parts of the world. This decline does not, however, apply uniformly to all of Latin America. Brazil and Mexico are still favored countries for U.S. investments.

foreign investments continue, this will almost certainly lead to a reduction in the U.S. share of the Latin American market. Investments in Latin America, as elsewhere, produce for the countries making them an increase in exports since the foreign firms in Latin America are substantial consumers of goods imported from their own country. Every £100 of direct private investment by Great Britain in Nigeria generated about £39 of increased trade with that country. This effect is apparently the greater according to the degree to which the industry of the country in which investments are made is under-developed, and the ratio in Latin America is unlikely to be as large as in Nigeria. Nonetheless, Japanese, German, British, and Italian investments in Latin America are undertaken in many instances precisely in order to protect trade interests and to advance them.

During the sixties the U.S. trade position was strengthened by the Alliance for Progress whose tied loans led to purchases in the United States that otherwise might have gone to other countries. Unfortunately, available data do not seem to provide any clear answer to the question of how much trade the United States gained from its aid activities. Nonetheless, as U.S. aid and the practice of tying aid decline, and as multilateral aid replaces bilateral aid, it is likely that some negative effect on the U.S. trade position will occur.[6]

The increased physical presence of the nonhemispheric powers achieved by postwar migrations ceased to be reinforced in the late sixties when the flow of workers from Spain, Portugal, Italy, Greece, and Turkey was diverted by opportunities in Western Europe. These opportunities have now declined, but it is not likely, given European and Japanese prosperity, that there will be a new major wave of migration to Latin America in the seventies. Nonetheless, the presence in Latin America of first, second, and third generation migrants who maintain a close identity with their country (and language) of origin, will continue to provide some commercial and financial advantages to these countries.[7] Japan especially has appreciated this. Although hard pressed at home for skilled workers and technicians, she has arranged the migration of technical personnel to Brazil and helped to establish them in Brazilian enterprises where their influence will favor purchases from Japan.

The U.S. trade (and perhaps even investment) position in Latin America

---

6. When the United States began to tie aid in 1960, only 41 percent of AID assistance was used to buy U.S. commodities. By 1968 this figure had risen to 98 percent. The campaign for untying aid was supported in 1970 in the OECD by the United States and was opposed by Canada, France, and Japan.

7. Thus, in 1970 Italy ranked third (to the United States and Germany) in the Argentine market, and Japan third (to the United States and Germany) in the Brazilian market.

may be eased by increasing European preoccupation with trade within the EEC and with new opportunities that may open in the seventies in the Soviet Union and China.[8] Those industrial countries that are not associated with important regional economic groupings may find themselves increasingly drawn together.[9] If, in addition, the United States finally gets around to providing Latin America with the tariff concessions promised some time ago, the United States may develop a special entrée to Latin American markets more effective than its aid programs. Its effectiveness is likely, however, to be diminished by the growing ability of the nonhemispheric countries, as the decade moves on, to compete more effectively in manufacturing fields in which U.S. technology and productivity formerly had a marked advantage. Nonetheless, the current U.S. trade and investment position in Latin America will, despite further declines, almost certainly continue to make the United States the single most important foreign economic power in Latin America throughout the decade.

The current U.S. trade position and its position in the seventies relative to the nonhemispheric countries are alleviated to some extent by a factor sometimes overlooked. The position of the United States is usually calculated in terms of exports from the United States proper, but many U.S. firms operate in Canada, in Europe, and in Latin America itself, and these firms sell their commodities to Latin America.[10] Thus, from the standpoint of U.S. economic interests, a certain amount of the trade of Canada and Europe and sales within Latin America itself must be viewed as at least ancillary to if not an integral part of what is usually called U.S. trade with Latin America.[11]

Probably more essential than the foregoing factors to the future balance of the nonhemispheric and the U.S. presence in Latin America are certain larger

---

8. This may also render more unlikely a renewal in the seventies by France and Italy of those initiatives taken in 1964–1965 to stem the tide of U.S. dominance in Latin America.

9. LAFTA and CACM are likely in the long run to increase the amount of intra-Latin American trade, but this will affect the nonhemispheric competitors of the United States as well as the United States. It is true, nonetheless, that European traders have lost less from CACM than has the United States.

10. In 1966 United States manufacturing affiliates in Latin America had $5.9 billion in local sales, that is, about $1.5 billion more than U.S. exports to Latin America for that year.

11. A decline in the U.S. share of the Latin American market has also to be interpreted in light of the relatively small role international trade plays in the United States GNP—about 4 percent as compared with 10–35 percent for the principal industrial nations. Exports as a percent of GNP were (1968–1969): Japan 10, France 11, Italy 14, Britain 16, West Germany 19, Netherlands 35, Belgium 40. Since, however, U.S. exports comprise almost 17 percent of the exports of the non-Communist world, even a modest U.S. trade deficit can create difficulties for the U.S. balance of payments.

political or political-economic developments that emerged primarily in the sixties and whose final course has not yet been run.

The Latin American interest in political and economic diversification that played so important a role in the mid-sixties will almost certainly continue to play a significant role in the present decade. Apart from politically inspired motives, the U.S. economic presence will continue to loom large enough to provide the necessary stimulus. However, the partial success of Latin America's drive toward diversification will probably deprive this interest of the strong emotional motivation and appeal that it had in the mid-sixties. In the coming years, Latin American leaders will probably be more cautious in their dealings with the Soviet Union, China, the European countries, and Japan than they were in the sixties when they were misled by gestures made by General de Gaulle and President Saragat, and looked forward to much more in the way of economic assistance and trade than they in fact received. The Latin American states still want increased trade with and investment from the nonhemispheric powers, but they are likely to avoid slighting opportunities in the United States. However, if the political left and intense nationalism continue to grow, both political passions and political expediency may lead in some instances to a decline in economic relations with the United States, even when it injures economic interests.

There will no doubt be some interaction between domestic development in the Latin American states and U.S. policy toward Latin America. However, a U.S. policy in the seventies that provides less economic aid and reacts more sharply to some Latin American actions (uncompensated expropriations, for example), may not exacerbate U.S.-Latin American relations provided it affords Latin America satisfactory opportunities for trade and investment. It may lead to less good neighbor rhetoric than in the sixties, but also to fewer of the day-to-day all-pervasive forms of irritation and dissatisfaction that stemmed from U.S. large-scale assistance in the early sixties and the tutelary and managerial relations that accompanied it. Unless it becomes severely punitive rather than simply hardheaded and self-interested, U.S. policy is not likely to be a major determinant of whether or not radical nationalism or Marxism spreads in Latin America during the seventies.

Just as Western Europe and Japan played a major role in the sixties in providing Latin America with new alternatives or additions to U.S. relations, so the Soviet Union and China will almost certainly play an increased role in the seventies. This should not be interpreted solely in terms of political penetration and economic assistance. The Soviets and, increasingly, the Chinese are major powers and given their apparent interest in benefiting from the international division of labor, it is likely that they will find economic relations with Latin America advantageous to them. Even a modest incursion into the Latin American market by countries of this size will by the late seventies involve a not trivial redistribution of trade shares. The Soviet Union and China may for the moment find economic penetration hindered by their inability to provide quality goods at competitive prices, but it would be dangerous to assume that this condition will continue indefinitely. By the late seventies the Soviet Union will have had enough experience in international nonsocialist markets to provide competition even where political considerations and special concessions do not smooth their path. The Russians are already showing increased flexibility and a willingness to drop their former exclusive reliance on barter deals.

For the present, Soviet interests in Third World areas would be modest were it not that these relations are an important aspect of her concerns with the United States and China. It is likely that the Soviets will continue to be particularly active in areas which border on the Soviet Union and China, or are contiguous to areas that do, that is, especially in the Middle East and South Asia. These preoccupations will limit Soviet assistance to Latin America. China is already exceeding Soviet disbursements and offers in a number of Third World areas. Since, however, the Soviets are likely to confine highly concessionary relations in Latin America to countries that follow a Marxist or "noncapitalist" line and show some sympathy for her foreign policy positions, she will not have to support, at least for the time being, a continent-wide effort in Latin America, as did the United States in the sixties.

It is unlikely that in the seventies the Soviet Union will find it necessary to try to exploit the Latin American states for prime Soviet security objectives. In 1962 Cuba provided the Soviets with a chance to lessen strategic imbalance and thus to serve a high priority security concern. However, in the seventies, under conditions of strategic parity with the United States, urgent military use of a Third World country, particularly a Latin American country, is not so likely to occur. This, however, certainly does not mean that Latin American states may not be used by the Russians for national security purposes. It only means that these purposes will not be quite so vital as those that were probably at stake in Cuba in 1962, and that therefore the risks to be taken and the costs to be paid will have to be in proportion to the benefits that the Soviets can expect to derive.

Soviet attempts to eliminate or discredit anti-Soviet left groups in Latin America may be supplemented in some instances by attempts to win over far left political movements by providing discreet support even at the risk of jeopardizing government-to-government relations. The apparent Soviet willingness to get involved in Ecuador, in Mexico, and in Costa Rica in domestic affairs suggests a Soviet judgment that they cannot pursue a purely "correct" policy without risking the loss of influence in political circles that they do not want to write off.

Soviet willingness to risk their diplomatic relations[12] may in part be motivated by a lack of confidence that they can, at least within the limits of the costs they are willing to bear, displace in any real way the influence of the United States and the larger nonhemispheric powers. The Russians cannot now provide either the capital, the trade, or the types of cultural contacts required by the Latin American states. The United States, West Germany, Japan, and where cultural relations are also involved, Italy, Britain, and France, will continue to be more useful to Latin America than the Soviets. Perhaps for this reason the Soviets do not feel they are risking a great deal, particularly given a tendency for some states to tolerate more interference from the Soviets than they do from other countries.

Three factors may in the long run assist the Russians. As the decade moves on, Soviet ability to provide capital assistance and to absorb Third World semi-manufactured and manufactured goods (as well as raw materials) will probably improve. Second, the large role that government and semi-autonomous government corporations play in Latin economies may give the Soviets some advantage as compared with Western private enterprise. Third, Latin American countries with anti-capitalist leanings will continue to avoid a too great dependence on capitalist states suspected, even when there is no foundation for this, of being secretly hostile to them. Latin American expropriations, particularly, may lead some Latin American governments to feel that sooner or later in one form or another, the United States or other Western powers will seek restitution. In any case, relations with the Soviet Union may be a useful means for undercutting the political appeal of party rivals on the left.

The Soviets may eventually use their political influence and their economic and military assistance programs to obtain bases in Latin American countries. Bases would be useful to the Soviet Union, although it is apparent that her opportunities to "show the flag" are plentiful without their expense. Chile had good reasons to conform to President Allende's statement that Chile will not permit a foreign country to establish bases. However, future Latin American crises may provide opportunities for the Soviets if they wish to take them. Agreements have been reported between the Russians and the

---

12. It is, of course, difficult to determine whether what we observe is two (partly incompatible) strains in Soviet policy or the rivalry of their diplomatic and security services.

Peruvians for the construction of a Peruvian fishing port. Such ventures could no doubt provide the Soviets with useful experience in South American West Coast waters and might provide an opportunity for naval utilization if political and economic relations of the countries involved deteriorate to the point where a willingness to bail them out might enable the Russians to get concessions of this sort.[13]

There are some offsetting difficulties that may suggest caution to the Soviets. Although the changeable character of Latin American politics often permits rapid gains for the outsider, political instability equally risks losses. Soviet credits granted to Chile in 1966, apparently to be applied to the construction of a large fishing port at Valparaiso, were still unutilized at Allende's death. In addition, Soviet ambitions to be the patrons of the Third World in the seventies will be handicapped by substantial residues of an iron curtain mentality that complicates relations with other people. Another limitation on Soviet Latin American ambitions is the greater cultural prestige of the Western nations. In Latin America the cultural affinities of the middle and upper classes with Western Europe and the United States can hardly be offset by Soviet offerings. It is difficult to know to what extent a major power can exercise an enduring and substantial influence of a noncoercive character over another nation when their cultural contact is limited and when the cultural prestige or importance of the big power is not very great for the smaller one. The political role of Western culture in the Third World may alter as time goes on, but it is unlikely that in the decade of the seventies the U.S.S.R. will be able to operate as freely as it would were it not handicapped by its limited ability to associate cultural affinities with economic and possibly military ties.

There is a fourth difficulty that the Soviet Union increasingly meets as it expands its relations in the Third World. Like the United States, the U.S.S.R. as a big power pursues activities in one part of the world that conflict with objectives elsewhere. Thus, Soviet attempts on behalf of East Germany to limit West German participation in U.N. aid activities were resented by some Latin American and other Third World countries that received West German aid.

The United States, were it to combine with Canada, West Germany, Japan, and Italy, could provide considerable leverage for the protection of such common economic and political interests in Latin America as these countries

---

13. The United States might find it easier to prevent this by dealing with the U.S.S.R. rather than by trying to compete with it for influence in specific local situations.

have. But it is not clear how much Canada, Western Europe, and Japan will attempt primarily to benefit from Latin American disaffection with the United States and how much they will prefer joint action. The United States might be able to make concessions to nonhemispheric trading and investment interests in Latin America in order to ensure cooperation on what it views as its most essential economic and political interests in the southern continent. The United States ability to achieve some measure of cooperation would, of course, depend on judgments by the nonhemispheric countries that their own interests, and not only those of the United States, are involved.[14] Latin American left and radical nationalists have sometimes attempted to convey that only the United States stands to lose by their accession to power, but it is evident that this was not entirely convincing in Cuba. In the sixties the United States had little success in eliciting European cooperation for its Latin American programs and policies. In the seventies the European powers and Japan may be too preoccupied in the competition to replace United States economic and political influence to be much more willing to cooperate with the United States. Still, their own position in Latin America may eventually seem to them to be not so different from that of the United States and this might provide the basis for greater unity of policy than existed in the past decade.

---

14. The investments of Germany, Japan, and Italy in Latin America are, taken individually, far less than those of the United States. On the other hand, their investments in Latin America are in each case a much larger part of their total investments abroad than is true for the United States, a not unimportant matter, especially for Germany already rendered sensitive by losses suffered in Latin America in two World Wars.

Chapter Thirteen

CONFLICT AND COOPERATION
AMONG LATIN AMERICAN STATES

David F. Ronfeldt and Luigi R. Einaudi

During this century Latin America has been one of the most harmonious regions of the world. While occasional disputes have marred the record of peaceful relations, the three decades stretching between the Peru-Ecuador conflict of 1941 and the Honduras-El Salvador clash of 1969 provided occasional smoke but little fire. Meanwhile, a number of governments have promoted regional economic integration and ventured haltingly toward the collective organization of political cooperation.

This history of regional peace and cooperation is often attributed to the relatively common language, cultural, and historical backgrounds of the Latin American countries. But the differences among Latin American states are sufficient to raise doubts whether the term "Latin America" conveys much that is meaningful. The great natural diversity of Latin America is particularly obvious with the rise of several English-speaking countries in the Caribbean. But the areas traditionally labeled "Latin America" were always diverse. The nearly 100 million Portuguese-speaking people of Brazil, inhabiting a continental region geographically if not spiritually closer to Africa than to North America, have very little in common with the million Spanish-speaking former Colombians who straddle the Panama Canal. Argentina has far closer historical ties to Europe than to most of its Latin American "sister states." Nor do Peruvians, Guatemalans, Paraguayans, and Mexicans have very much in common geographically, politically, socially, or even culturally, despite the superficial ethnic similarities deriving from their heavily "Indian" populations—which also have little in common other than the very "non-Europeanness" that led them to be mistakenly identified as "Indians" in the first place. Indeed, it has often seemed as though the one thing Latin American countries have had in common was the United States.

Factors other than shared characteristics, then, are needed to account for the course of comparatively harmonious relations during recent decades. It seems likely that two significant factors are:

- an international context based in part on the regional predominance of the United States; and
- a relatively low level of interactions between Latin American countries, combined with equally low interests and capabilities to affect each other's central concerns.

Since the 1940s these conditions have limited greatly the potential for political, economic, and military conflicts within the region—while also limiting the levels of cooperation and integration that might be attained. And both conditions are now rapidly changing.

Changes in the International Context of the Latin American Countries

The foreign policy stances of the Latin American countries toward outside powers and each other are strongly conditioned by the nature of the international context. A number of trends are making this general environment considerably different from the 1950s and 1960s.

New Opportunities
From the Latin American perspective, the fundamental changes in the global environment in recent decades are the decline of political-military bipolarity, the lessening of U.S. economic hegemony within the hemisphere, and the related growth of new opportunities for international political and economic relations. These changes mean that the diversification of political, economic, and security relations with a variety of foreign powers has more to offer and entails fewer risks for Latin American nations than at any time since World War II. This particularly applies to diplomatic relations, trade, technology transfer, training, and related forms of international communications.

The changed world environment is reflected, for example, in the justifications of the Costa Rican government for inviting diplomatic relations with the U.S.S.R., and of leaders in Brazil for generally expanding economic relations with the Communist countries—to provide two examples involving governments that remain quite friendly toward the United States, and are also wary of potential military security problems with the U.S.S.R. In addition, the benefits of diversified foreign relations may be domestic as well as international. The increasingly independent foreign policies of Argentina, Mexico, and Peru toward the Communist worlds suggest that prospects of pleasing and/or dividing dissident political elements outweight the possibilities of international subversion.

Friends and Enemies

Changing perceptions of "friends" and "enemies" underlie this trend toward diversification. From the 1940s through the 1960s most Latin American governments shared perceptions of common external enemies with the United States: such as Nazi Germany, Communist Russia, and later Cuba under Castro. These perceptions, though they varied greatly from country to country, helped to unify Latin American foreign policies toward each other and toward the United States.

For the 1970s, however, few Latin American government leaders see clear external enemies that might have such regionally unifying effects. Brazil is intensely anti-Communist and Cuba remains vividly anti-American; but these are major exceptions. Otherwise, though the practice has been broken by Costa Rica, only the governments of a number of small Central American and Caribbean island nations continue to shun diplomatic relations with the Soviet Union as potentially dangerous. In the larger countries, however, relations with virtually all the industrialized countries, including the United States and the U.S.S.R., are regarded with increasing ambivalence, for they present both opportunities and obstacles for national economic progress. Thus the unifying strand in regional foreign policies has tended to become anti-imperialism and anti-dependency, rather than anti-Fascism, anti-Communism, or even anti-Americanism.

This new perspective can be illustrated by considering attitudes toward the United States. Despite general patterns of close friendship since World War II, most Latin American governments have regarded the United States as a source of many economic problems. Now, however, some governments tend to view general U.S. economic hegemony, and sometimes the specific activities of particular U.S. firms, as problems or even limited "threats" not only for economic development but also for national security. These tendencies are clearest where national security doctrines are linked closely to economic development policies, and where radical reformists have entered office.[1]

---

1. The I.P.C. affair in Peru and the I.T.T. affair in Chile provide the current leading examples. Significant Argentine arguments that identify foreign economic penetrations as potential aggressions against national security are voiced in Osiris G. Villegas, *Políticas y Estrategias para el Desarrollo y la Seguridad Nacional*, Ediciones Pleamar, Buenos Aires, 1969, though the United States is not specifically identified as a threat or aggressor.

Typically, however, measures against certain U.S. business activities and against presumed U.S. government-business alliances in certain sectors are combined with a welcoming of U.S. business investments in other sectors or on other terms.[2] That is, the threat perception is limited, and coexists with desires for continuing cooperation and friendship. To some extent, the increased presence of foreign powers other than the United States will cushion the anti-U.S. focus of much Latin American nationalism. Moreover, it is clear that expropriations and other measures against U.S. investments derive not simply from anti-Americanism or anti-capitalism, but also from the clearly rising capacities of the Latin American governments and private sectors to master their own affairs.

Along with such modifications of external threat perceptions, many new leaders of Latin American governments are also rejecting the uncritical emulation of external "models" for the 1970s. In previous decades, admiration for Italian fascism, for Soviet or Chinese communism, and most commonly for Western liberal democracy, variously motivated the development programs of Latin American intellectual and political leaders, and to some extent guided their foreign policies. Now, however, they insist upon the need to institute locally-inspired systems that may draw upon certain practices found in liberal democracies as well as in European socialist and even communist patterns, but that deliberately reflect local traditions.[3] One likely outcome is a continuing turn to corporative political systems, for which Latin American political culture and political thought are historically well-suited.

The Foreign Presence

The United States remains the preponderant hemispheric power. In contrast to the heavy U.S. presence in the 1950s and 1960s, however, U.S. power and influence—and therefore its traditional leverage—in Latin America are weakening and can be increasingly countered. The decline in U.S. aid and assistance programs, the increased presence of nonhemispheric foreign powers, the trends toward international multipolarity and strategic parity, the growing capabilities of the Latin American governments, the emergence of regional

---

2. Objections to rigid anti-expropriation measures by the United States Government are not limited to local nationalist elites. Some leaders of influential U.S. business sectors also believe these measures have detrimental effects on U.S. investment opportunities.

3. The quest for local solutions to national problems has been recently voiced by leaders as diverse as Echeverría in Mexico, Velasco in Peru, Médici in Brazil, and Allende in Chile, although the latter was frequently caught between more doctrinaire extremes which led to his undoing. Liberal democracy as an organizing principle is undergoing stiff challenge in Colombia, Uruguay, and Venezuela.

powers, and the perceptions of new political elites confirm this relative weakening.

The relative changes in U.S. power and influence are redounding to the benefit of a variety of nonhemispheric nations, but not to any one of them in particular. Given Latin America's diverse economic and technological requirements, almost all foreign powers have something to offer. As described thoroughly in the preceding essay by Herbert Goldhamer, U.S. hegemony during the 1950s and 1960s was primarily the result of World War II, which interrupted Latin American access to many European trading partners. As Europe's industrial and manufacturing capacities have recovered, so have their trade and investment relations with Latin America. Western Europe and Japan have gained the most. Japan shows a potential for developing strong economic interests in some countries, particularly in Mexico, Peru, and Brazil; but the expansion of her economic relations will be slowed by the necessity to build modern ports on Mexico's Pacific coast, and to construct a (Japanese-financed) pipeline over the Andes in Peru. In a competitive environment the Soviet Union shows only moderate, if not relatively low, potential for significantly expanding its still minor economic relations with Latin America outside of Cuba. Latin American governments seek relations with the U.S.S.R. more as an exercise in political sovereignty and in the search for auxiliary trading partners than in the expectation of developing major economic or political relationships.

Most Latin American governments continue to have very strong interests in U.S. export markets, investment capital, technology and related training, and in American tourists. Whereas economic development and political changes of the 1960s have fostered increased national control over primary sectors, basic industries, and the financial and telecommunications sectors, this is far from implying the demise of private activity or interests in relations with the United States. Instead, recent expropriations and nationalizations in countries as different as Peru and Venezuela may presage a strengthening of state capitalism, as has been the case in Mexico, rather than a turn to socialism.

Moreover, a potentially strong U.S. presence is still desired for political and security reasons. As Latin American nations become more concerned with their neighbors, they will continue to look to the United States as a major potential mediator and balancer in case of regional conflict. They will become extremely worried lest U.S. activities appear to upset the regional balances of power. Argentine reactions in particular to close U.S.-Brazilian relations illustrate this process, as do Latin American desires for continuing U.S. participation in a reformed inter-American system, including the O.A.S.

The Region's Value

Latin America's international "value" may be changing in ways that will significantly affect relations among its countries. For some time during and after World War II Latin America was commonly regarded as a valuable wartime reserve of foodstuffs and raw materials for the United States and its allies. New war technologies have practically obviated this geopolitical consideration. Latin America is remote from central nuclear war scenarios, and thus relatively unimportant as a strategic objective for the major foreign powers. For the 1970s, however, the strategic "value" of Latin America to the foreign powers is being determined somewhat less by Cold War perspectives, and more by energy crisis and other economic considerations. Recent and possible future discoveries of petroleum, not to mention other mineral resources, in the Andes and upper Amazon areas once again raise the interest that Latin American leaders expect the United States, Japan, and other industrialized nations to have in their countries, especially if problems persist in the Middle East and Persian Gulf areas. The implications of these developments for relations inside and outside the Latin American region are quite uncertain, but will surely enhance local interests in the control of large, sparsely populated border areas where significant natural resources may be found.

Some Implications

Together these interrelated trends amount to a striking change in the world context of the Latin American countries. Three related implications seem to stand out for the strategies and policies to be adopted by their varying governments in the decade ahead. First, the new external context will probably intensify the concerns among the Latin American nations for their relations with each other. Indeed, the weakening of the U.S. presence in particular appears to be indirectly enhancing the significance attached to intraregional interactions in local foreign policy formulations on issues ranging from Andean Pact cooperation to the resurgence of old Argentine-Brazilian rivalries. The development of trade relations with the Orient will likely increase Brazil's interests in overland routes from its interior to certain Pacific ports, as well as in seagoing routes through the Panama Canal. Depending upon the character of the trade relations that develop, this general tendency may stimulate increasing Brazilian attention to conditions in countries on the trade routes.

Second, the changes in the world context will facilitate considerable flexibility among the Latin American nations in their dealings not only with the outside world, but also with each other. If U.S. power had lessened extensively while the old political-military bipolarity persisted, regional divisions might have led to rival ideological camps. The new world trends toward political and economic multipolarity, however, would seem to make constantly shifting intraregional alliances on specific issues a much more likely outcome.

Latin American governments, whether rightist, leftist, or centrist, can be expected to be quite flexible also in their dealings with the United States. On the one hand, conservative governments can more easily afford a nationalistic posture of independence from, and even opposition to the U.S. on some issues. The last Velasco Ybarra government in Ecuador, which combined conservative policies at home with defiance of U.S. fishing activities, showed how this can be done. It would not be surprising if the relatively conservative military government of Brazil also began to identify less with U.S. policies. Brazil has tended to vote closely with the U.S. on Cold War issues, but it has recently exhibited considerable independence on other issues. Brazil's strong allegiance to the U.S. has derived to a significant extent from persisting bipolar perspectives on worldwide political conditions. As the country's leaders become increasingly familiar with the opportunities offered by trends toward multipolarity, they may well act with greater independence on many issues, even while continuing to treat the U.S. as a major ally.

On the other hand, radical and highly reformist governments can now more readily afford to cooperate with the U.S. The dynamic Peruvian government, which seems to represent more a new center than a new left in Latin American politics, is highly attuned both to the opportunities for increased national independence and to the continuing need for good if not always close relations with the U.S. Even the Allende government, operating largely according to old left ideological perspectives, sought constructive relations with the U.S. In contrast, the Cuban leaders seized power in an area of very strong U.S. power and influence at a time when bipolar processes prevailed; yet continued erosion of bipolarity may over time induce modification of their perspectives on Cuban-U.S. relationships. Today, changed world and regional contexts increase the incentives for a nationalistic multilateralism that includes cooperative relations with the United States on some if not many issues, and reduces the incentives for either very close cooperation with or very strong rejection of the U.S.

Third, while in many respects improving the incentives and bases for intraregional cooperation and integration, the nature of the world context may facilitate local conflicts of interest to become as prominent as historic harmonies of interest. The lessening of the U.S. presence may actually have disturbing rather than integrative effects, for in the past strong U.S. power and influence often served to mute local rivalries and potential conflicts.

Indeed, with the exception of Guatemala during the early 1950s and of Cuba during the 1960s, Latin America has experienced few "confrontations by proxy" between major world powers. By the end of the 1960s, however, the Western European countries and Japan had regained the levels of activity existing before World War II. During the 1970s, therefore, many of the activities of the individual Latin American countries seem likely once again to reflect the imprint of international competition, in ways that will certainly encourage regional diversity, if not conflict. Recent O.A.S. meetings—where Argentine, Brazilian, and Mexican activities have been criticized along with those of the United States—may reflect this change. These stronger Latin American countries are more likely to compete for regional leadership and local spheres of influence; and in general it would not be surprising if political, economic, and even military conflicts across some local borders occasionally took place, as they did during the 1930s and early 1940s. But any such predictions depend upon the regional as well as the world context of the individual countries, and it is to that topic that we now turn.

Trends within the Regional Context
of the Latin American Nations

In striking contrast to recent decades, interactions among the individual Latin American countries are diversifying at a rapid rate, and reaching a substantial level. Whereas just a generation ago most major lines of communication flowed between the United States and individual Latin American countries, now press communications reveal a substantial process of "Latin Americanization." The growth of regional news services, such as the Catholic Inter-Press Service, the Argentina-based *Latin* and even Cuba-based *Prensa Latina,* is effectively challenging the primacy of both U.P.I. and A.P. and their European competitors such as Agence France-Presse and Reuters. Moreover, local newspapers and magazines have been expanding the proportions of space devoted to intraregional issues. People are moving across borders too: large numbers of Chileans have moved into Argentina, Colombians into Venezuela, Salvadoreans into Honduras, and Brazilians into Bolivia, Paraguay, Uruguay, and even Peru.

Meanwhile, governments and entrepreneurs from some countries, especially Mexico, Brazil, and Argentina, are actively competing for markets and investments in their neighbors. Intraregional trade is growing, stimulated by the multinational business corporations. Commissions for bilateral and regional planning on a variety of sensitive economic issues are spreading, as evidenced by the Andean Pact, Brazil-Bolivian economic relations, the development of the River Plate system, and attempts to establish a common economic front vis-à-vis the industrialized nations, an endeavor which stimulated the emergence of the Special Coordinating Commission for Latin America (CECLA). The extension of the Brazilian road system to its frontiers portends the linking together of a continental infrastructure for communication and trade that could revolutionize population and transportation patterns in an area where a very high proportion of goods are now shipped by sea between countries. In the diplomatic arena, heads of state are visiting neighboring nations for the first time, and foreign affairs ministries in Mexico and South America are expanding their capabilities to pay attention to regional matters. Military and security contacts are also increasing, highlighted by Mexican training missions in Central America, by Argentine and Brazilian missions in the smaller buffer nations between them, and by continuing exchanges of officers and students among traditional allies such as Peru and Venezuela.

Nationalism and Ideological Differentiation

This remarkable growth in intraregional interactions is generating new interests and capabilities, both public and private, for the Latin American countries to affect each other directly. In the process their governments are "turning outward" toward their neighbors, even as they become more clearly differentiated from each other. Intraregional relations appear to be assuming an attention in local foreign policy formulation that may challenge the priority customarily accorded to relations with the United States and non-hemispheric powers in the past.

These developments may foster the forging of a regional consciousness and new institutions. During the 1960s Christian Democratic leaders were perhaps the most outspoken proponents of the thesis that strength comes through unity, and that Latin America could carry increased weight in world councils only to the extent that it did not allow itself to become "Balkanized" through the pursuit of bilateral advantage. It is increasingly recognized today that Latin America, if it is to take its rightful place on the world stage, may in the long run need to emulate the process of formal and informal integration that has taken place in Europe since World War II.

While the economic future of Latin America over the near term seems more closely linked to development of the national markets of the individual countries rather than to the establishment of common markets, regional cooperation is becoming increasingly organized as regards foreign investment. The Andean Code is an early manifestation of this. And if it is clear that it is impossible to establish a unanimous ideological front between countries as diverse as Colombia, Peru, and Chile, it is nonetheless equally clear that Latin American leaders consider improvements in technical information exchanges and forms of regional cooperation like CECLA to be essential in order to at least partially counterbalance the power of the major international economic corporations. Within the public sector, for example, the national petroleum agencies meet regionally through the Latin American Regional Association of State Petroleum Agencies (ARPEL) and exchange data and even equipment.

There can be no denying either the increased regional self-consciousness of younger political elites, nor the contribution toward this end of the current emphasis on multilateral discussions and international agencies. But it seems unlikely that moves toward regional or even subregional unity will overcome the nationalism of individual sovereignties much before the turn of the century, if then. Instead, as nations come into closer contact, nationalism also frequently tends to emphasize those characteristics that differentiate one country from another. As one Latin American historian has commented, the national history of each Latin American republic since independence tends to be an "anti-history" of the other republics, with different interpretations of shared events helping to foment mutual suspicions if not animosity. The spread of nationalism thus sometimes creates new tensions along with the more positive values of development and social consciousness. In a region studded with historic rivalries and deep-seated mutual suspicions, the danger is ever present that national difficulties could be demagogically exploited and contribute to international tensions. In addition, there are a number of other trends that foreshadow increased interstate tensions, if not outright conflicts.

As noted earlier, the trend toward local ideological differentiation is associated with the decline and modification of liberal democracy as an ideal. During the 1960s, liberal democratic experiments did not take root in Argentina, Brazil, and Peru; and their durability is not even assured in Colombia, Uruguay, and Venezuela. Traditional debates persist among partisans of liberal democracy and capitalism, and proponents of socialism or communism; but now anti-liberal voices are more prominent, and are reflected in the very different governments of Perón's Argentina, Médici's Brazil, Castro's Cuba, Torrijos's Panama, and Velasco's Peru. While Mexico and Peru provide leading examples of flexible approaches to local issues, these differing approaches may strengthen the potential for regional tensions.

Security and Geopolitics
Regional security threat perceptions have shifted in a number of countries. During the 1960s Cuba was regarded, directly or indirectly, as a subversive threat by a variety of Latin American governments. Venezuela even consid-

ered a declaration of war. Now, however, Cuba has become quite secure in defensive military capabilities, and has greatly reduced its export of revolution. Meanwhile, governments have also increased their capacities to cope with Castro-type insurgent activities. As a result, Cuba no longer represents the common concern of the 1960s, and internal security conditions are considered manageable.

As a result, many governments, especially in South America, are turning once again to traditional missions of external defense, and to a focus on their neighbors as rivals for regional leadership, natural resources, economic markets, investments, and the control of border domains that could become the stuff of local conflicts rather than of regional integration. Indeed, there appears to be a resurgence of "frontier-minded" military nationalism, fed by concern for ocean resources and the spreading claim to a 200-mile limit.

Reflecting these trends, local "geopolitical" analyses are becoming prominent elements in local national security doctrines and foreign policy processes. Indeed, Latin American leaders now appear to be undergoing the concern for geopolitics that was experienced in Europe and the United States during the late nineteenth and early twentieth centuries. This trend is particularly pronounced in Argentina and Brazil, and relates clearly to their governments' and militaries' ambitions for regional leadership and strength.[4]

In general, geopolitical analyses reinforce doctrines that national development and national security are highly interdependent, and that therefore the military merits major political roles. Geopolitical thinkers in Brazil emphasize the prospects of strong regional as well as global roles for their country, and confirm the necessity for aggressive—even though defensive—foreign policies toward their South American neighbors, and urge the rapid occupation and

---

4. For example, an Argentine press has recently published a series of books on the topic, including Jorge E. Atencio, *Qué es la Geopolítica,* Ediciones Pleamar, Buenos Aires, 1965; Pierre Celerier, *Geopolítica, y Geostrategia,* Ediciones Pleamar, Buenos Aires, 1965; Osiris G. Villegas, *Políticas y Estrategias para el Desarrollo y la Seguridad Nacional,* Ediciones Pleamar, Buenos Aires, 1969; Justo P. Briano, *Geopolítica y Geostrategia Americana,* Ediciones Pleamar, Buenos Aires, 1966. Another work is Vivian Trias, *Imperialismo y Geopolítica en América Latina,* Editorial Jorge Alvarez, Buenos Aires, 1969. Nicholas J. Spykman, *Estados Unidos frente al mundo,* Editorial Fondo de Cultura Económica (a translation of his *America's Strategy in World Politics: The United States and the Balance of Power,* Harcourt, Brace and Company, New York, 1942), has received wide circulation. The Brazilian government's concern with regional geopolitics is reflected especially in General Golbery do Couto e Silva, *Geopolítica do Brasil,* Livraria José Olympio, Rio de Janeiro, 1967, though its guiding principles are being reexamined in light of recent world developments. Lewis A. Tambs, "Latin American Geopolitics: A Basic Bibliography," *Revista Geográfica* (Rio de Janeiro), #73, Diciembre 1970, pp. 71–105, provides a useful guide.

development of frontier regions. In Argentina, geopolitical thinkers admire their country's potential for regional and even world power, but emphasize the priority of national development ("putting one's own house in order first"), both as a precondition for security against internal and external threats, and as a prelude to foreign policy strength and leadership within the hemisphere. Particular issues that occupy the attention of geopolitical analysts in both countries are conflicting interests in the hydroelectric development of the Plate river systems, and diverging interests in economic relations with Bolivia and with Paraguay and Uruguay, which have historically served as "buffer" countries between them.

These changing geopolitical perspectives and international pressures are turning the attention of government elites to the development and security of large frontier areas that are isolated, sparsely populated, and that may contain abundant natural resources, such as petroleum. Many military officers in Argentina argue, for example, that the development of Patagonia is a vital precondition for eventual integration with Chile, while development of the northern provinces is needed for national security against Brazil. Other cases include: Colombia's Guajira peninsula claimed by Venezuela, Guyanese territory claimed by Venezuela, the oil-rich Amazon territories of Colombia, Ecuador, and Peru, Bolivia's Santa Cruz region, and the Paraguayan Chaco. The concern for frontier areas, often more pronounced among military than civilian elites, reinforces the concern for relations with the bordering nation, especially since such areas have been the issue of interstate tensions, if not outright conflicts, in the past.

Such developments will accentuate the trend toward diversity among the Latin American countries, but need not lead to hostility. Other trends counteract any emergence of conflicts. In particular, the combination of limited economic resources and continuing uneven development leads to a practical mandate to avoid heavy arms purchases that could in turn escalate into sources of conflict. In fact, the costliness of maintaining modern military establishments seems likely to foster at least some tacit limitations on arms acquisitions, which remain at a low level compared to the rest of the world anyway. In addition, the ever present dangers of foreign manipulation of local security environments, whether through terrorism or political and economic pressures, will inevitably foster some need for informal cooperation and information exchange in security matters as a counter to historic mutual suspicions.

Subregional Powers

These varied and often contradictory trends are visible in the controversies over the possible emergence of Brazil and other countries as subregional competitive powers that seek to bend their neighbors and establish local spheres of influence.

In the Caribbean area Mexico and Venezuela may be identified in some respects as subregional powers, perhaps to be joined eventually by Cuba. Mexican entrepreneurs, supported by their government, are rather actively seeking markets and investments in Central America, as are Venezuelan investors in the offshore islands. So far, however, their governments do not pursue aggressive, outward political and security policies toward their neighbors. The Mexican government has expanded a little its security relations with the Central American countries, and the Venezuelan government is developing some security interests and capabilities among its troubled offshore islands. Yet these governments leave Caribbean security as a whole to the United States and partly to the diminishing British forces. As a complicating factor, Venezuela's national security perspectives are affected by its geographic location between the Caribbean area and South America. Indeed, Venezuelan military capabilities are perhaps as likely to be oriented to protecting interests against Brazil, Colombia, or Guyana as to supporting interests in the Caribbean. Elsewhere in the Caribbean, a normalization of Cuban relations with Latin America in the years ahead may motivate the Cuban government to adopt more aggressive conventional diplomatic and economic policies, perhaps matching Venezuelan and Mexican levels of activity. Guatemala is a significant contender for a Central American sphere of influence, and in the future it would not be surprising if a highly nationalistic government sought leadership in Central American affairs.

In South America, geographic and historic conditions induce more aggressive foreign policies. As in the past, Brazilian-Argentine rivalry will continue to be a major factor; and indeed, at least psychologically, some Spanish-speaking countries seem to fear Brazil's rise almost as much as they currently suspect U.S. domination.[5]

Brazil's development underscores the variety of contemporary approaches to Latin America's problems, and thereby also the short-term trend toward diversity. Brazil is strategically located, sharing borders with every South American country except Chile and Ecuador. Of the South American countries it is probably the only one to credibly aspire to world power status by the end of the century. Brazil certainly has the advantage in location and resource base, as well as in infrastructure and organization, and is beginning to achieve undisputed regional power status.

---

5. Dirección de Estrategia, "Relaciones argentino-brasileñas," *Estrategia* (Buenos Aires), #5, January-February 1970, pp. 48–57, provides an example of such concerns, which are also prominent among leaders of the Andean Pact countries.

Among Brazil's neighbors, Argentina has strong regional ambitions of its own and is quick to feel slighted by any hint of favored U.S. treatment of Brazil. Argentine leaders realize that the nation has many internal problems to resolve before it can compete successfully with Brazil. Yet, whereas Brazilian leadership is convinced that Brazil can become a major power on its own, Argentine leaders perceive that regional cooperation and integration may be essential to enable Argentina to become a regional power. Thus, while Brazil has consistently opposed any groupings that would check the expansion of its power, Argentina has just as consistently sought federations or alliances to counter Brazilian influence. Today, for example, Argentina seems well disposed toward the Andean subregional group, whereas Brazil remains distantly cool.

While recognizing that the potential for tension is there, it is important not to overstate these differences. Within Brazil, sensitivity to charges of pro-Americanism and favoritism may increase tendencies to prove Brazilian independence through the advocacy of positions conflicting with those of the United States (as has happened with Brazil's espousal of a 200-mile claim to territorial waters). Moreover, though they fear Brazilian expansionism, few if any Spanish-speaking countries seem interested in accepting Argentine leadership. Nonetheless, any supposed U.S. favoritism toward Brazil could well contribute to increased anti-Brazilian alliances among the countries of Spanish-speaking South America, possibly with anti-U.S. overtones. In the longer run, however, Brazil is both too important to the future of Latin America as a whole and too diplomatically skilled to allow herself to be alienated from her neighbors.

If, referring to nations as a whole, we can say that Brazil constitutes a geopolitical "strong spot," then Bolivia (not to mention Paraguay and Uruguay, the other "buffer" countries) appears to be a major "weak spot." Geographically and politically it is very fragmented. Moreover, Bolivian governments and economic activities have historically been highly penetrated by, and dependent upon, foreign nations. During the 1950s and 1960s, the United States was the major foreign presence. Currently, Argentine and Brazilian interests in, and competition for, influence are increasing. Indeed, in Bolivia's case, it may be only natural for reductions in U.S. presence to be followed by expansion of the presence of other outside powers, in this case Latin American ones, who are seeking resources, markets, and political stability.

A primary effect of the international environment of the 1970s may thus well be to restore an awareness of the more traditional aspects of "power politics" among the Latin American countries themselves. The lowered political and military profile of the United States in Latin America, and the increase in European and Russian diplomatic, economic, and military activities are similarly likely to contribute to heightened Latin American interest in regional conflict environments and in the national characteristics, aspirations, and fears of their individual countries. Yet domestic fears of violent subversion may (depending on perceptions of the international repercussions and external encouragement for subversive activities) contribute to increased cooperation among the Latin American countries themselves.

Regional cooperation has certainly developed on economic matters. Integration, particularly at a subregional level (as in the Andean Group or the Central American Common Market), has made sufficient headway to emphasize national interdependence. Though the process of integration also brings national rivalries to the forefront by highlighting economic competition and expansion, its major long-term effect may well be to emphasize the needs of Latin American countries, individually and collectively, to define their own interests and patterns of development vis-à-vis the outside world.

Conclusion

Compared to the 1950s and 1960s, then, we can expect Latin America to provide a substantially different panorama of intraregional relations during the 1970s. In many respects the opportunities for higher levels of regional cooperation and integration are clearly presenting themselves. Yet at the same time it also appears that potentials for limited political, economic, and even military conflicts over some issues are also rising. Latin American government leaders and political analysts appear to be thoroughly aware of these trends.[6]

Whether conflict or cooperation (or both) is more likely is not clear. But the strengthening of governmental capacities and national identities, in a context of emerging multipolarity, seems likely to make local diversity and nationalism the prevailing features of the Latin American scene. No one nation is likely to establish regional dominance, and subregional alliances based on specific economic and security interests rather than on over-arching ideology seem likely to become the chief form of cooperation.

It is worth emphasizing that diversity need not imply conflict. Sometimes

---

6. In contrast, U.S. scholars and analysts seem barely aware of the probable significance of intra-Latin American relations as a research topic for the 1970s. For an exception, see Weston H. Agor and Andrés Suárez, "The Emerging Latin American Political Subsystem," in Douglas A. Chalmers, ed., *Changing Latin America,* Proceedings of the Academy of Political Science, Vol. 30, No. 4, 1972, pp. 153–66.

national differences help foster cooperation as a means of avoiding or mini-mizing conflict. Certainly the presence of differentiated nations within a given geographic region need not induce military conflict. Differences may be resolved—even struggled over—through a variety of means, of which force is but one. Indeed, with the rise of economic interdependence and other forms of transnational activity, it may well be that economic competition will be the most frequent outcome of diversity in a region like Latin America, where economies are largely competitive rather than complementary.

Politically, the internal differentiation of Latin America will present a severe test of the vitality of the inter-American system, particularly as Latin American differences may occasionally appear magnified in the absence of U.S. predominance. Within this framework, the Organization of American States, long in decline in comparison to the United Nations during the period of U.S. predominance, may retain significance mainly as an instrument for the exposition of the differences among Latin American countries themselves, and for the forging of a new regional consciousness that may in the longer run replace the current trend toward diversity with one toward unity.

Chapter Fourteen

A NOTE ON U.S. GOVERNMENT
EXCHANGE PROGRAMS

Luigi R. Einaudi

As emphasized in the Conclusion, communication between the United States and Latin America has frequently been poor. Without a sound grounding in mutual understanding, the two Americas are seriously handicapped in any effort to identify and maximize mutual interests. This note explores a few aspects of one instrument of international communication: the exchange of persons under governmental auspices.

The General Setting

Government programs account for only part of the travel, study, and work opportunities that make up the international experience of the world's peoples, much of which is sponsored privately, by business concerns, foundations, individuals, and voluntary associations. The importance of government programs, however, lies in their reflection of public policy, and in the potential impact of participants on that policy. In the United States, the Bureau of Educational and Cultural Affairs of the Department of State administers the Mutual Educational and Cultural Exchange Act of 1961. Important international training and exchange activities are also undertaken, however, by such other agencies as the Department of Defense and the Agency for International Development (AID). Together, these governmental exchange programs constitute an important part of America's interaction with the outside world.

The environment in the United States and in Latin America for exchange programs is very different in the 1970s from what it was earlier. In the United States, the reorientation toward domestic problems creates major environmental and bureaucratic problems. Environmentally, it lessens the influence of individuals and organizations concerned with foreign affairs and able to support cultural exchange programs. Bureaucratically, the reduction in activities of agencies such as AID implies a decline in programs of a technical training nature. U.S. training of foreign military officers has been frequently criticized. On the positive side, increased U.S. concern with its own domestic problems may favorably impress visitors who might previously have been repelled by the guileless ethnocentrism of much American advice to foreigners.

In Latin America, one of the major contemporary trends is the continuing growth of the institutions associated with modern industrial societies. Public bureaucracies, universities, military forces, all are increasing the importance of government in Latin American life, which is becoming increasingly urbanized and industrial. Consistent with this greater institutional complexity and growth, Latin American countries are demonstrating increased self-assertiveness and sophistication, often tinged with nationalism. Clashes of interest with the United States are increasingly reflected in the activities of official governmental entities and major private institutions.

In this atmosphere, cultural programs, including exchanges of persons, should increase in importance among instruments available to U.S. policy makers, if only because of the relative decline of U.S. military and economic programs. But there is also an increased need to establish communication on a broad basis that takes into consideration the spread of nationalism and the increasing sophistication of Latin America. Among the many purposes of cultural programs, the most important operational objective is to improve the general environment for long-term constructive relations.

To achieve this objective, programs should be professional and politically nonpartisan. They should express mutuality of interests and style. And they should seek to increase the acceptance of Latin America's own national aspirations in the United States as well as Latin American understanding of the United States. Perhaps the best programs will be those that will take into consideration the increased parallelism between the modern sectors and institutions of Latin America and the United States. Cultural programs should retain elements focused on traditional cultural activities, such as music and the arts, but should be broadened to include intellectual and professional dialogue on matters of public importance, and should receive increased attention within the U.S. foreign policy community, including Congress.[1]

---

1. Another aspect of official U.S. interaction with foreigners merits brief mention because of its negative impact. Visa regulations preventing or restricting travel to the United States by Latin Americans suspected of "Anti-American" views, though less arbitrarily enforced today than in the past, seriously cloud the democratic image of the United States, and should be largely done away with.

Past Performance and Future Requirements

Past U.S. government activities have contributed significantly to the changes in Latin America described elsewhere in this volume. The Alliance for Progress contributed fundamentally to the ideological ferment that led to the emergence of new development priorities within Latin American political elites, and some U.S. programs, at least, played important roles in the process of institutional development. But U.S. programs have also failed to keep up.

• AID is declining just when the generation of new technocrats trained under the Alliance have begun to move into government institutions and make their weight felt.

• U.S. cultural exchange programs have become increasingly marginal in their contribution, as political controversy and the relatively poor quality of many individual grantees have limited their involvement in sensitive areas and institutions.

• Our military training has been more institutionally linked than other types of assistance, but it continues to focus heavily on technical subjects that Latin American countries are increasingly able to handle on their own.

Instead of adapting programs to the increased sophistication of Latin American institutions and public life, the tendency has been to look for ways to preserve established programs and procedures. Even in the Fulbright program, provincial universities and noncontroversial subject matter have been the rule rather than the exception. As a result, all too frequently there is little or no direct contact between the decision-making centers and key social communicators of Latin America and of the United States.

From a Latin American viewpoint, U.S. programs are frequently not serving contemporary needs. Greater local capacity is but one source of the frequently encountered Latin American desire for improved coordination of foreign training. Shortages of foreign currency also require that persons traveling abroad have experiences that do not duplicate what is available locally and that offer some likelihood of contributing to current or future development needs.

Some Suggestions for the Future

Viewed most broadly, of course, exchanges affect a whole range of public and private relationships. The U.S. government cannot monopolize international communications, and frequently should only facilitate contacts among equivalent institutions and professionals in the United States and abroad. Indeed, most of the comments that follow apply primarily to public support for private or quasi-private activities, a traditional focus of information and cultural exchange programs. But consideration should also be given to improved government-to-government communications just below the highest policy levels, including regular exchanges of personnel and occasional bilateral conferences among U.S. and Latin American public officials concerned with foreign policy, national security, and development planning. Conversations on long-term policy directions and international problems have long been a standard dimension of alliance relationships in the Atlantic community, and could, if extended to Latin America, help overcome some of the uncertainty and frustrations associated with the accumulation of immediate problems and lack of recognition.

In view of these considerations, U.S. exchange programs with Latin America should be reoriented along the following lines:

● Exchanges should emphasize *institutions.* U.S. fears of loss of "control" and of Latin American nepotism have delayed recognition of the need to give leading Latin American institutions a major voice in the selection of programs and individuals. Quality people are still a key to successful exchanges, but the utilization of exchangees' knowledge and their reentry into their own societies will be greatly facilitated if they have viable connections with important institutions.

● Exchanges, even short-term visits, should emphasize *professional content,* and should support the development of skills and dialogue among persons faced with similar problems, both in North and South America. State Department Visitor Program grants, for example, could be used to follow up technical training previously made available through AID under the Alliance for Progress. The Government Affairs Institute (GAI) is hindered in developing programs for short-term visitors by erratic communication both with embassies and with potentially interested individuals in U.S. universities and other professional organizations.

● Exchanges should include a mix of *junior* professionals, who would be exchanged on a long-term basis, supplemented by high-quality *senior* personnel, who would engage in more specific short-term projects. As things now stand, the best junior and senior people are both frequently missed, the young because they are difficult to identify and frequently do not come forward because they do not believe they have the required "status," while those who are well established sometimes find it difficult to commit themselves for extended periods of time.

● U.S. government exchange programs should be used to educate North Americans about the profound changes taking place in Latin American life, as well as Latin Americans about the United States. Improved bilateralism would lead to greater Latin American contributions, including the sharing of administrative responsibilities that would help ensure mutuality of interests.

These recommendations are neither new nor particularly earthshaking. To some extent they reflect changes now taking place as more adventurous policy makers and administrators take advantage of opportunities on a country-by-country basis.[2] To implement these principles more generally and transform them into operating realities, however, will require a number of prerequisites. The following stand out:

● Cultural programs are already receiving a higher priority as the decline in both AID and military assistance gives cultural exchanges greater relative weight in U.S. activities. This change, however, should be made explicit to underscore their potential for improving understanding of Latin America even within the U.S. government, as well as for hemispheric communications in general.

● Cultural affairs officers should have some professional qualifications in development problems. More importantly, they should be encouraged to act as facilitators of communications between professionals on both sides. To be effective, this approach may require that the U.S. Foreign Service become more actively involved—as an interpreter between cultures—than traditional concepts of diplomacy and passive political reporting have hitherto encouraged.

● Improved identification of both Latin American and U.S. institutions and potential communicators is a primary requirement. Past Fulbright grantees or Short-Term American Grantees (STAGS) provide a possible source of information and personnel, as do the experiences of the Inter-American Foundation, the Eisenhower Exchange Fellowship Program, and the International Executive Service Corps, among others.

● Cultural exchange activities can achieve their full potential only if they are politically nonpartisan. By promoting U.S. identification with the processes of change and development, exchanges can contribute to the key political goal of a constructive environment for U.S.-Latin American relations. But they can do this only if they reflect Latin American as well as U.S. interests, and particularly if they are not tied to immediate U.S. goals in what

---

2. To a large extent, they also reflect the evolution of private programs, such as the Social Science Research Council's Foreign Area Fellowship Program, which has recently sought to emphasize collaborative research and institutional commitment. See Bryce Wood, "Scholarly Exchanges Between Latin America and the United States," in Douglas A. Chalmers, ed., *Changing Latin America,* Proceedings of the Academy of Political Science, Columbia University, Vol. 30, No. 4, 1972, pp. 123–40.

would appear outside the government as a new "control mechanism." If this political paradox goes unrecognized and exchanges are subordinated to short-term unilateral interests, they will not gain acceptance in either North or South America in the intellectual and professional communities so important to the perspectives of future leaders.

The basic prescription, therefore, is that exchanges not be linked to propaganda, make full use of both governmental and independent profession-als, and focus on assisting Latin America's institutional development to the extent our great but limited capabilities allow.

VI. CONCLUSION

15. Latin America's Development and the United States

Chapter Fifteen

LATIN AMERICA'S DEVELOPMENT
AND THE UNITED STATES

Luigi R. Einaudi

The containment of revolutionary violence has not stopped change in Latin America: indeed, as the essays in this volume demonstrate, local and international relationships are being transformed—often in unexpected ways. The purpose of this brief concluding chapter is to highlight some of the major features of this process of change, to relate them to the rather different situation of the United States, and to suggest some activities that might help the two Americas keep in touch during this period of general redefinition.

The Latin American
Revolution Institutionalized

During the 1960s, it sometimes seemed as though Latin American governments would be swept aside by a resurgent revolutionary tradition, ignited by the dreams of Cuban revolutionaries and sweeping the hemisphere in a series of guerrilla uprisings led by young romantics who saw in armed rebellion the only clear answer to Latin America's problems. In an optimistic and generous, but also confused and somewhat defensive echo, many similar slogans were enshrined in the framework of the Alliance for Progress, making "revolution" the catchword of the decade in Latin America.

Predictably, the enthusiasms of the sixties led more often to failure than to success. The visionaries of the 1960s have yielded, where they have survived, to less dramatic yet perhaps more enduring efforts. For whether reforms have been sought through electoral politics (as in Chile), through the direct imposition of change from above (as in Peru), or as indirect consequences of rapid economic growth (as in Brazil), the *fundamental trend of the 1970s is the translation of the impulse toward change into the programs and activities of central governments. Previous "outside" strategies of voluntaristic violence have been replaced by "inside" strategies designed to reorient national institutions from within rather than replace them.* As a result, the leaders of change today are frequently representatives of the very institutions that have traditionally dominated Latin American life: the Church, the military, "traditional" political parties, and the very central government establishments once criticized as obstinate defenders of the status quo.

No social process is without exceptions and difficulties. The ultimate collapse of Chile's constitutional order and the death of Salvador Allende in September, 1973, underscored the fragility of political and economic life in societies undergoing rapid transformations. Yet underlying the partisan disputes and continuing uncertainties of Latin American life is a generalized commitment to independent national development that promises to be considerably more significant than the guerrilla uprisings of a decade ago, or the temporary retrenchments of the present.

Underpinning this new commitment to national development is a growth of institutions that escapes many of the simpler generalizations through which we have become accustomed to view "Latin America." The spread of education and industrialization has transformed old institutions and created new ones. Throughout Latin America we find planning institutes, research centers, and similar manifestations of growing economic and intellectual modernity. A new generation of political leaders and government technocrats, politically socialized since World War II and frequently educated in the leading universities of the industrialized world, are applying innovative techniques to the solution of Latin America's problems and to the search for a revitalized international role, freer from external domination than in the past.

Generalizations such as these are dangerous in an area as varied as Latin America. They can be particularly misleading because of the poor mental hygiene displayed by use of the singular, as in "the Church," "the military," or "Latin America" for what are clearly plural phenomena within as well as among countries. Many of the developments discussed in this volume apply more to the larger rather than the smaller countries of Latin America. But the general nature of the trends we are discussing can be illustrated as follows:

• Catholic authorities have abandoned their traditional legitimization of secular authority, adopting instead a role of independent social criticism, denouncing injustices in accord with a "prophetic mission" that profoundly alters the political environment in favor of change. Underpinning this evolution, publicly but rather inaccurately dramatized by the activities of radicalized priests, is the emergence of National Bishops' Conferences that establish guidelines for each country's Catholic communities. The deliberations of these conferences are supported by Catholic study groups, research centers, and a growing number of scholarly and semi-scholarly publications.

• Military forces are increasingly concerned with the nexus between security, their primary mission, and development. National war colleges, considered twenty years ago primarily as centers for the transmission of U.S. military doctrines, have played a major role in the elaboration of indigenous doctrines, as has been most evident in Peru and Brazil. Argentina even has an independent Institute of Strategic Studies, which surpasses its own war college in the constant elaboration and public dissemination of materials on civil-military relations and national development. But this phenomenon has not been limited to the larger countries: Venezuela and now Guatemala have recently founded centers of "higher military studies."

• The spread of planning institutes and statistical offices in government ministries reflects the increased concern, and to some extent capacity, of Latin American leaders for dealing with socioeconomic problems. Public and quasi-public corporations have risen, not only in countries like Chile, which under Allende sought explicitly "socialist" solutions, or Peru, which is experimenting with "participationist" formulas, but in the larger countries following more "traditional" forms of economic development, such as Argentina, Brazil, and Mexico.

• Public bureaucracies are gaining in strength and responsibility, have improved internal training procedures, and display other signs of increasing rationalization. The foreign service training institutes ("diplomatic academies") within foreign ministries have become prerequisites for the diplomatic career and have improved in quality. Public bureaucracies are also increasing their regional linkages. Information and training activities related to petroleum exploration and production, for example, are now fostered by ARPEL, the Latin American association of state oil companies.

• Universities have proliferated and diversified. Over the past decade significant advances have been made in graduate studies and in the development of independent local research centers. Schools of public administration have sprung up to provide a source of public servants whose qualifications extend beyond partisan political militancy.

These developments suggest that to understand the course of Latin America in the years ahead it will be essential to focus on institutional processes and elite perspectives. Mass pressures will certainly continue, and will in many cases fundamentally affect the directions of change, but mass participation will normally occur through institutions and elections, rather than through voluntaristic uprisings and guerrilla violence. Relevant institutions are both public (military forces, government bureaucracies, planning institutes, and national universities) and private (the Church, political parties, private universities, trade unions, and major corporations). Significantly, semi-autonomous public agencies are also assuming major roles in key areas of economic activity, such as petroleum, banking, and heavy industry.

Some Consequences of Institutional Change

In sum, a basic feature of Latin American life today is increased institutional development and sophistication. This pattern of state-related institutional growth does not mean that the "free enterprise system" is being supplanted by "socialism," or even that Latin America is abandoning all of its traditional ways. The nature of emerging systems, their nomenclature, and their actual accomplishments will continue to vary greatly from country to country. But institutional development helps explain the recent decline of three of the major characteristics of past Latin American politics: dictators, oligarchies, and political instability.

The lessened power of individual *caudillos* may be exemplified by the evolution of military institutions. Despite the ever-present rewards for strong individual leadership, military leaders are now checked by the need to deal with their fellow officers within an institutional framework. Generals, not colonels or majors, command, and the road to personal power even for a general has become less a function of individual popularity or troop command than of technical competence and bureaucratic skill.

The lessening of oligarchical forms derives in part from the presence of new actors in the political game and greater diversification among old actors. Modern institutions are less subject to elitist manipulation, and provide channels for elements of the middle classes and the professions to make their views felt.

Lessened instability may not affect leading government officeholders, as these frequently still change rapidly, but takes the form of fewer chances of radical upheaval through revolution from below, and of increased bureaucratic stability. As in the United States, public policy and institutional relationships are acquiring a continuity that transcends specific regimes and narrow partisan limits.

Taken as a whole, these changes also follow from increased dispersion of power among different groups, no one of which has the power on its own to dominate the rest. The decision of many Catholic leaders to seek an independent and frequently critical posture, for example, contributes to public debate rather than to the emergence of a new single dominant power center, or "counter-elite." The weakening of traditional "parties of notables" and the still hesitant emergence of mass-based parties, and the erosion of the elite environment that made of universities an adjunct of narrowly based political orders, are other indications of increased fluidity and dispersion of political influence. This process also makes alienated elements among students or the urbanized poor harder to organize or to bring to bear directly on political processes.

The dispersion of power among several groups, some with an increased capacity to make their own demands on the political system, can be symbolized by the transition of several military forces from political "arbiters" to policy makers. In the past, officers tended to participate in politics on the call of others or to mediate conservatively among other contenders for power. Today, officers insist that military institutions as a whole be recognized as actors in their own right, capable of generating national initiatives. Yet at the same time, given the extreme diversity of political forces and the requirements of knowledge and technology underlying effective policy, neither the military nor any other group can govern for long alone.

One result seems likely to be a variety of different interrelationships linking contending interest groups. Exactly what form these coalitions will take under differing political and economic circumstances remains an issue difficult to define satisfactorily. One thing seems clear: no simple distinction between "military" and "civilian" government seems likely to hold.

Another question relates to the long-term capacity of governments and institutions to maintain popular confidence. The failures of the guerrilla movements and Cuba's limited economic growth and lack of national independence are contributing to a sense of caution even among radicals and thereby defusing some of the revolutionary voluntarism that was so predominant a characteristic of the hemispheric scene in the early sixties. How long will these sobering lessons be remembered if government initiatives currently under way fail to meet expectations?

Some Directions of Change

The institutional channeling of change is to some extent a guarantee of stability and of social control—but it also contributes to increased experimentation on the part of governments. Latin America's governments are operating in a context of increased nationalism, of general diversification of linkages with foreign powers, and of an accentuation of diversity within the Latin American region as well as within the countries themselves. Most importantly, concern over national identity is challenging the more conventional interest in economic growth.

These developments are reflected in three foci of governmental activity. The first involves a growing effort to increase exports, particularly of non-traditional manufactures and semi-manufactures, as a means of increasing the availability of foreign exchange and thereby maintaining the pace of industrial growth. Set against this innovative attempt to relieve a growth bottle-neck is the likelihood that continuing unemployment and concentrated poverty will lead to increased efforts at income redistribution, a policy goal that may frequently conflict with growth. Finally, governments are attempting to seek new arrangements in foreign economic relations, driving harder bargains in negotiations over trade and foreign investment, and seeking lower cost and politically more acceptable institutional arrangements. Not infrequently, state enterprises will seek to participate in these arrangements, or to acquire technology and management independent of direct foreign control.

The prospects for these initiatives are mixed. Industrial efficiency is greater than commonly believed, and could contribute to a major expansion of nontraditional exports. But until Latin American economies show greater capacity to mobilize savings for capital formation (as Brazil has done in just the last few years), overall growth prospects must be described as modest. Nonetheless, of the three goals just mentioned, industrial growth through export promotion, income redistribution, and control over foreign involvements and influence, two are not growth goals in themselves. This suggests at least one important implication—that rates of increase in GNP are not likely to be adequate indicators of the success of government economic policies. Latin American governments are to a significant extent going to measure their success by their capacity to achieve more equitable income distribution and greater control over their domestic economies.

Considerable uncertainty, and a need to clarify concepts and obtain improved data, prevent a clearer projection of general regional trends. Nationalism clearly can be a positive factor in many ways: it underlies the self-respect needed to participate in a more relaxed fashion in the world. It also has a democratic component of concern for the integration of marginal population elements into national life. On the other hand, nationalism can become a source of friction and of escalation of potential conflicts. The evolution of regional subgroupings and of the national security policies of the individual Latin American states are topics on which there has been little systematic research, despite the increasing regional weight of Brazil and of the leading Spanish-speaking republics, particularly Argentina, Peru, and Mexico, and the international repercussions of events in Cuba, Chile, and Panama. Nonetheless, the strengthening of governmental capacities and national identities seems likely in the long run to lead to increased cooperation among Latin

American countries on common economic and security interests vis-à-vis the outside world, which is itself becoming increasingly differentiated with the decline of bipolarity.

Several of the Latin American trends discussed above, therefore, will decisively condition the international environment. Among these, the following seem most worthy of emphasis:

- Latin America's social and economic inequalities will continue and will occasionally provide fuel for political unrest, but will not prevent overall institutional continuity.

- Governments and elites in Latin America will be less subject to external manipulation than in the past.

- Most Latin American governments are likely to seek to maximize their national potentials through policies conducive to greater industrialization.

- The emphasis on industrialization will increasingly make the theme of trade, not aid, a central issue in inter-American relations.

- The call for improved terms of trade and economic relations will be supported *institutionally* by Latin America's own development and consequent desire for lessened dependence, and *internationally* by competition among the major industrial powers, whose activities provide Latin America with more varied options—both politically and economically—than in the past.

Taken as a whole, these trends derive essentially from Latin America's continuing growth and have considerable positive potential. How the United States responds to them may affect developments, even decisively in some cases, but cannot alter their presence. In addition, of course, U.S. government policies will depend not merely on these trends and on the relative weights assigned to specific American interests in Latin America itself, but on the evolution of American domestic policies and foreign relations as a whole.

The remainder of this conclusion, therefore, considers some important aspects of change in the United States, presents a few general considerations affecting the evolution of U.S. policies toward Latin America, and concludes with some suggestions on possible future directions.

Change in the United States

How will the United States respond to Latin America's continuing development? The policy statements of the Nixon Administration toward Latin America have been relatively vague. The President in 1969 called for a "mature partnership," but neither he nor other spokesmen have gone much beyond appeals for lessened U.S. "paternalism," and government behavior has been chiefly characterized by inaction. This lack of explicit definition has contributed to a good deal of uncertainty about American intentions. This confusion about U.S. Latin American policy is compounded by the fact that intellectual observers and practicing politicians—in North and South America alike—sometimes still appear to be reacting with the reflexes of the past. The tendency is still strong, for example, for North Americans to consider Latin American criticism of the U.S.A. as somehow related to "communist" activity, or to encourage Latin America to follow U.S. prescriptions for economic development and "democracy." Similarly, many Latin Americans are quick to denounce U.S. activities, or even developments in their own countries they do not understand or like, as manifestations of American "imperialism."

Indeed, many observers of U.S. policy suspect that recent changes in American activities in Latin America do not represent fundamental changes in American perceptions or policy, but constitute rather a tactical shift, the adoption of new (and generally more intelligent) "forms of control" by the United States over Latin America. According to this view, the United States, or at least its ruling groups, have a permanent interest, largely economic, in maintaining hegemony over Latin America. The means required to maintain this domination change with changing circumstances. We saw in Chapter Two that youthful Latin American radicals argued in the 1950s that the emergence of the Good Neighbor policy under Franklin Delano Roosevelt had represented a tactical shift, required by the ineffectiveness of Dollar Diplomacy and the Big Stick in advancing U.S. economic interests. Under the impact of the Cold War, the overt noninterventionism of the Good Neighbor was supplemented by covert intervention and finally by the strengthening of military and police forces under the screen of the "developmentalist" legitimacy provided by the Alliance for Progress. Continuing this line of reasoning, the often crude interventionism of the 1950s and 1960s is today seen to be similarly giving way to fresh tactics. According to these analyses, subtle new "forms" of control," known generally as the "low profile," are being developed to enable the United States to continue its domination. These new tactics are said to include indirect economic pressures, chiefly exercised through international financial institutions, and the delegation of direct interventionism to the more powerful Latin American nations, such as Brazil, which, having been drawn into the U.S. orbit by prior economic and military programs, are now capable of acting as indirect executors of American intentions.

The sweep of this argument is breathtaking. Though some might find it appealing for that very reason, I am somewhat troubled by its failure to discriminate between different American interests and agencies, public and private, and by its assumptions of unified rationality and control over time. To be sure, there is much in the argument that is more accurate than most Americans would care to admit. Some forms of intervention have indeed had to be modified or abandoned partly because they became counterproductive. Certainly, for example, I.T.T.'s attempts to foster U.S. government intervention in Chile in 1970 failed at least partly because the tactics advocated seemed unlikely to succeed. But the chief objection to this argument is that it overlooks some of the most important forces of change in contemporary U.S.-Latin American relations. Despite its assumption that changing Latin American conditions have forced tactical shifts on the part of the United States, the imperialist argument implies that Latin America has been and is likely to remain ultimately a pawn of U.S. manipulation.

Without minimizing the enormous differences in power between "the United States" globally considered, and the individual states of Latin America, Latin America's "margin of freedom" appears to be substantial and growing, and is overlooked by an overly great concentration on "dependence." The essays presented in this volume suggest that most countries have reached a point in which the state can exercise a decisive mediating role with respect to the impact of foreign influences, including the activities of private corporations as well as governments. In addition, the role of the U.S. government in foreign affairs has begun to change drastically, as American leaders moderate their aspirations. The realization that there are limits to U.S. power began with the Kennedy Administration's failure at Bahía de Cochinos in Cuba in 1961, and has been confirmed more recently by events in Vietnam. Indeed, Vietnam offers us a useful beginning from which to reconstruct something of what is actually happening to U.S. approaches to Latin America and the outside world.

The Political Crisis in the United States

Vietnam has for several years been the chief problem of U.S. foreign policy and the major focus of political attention. The logic of disengagement from the Vietnamese folly has led the U.S. government to seek more cooperative relations with both the Soviet Union and China. One result has been to accelerate a tendency toward world political and economic multipolarity already foreshadowed by the resurgence of Europe and Japan from the devastation of World War II, by the widening differences within the "socialist bloc," and by the refusal of many countries of the Third World to allow themselves to be drawn into a bipolar system. Understanding and participating constructively in the new international system now gradually replacing the broken post-World War II balance is understandably the first priority of U.S. foreign policy.

But the Vietnam war has also combined with the press of domestic problems within the United States to produce a generalized revulsion against "foreign entanglements" among the American public. One consequence, in addition to a climate of hostility and divided opinion that bedevils all concerned with foreign policy, has been great pressure on U.S. foreign assistance programs, economic as well as military, and the growing difficulty they have experienced in Congress throughout the past decade. In this environment, the Alliance for Progress, and with it much of the political-military interventionism characteristic of U.S. Latin American policy during the 1960s, has been quietly abandoned. This retreat from interventionism (no new Marine interventions, for example, since the Dominican affair in 1965) does not require as an explanation either a sudden growth of sympathetic understanding for Latin America or the emergence of a new U.S. "imperialist master plan." Rather more prosaically, the origins of current policy are to be found in a desire to avoid problems that might divert attention and resources from more important issues. The main objective of U.S. Latin American policy today, therefore, seems to be more negative than positive: to minimize conflict, if necessary through inaction.

Coming on the heels of the bureaucratized hyperactivism of the Alliance for Progress, this style is distinctly refreshing. It may even work relatively well for a while. But it cannot be a permanent approach to policy. Among the many issues that today require increased attention from the U.S. government are the entire range of economic relations within the hemisphere, both bilateral and multilateral, as well as the establishment of new patterns of political and military relations outside of the traditional but now slowly dissolving "assistance" framework. Specific problems that cannot be avoided much longer include the relationship between expropriation of U.S. proper-ties and U.S. policy towards the international lending agencies, an area in which executive indecision has already produced some congressional heavy-handedness; trade and investment policies, including transfers of arms and technology, but essentially focused on the place of direct American private investment in Latin American industries, and on the availability of American markets for nontraditional Latin American exports; and a host of other issues, including relations with Cuba, the future status of the Panama Canal, and the rise of Brazilian power in South America.

But it is one thing to be aware of the need to recast policy and quite another to in fact do so. President Nixon has characterized inter-American relations as a "sharp disappointment"; in his 1972 report to the Congress on U.S. foreign policy he said that

We have yet to work out with our friends a solution of the conflict between their desire for our help and their determination to be free of dependence upon us. The thrust for change in Latin America, and our response to it, have yet to shape themselves into a pattern permitting us to make as full a contribution as we wish and as our hemisphere friends expect.[1]

Earlier, in 1969, the Rockefeller Report was issued for public consideration, but not generally implemented. Its fate, like the continuing debates over U.S. policies throughout the world, not just in Latin America, suggests that the process of redefining America's roles abroad is likely to be thoroughly agonizing. For at least the past ten years, as the post-World War II bipartisan consensus on foreign policy began to break down, American national leaders have had great difficulty in formulating and then communicating policies commensurate with a true sense of both the limits and potentials of U.S. power and responsibilities.

The United States, in other words, is currently traversing a period of profound intellectual and moral uncertainty, internally and internationally. The Vietnam war and concern over domestic priorities have fostered divisions that frequently remain beyond the capacity of American leaders or political parties to articulate constructively. Lack of consensus in turn makes policy difficult to define or defend. Domestic support for the détente in the Cold War is matched by uncertainty over the basis and nature of emerging patterns of world politics and economics.

Lack of attention and confusion do not, however, necessarily imply that bureaucratic routines will take over and policy remain unchanged. Indeed, if current trends persist unchanged, bilateral economic and military assistance programs will go out of existence, at least as we have known them since World War II. From an American standpoint, the Alliance for Progress was in many respects a delayed application of the principles of U.S. responsibility and leadership expressed earlier in the Marshall Plan. To take another example, military assistance to Latin America was also largely a reflection of a global postwar policy of strengthening allies to enable them to operate jointly with U.S. forces in the face of a common enemy. The current process of redefinition of international relationships in all their phases will profoundly

---

1. *U.S. Foreign Policy for the 1970s: The Emerging Structure of Peace,* a report to the Congress by Richard M. Nixon, February 9, 1972, U.S. Government Printing Office, Washington, D.C., 1972, pp. 11–12.

condition U.S. policies toward Latin America, as well as toward the rest of the world. The import surcharge of August 15, 1971, which was applied to Latin America as well as to the more developed countries, is a harbinger of this process.

The Centrality of Economic Interests

Economic conflicts are a major theme of inter-American relations. And they are likely to remain so. But economic issues cannot be considered in isolation. Particularly in foreign affairs, U.S. corporations frequently gain their political influence by manipulating the symbols of nationalism, a topic much written about in the United States with regard to Latin America, but virtually ignored in thinking about the United States. Congressional nationalism does not, of course, always favor the operations of multinational enterprises, particularly when these utilize foreign factors to produce for the U.S. market. Nonetheless, rising protectionist sentiment in American labor and Congress, and recent legislation sponsored by Representative Henry B. Gonzalez, Democrat of Texas, suggest that economic nationalism may be replacing anti-Communism as an accepted standard of "toughness."

The 1972 Gonzalez Amendment extends the Hickenlooper principle to multilateral economic relations, by requiring U.S. representatives on international financial institutions to vote against loans to countries which have nationalized U.S. properties without first paying the compensation desired by the companies affected. This is, of course, not the language of the Amendment. But so long as there is no accepted external measure, the effect of the doctrine of "prompt, adequate and effective" compensation is precisely this: to make U.S. assistance policy dependent on the attitudes of major foreign investors in their relations with foreign countries. This is clearly not the desire of many in the Executive branch—but others, with a powerful assist from Congressional nationalism, still prevail. As a $26 million disaster relief loan to Peru in 1972 implied, such pressures can be partially overcome through other channels—but only at the cost of great effort.

The prominence of economic factors in U.S. policy toward Latin America is enhanced today by the absence of recognized countervailing political and security interests. In the past two decades, American leaders generally felt that the world situation required a friendly and developing Latin America— whether as a political ally against the U.S.S.R., or as a strategic reserve in case of actual conflict and reconstruction, or as a front line of defense against foreign Communist attempts to exploit the weaknesses of Latin American underdevelopment through subversion. For these political and security reasons, therefore, U.S. policy sought to foster Latin American development.

Inevitably, the United States—following a pattern that suited its resources and historical experience—sought to encourage Latin American development through "free enterprise" and U.S. private investment, as well as by providing public assistance. Sometimes, in fact, the American companies seemed reluctant to act on their own to make the investments favored by U.S. policies. It was President John F. Kennedy who argued a week before his death that

There is not enough available public capital either in the United States or in Latin America to carry development forward at the pace that is demanded. . . . *If encouraged,* private investment . . . can . . . provide the vital margin of success as it did in the development of all the nations of the West and most especially in the development of the United States of America.[2]

The point often missed in discussions of U.S. foreign policy and "imperialism" is precisely this: So long as a substantial consensus existed in the United States that development was necessary for security and that development in turn depended at least in part on American private capital, the defense and even advocacy of American private investment in Latin America was a concern affecting the security of the United States. Of course, American companies sometimes sought U.S. government protection or influence. But the driving force was frequently not the companies using the state to implement their desires; it was rather the state that actively encouraged such relations in the name of security. Business is not always just "business."

Today, without compelling reasons for such policies, the U.S. government's approach is essentially passive. Latin America, it is increasingly felt, does not threaten the United States. Moreover, while economic relationships may serve to lessen the likelihood of war with China or the Soviet Union by creating interdependence, economic relationships with Latin America may well be a source of political tensions. American private investments in Latin America, it is now felt, often create more political headaches than they resolve. Thus perhaps investment should no longer be encouraged. But the "rights" of U.S. investors as citizens entitled to the protection of their government cannot be ignored either, and may no longer be counterbalanced as much as in the past by security considerations or the political requirement for friendly relations.

U.S. governmental restraint toward the Chilean copper expropriations, for example, was almost certainly influenced by a desire to avoid a repetition of the mutual escalation that a decade earlier transformed economic and politi-

---

2. Remarks of the President to the Inter-American Press Association, as released by the Office of the White House Press Secretary, Miami Beach, Florida, November 18, 1963 (emphasis supplied).

cal problems with Cuba into a security crisis with the Soviet Union. But who else in Latin America can play such a card in an era of great power détente? Will what Washington considers an effort to "have with Latin America the relations it is prepared to have with us" thus turn out in practice to be a new form of mercantilism? Will U.S. policy become a hostage to the interests and activities of its private business concerns, backed by Congressional nationalism, untempered either by understanding of Latin America or by a broader sense of U.S. national interests?

Before accepting such a gloomy prospect, we should consider several additional perspectives. First, it is both inevitable and legitimate for the government of the United States to seek equitable treatment for its citizen-investors. Even so, it should be noted that President Nixon explicitly provided for other interests in his 1972 policy statement on expropriation:

Henceforth, should an American firm be expropriated without reasonable steps to provide prompt, adequate, and effective compensation, there is a presumption that the expropriating country would receive no new bilateral economic benefits, *unless major factors affecting our interests require us to do otherwise.*[3]

Secondly, as the Nixon statement implies, the means likely to be employed in defense of economic interests are likely also to be economic. Even so, their application may well be limited by the decline in U.S. strategic concern for Latin America, and by the collapse of the ideological rationale that had automatically linked investment to development to security. Limited economic pressures, however obnoxious, are clearly different in kind from political subversion or from the U.S. Marine Corps.

Thirdly, the U.S. government cannot limit its interest in Latin America exclusively to economic matters. Even if it were to do so, that decision would not necessarily automatically determine the content of policy. Differing economic interests frequently come into conflict. Should conflicts between some companies or even one company and a local government be allowed to endanger the operations of other companies? Should trade be sacrificed to investment? Access to raw materials, for example, is not necessarily determined by ownership of the means of production. Chilean copper continued to be marketed predominantly in the United States and other Western countries, even after the nationalization of Kennecott and Anaconda.

Finally, it is not clear that U.S. private economic activities are either inevitably damaging to Latin America, or that they are independent of growing Latin American regulatory capacities. Latin American governments

---

3. *U.S. Foreign Policy for the 1970s, op. cit.,* p. 76 (emphasis supplied).

have for some time been successfully imposing greater national controls over foreign economic activities. Transfer pricing, royalty and technology payments, profit remittances, taxation and management policies, all are coming under increasingly careful and informed scrutiny. In addition, multinational enterprises can be of considerable use in current attempts to increase Latin America's non-traditional exports.

Relations would be far easier, of course, if each side did not fear the other was playing a "zero-sum" game with few prospects for mutual advantage. In practice, many Latin Americans remain dubious about the ability of all but the strongest governments to keep up with the constantly changing forms of international economic relations. On the American side, there is some possibility that foreign investors may become discouraged by constantly changing "rules of the game," and that the investment climate may be affected negatively. Any "drying up" of new investments, however, would be the result, not of a coordinated "imperialist plot," but rather of the lessened attractiveness of investment in Latin America.

Many Latin Americans, influenced by the powerful impact of U.S. economic activities on their societies, seem to give credence to the notion that the United States must export capital for its own survival, and therefore discount such possibilities. However, opportunities for investment are so varied that even were the vague Leninist thesis on imperialism generally correct, the United States could still export capital through investments elsewhere, including "socialist" Eastern Europe, the Soviet Union, or even China. Were that to happen, that part of the U.S. entrepreneurial class active in Latin America would certainly suffer, but the United States and its economy, however labeled, would just as certainly survive. Latin America's relative importance in U.S. foreign trade has already declined. And while much of what the United States continues to import does fall into the "essential raw materials" category, access may not necessarily depend on continued U.S. ownership of the means of production.

Lessening U.S. strategic interest in Latin America may ironically also deprive Latin Americans of means of controlling the United States. The predictable responses elicited in the past, for example, by the fear of Communism, are no longer there. In fact, many Latin American leaders now complain privately that it is difficult to elicit any response at all from the United States government. Why should U.S. investors, faced with what they consider hostility, behave any differently? Just as importantly, why should U.S. labor leaders support activities by multinational enterprises they feel exploit cheap foreign labor to the detriment of employment in the United States?

Despite the Alliance for Progress, U.S. commitment to the development of foreign countries in general has weakened steadily since the 1950s. To take just one dimension: now that the advent of nuclear parity and the evolution of relations with the Soviet Union have altered the strategic perceptions of a generation ago, Latin America seems less important as a reservoir of industrial capacity and raw materials for reconstruction after a potential world war. In the longer run, of course, Latin America's growing industrialization and the dwindling world reserves of natural resources may lead to a reassertion of the importance of Latin American trade and raw materials to the United States. By then, however, economic relations, including access to raw materials, may already have been largely determined by the ground rules now emerging as Latin American countries seek to assert control over their resources before they are depleted. This is but one reason for following with care developments in countries like Peru, now taking the lead in exploring new forms of economic organization and cooperation.

These problems will require a constructive political environment for their resolution. Latin American governments, we have seen, are increasingly statist in their approach to economic problems. U.S. policy must consider these Latin American political and institutional factors as well as U.S. interests. To take but one example: the growing concern over the environment character-istic of the current decade could facilitate joint development and application of anti-pollution technology and resource utilization patterns on a coopera-tive basis with Latin America before it repeats our worst mistakes. But U.S. industry cannot normally afford to share its experience with the Third World without economic incentives. In this as in other areas there is a fundamental role for the U.S. government in promoting first dialogue and awareness, and then policies to maximize common interests.

But there is no guarantee that cooperation will come automatically, without effort on both sides. As Raymond Aron once commented, when men do not decide, events decide for them. And events seem to be slowly but inexorably driving the two Americas apart.

The Future

The best means to ensure the ability to identify the interests we are most likely to share with Latin America (and thereby also to maximize our capacity to defend those interests over which we may enter into conflict) is a continuing dialogue with the Latin American countries.

From this viewpoint, one of the most dangerous heritages of the seventies may well be the lack of dialogue in the sixties. Vietnam and Cuba have not only affected direct dialogue between Americans and Latin Americans but have also damaged the links of the U.S. government to potential interpreters in the U.S. intellectual community, and weakened both through a process of mutual alienation. In addition, the resistance, frequently but not always polarized along ideological lines, of many American liberals and Latin American nationalists to what they consider an overweening American presence and a naive desire to impose American solutions—which would be a somewhat unfair but not altogether inaccurate rendering of one aspect of the Alliance for Progress—has hindered a search for alternative patterns of relations. And there has been a time lag—in the American public as well as in Latin America—in perceiving the U.S. government's increased awareness of this issue.

For these and other reasons, despite our incredible technological progress, communications between the developing Latin American institutions and the United States tend on the whole to be poor. Latin America's growing development, the rise of nationalism, the increased diversity of Latin America's foreign links, and the uncertainty of the exact ways in which we ourselves should define our interests there, all suggest a need to develop what President Nixon has called a more mature relationship. But they also create a prior requirement for exchange of views to identify the forms this relationship should take as it is divested of the tutelary dimensions of prior policy.

The transition of Argentina and Brazil from being aid recipients to the status of aid givers illustrates some interesting problems in communication. To some extent, Argentina and Brazil, by participating in U.S. aid programs, were thereby engaged in a dialogue with the U.S. government. This dialogue—always somewhat conflicted—may be significantly affected by the termination of the aid relationship. In these countries, as also in Mexico which has avoided many bilateral relationships, and in other Latin American countries as they too become increasingly industrialized, there will be a need for the maintenance of communication in matters of common interest, including technology and economic policies generally.

While many Latin Americans worry about the danger of U.S. "penetration," most still seek U.S. understanding and would favor strengthened professional relationships and communications among U.S. and Latin American national institutions, both public and private. Simultaneously, however, past and current controversies have frequently contributed—on both sides—to diminished interaction and to what in the United States has been called a "low profile" policy. To the extent that the low profile is understood as the abandonment of attempts to impose U.S. solutions on Latin American problems and to lay the basis for a more mature relationship, such a policy guideline is clearly desirable. To the extent, however, that it paralyzes individual initiative and contributes to a decline in the interaction necessary for understanding, it is just as clearly undesirable. To some extent, we may be faced with a practical contradiction between the goals of nonintervention and cooperation: If Americans can only cooperate in an overbearing and counter-productive fashion, then it may be preferable not to try. But this view is probably an overreaction to criticism and to mistakes of the past. If the western hemisphere is to have a future conducive to the common interests of its countries, that future must be built, and the building of anything worth-while inevitably entails a certain amount of friction.

In many ways, therefore, the central intellectual challenge of the 1970s for the United States and Latin America may well be the development of relationships outside of the traditional assistance-intervention framework. These relationships should enable Latin America to shape its own paths of development and define its own interests, while encouraging a continuing rediscovery of common interests within this changing inter-American context. Only if it recognizes the changes that are taking place can a new policy consensus, when it is finally forged, incorporate the improved consciousness of mutual interests necessary to give it some stability.

In the interim, the old principle of nonintervention may still prove a useful reference point—despite its unattainability—in providing Latin America great-er latitude and in developing a basis for greater cooperation in the future. The cornerstone of policy would be the reaffirmation of the principle of noninter-ference in Latin American affairs, with the United States explicitly recog-nizing the right of states to give themselves any form of political or economic organization that they see fit. A major corollary of this doctrine would be that the United States recognize all regimes in Latin America, whether communist or fascist, socialist or oligarchical, democratic or dictatorial, military or civilian. Secondly, the United States would do away with the discriminatory treatment embodied most vividly in the maze of restrictions currently affecting U.S. assistance programs to Latin America—even if the price were the termination of all assistance.

The outline of such a policy could be roughly as follows:

Diplomatically, to extend automatic recognition to any government in control of its national territory.

Politically, to seek constructive relations by emphasizing the advancement of common interests while simultaneously recognizing that the evolution of a more harmonious world order, and hence U.S. security and prosperity as well, depend on the mutual acceptance of diversity.

Militarily, to cooperate on a technical and quasi-commercial basis through sales of such equipment and services as the United States makes available elsewhere, but terminating concessional military and police assistance programs.[4]

Economically, to extend nondiscriminatory treatment to Latin America, but otherwise to treat trade and investment as primarily private matters, while seeking to offset major imbalances through multilateral programs and bilateral consultations.

Culturally, to foster greater understanding of Latin America in the United States, and to increase nonpartisan professional exchanges and training of governmental and private personnel from both North and South.[5]

I do not advocate this general orientation as a panacea. The problems and even direct conflicts of interest between the Americas are too many to be papered over or solved with slogans. But I believe that without an atmosphere of "respectful and correct relations" we cannot hope to approach the issues that divide us or to construct a new pattern more in harmony with our aspirations.

The collapse of the simplistic design of the Alliance for Progress has coincided with the erosion of the Cold War and the post-World War II international political and economic system. What is left is variety, multipolarity, and a good deal of confusion. Future U.S. Latin American policy will inevitably reflect the broader principles of the post-Vietnam world. But what sense of purpose will infuse specific approaches to Latin America? Commercialism is too petty, and "the common good" doesn't sound very convincing—at least in the absence of a common enemy—particularly in the light of accumulating evidence about conflicts of interests within the hemisphere, and the difficulties of unilaterally imposing "rational" solutions.

Past U.S. policy toward Latin America, like today's relative indifference, frequently had little to do with Latin America. Indeed, that was one of its chief problems, and has led to many contemporary tensions. Concerned with blocking the advance of Communism, U.S. leaders tended to interpret events in countries they did not understand as part of a worldwide Soviet conspiracy. Not understanding the problem, they naturally sought to resolve it by applying U.S. solutions. Today, with the urgency gone and with Vietnam-

---

4. A more thorough development of this approach will be found in Luigi R. Einaudi, Hans Heymann, Jr., David Ronfeldt, and Cesar Sereseres, *Arms Transfers to Latin America: Toward a Policy of Mutual Respect,* R-1173-DOS, The Rand Corporation, Santa Monica, California, June 1973, especially pp. 62–69.

5. Chapter Fourteen provides additional considerations on this subject, which stands out as a virtual prerequisite to the improved communication between Latin America and the United States that must underlie constructive relations in other areas.

induced beginnings of wisdom about the limits of U.S. power, U.S. leaders, to the extent they are prepared to think at all about Latin America, also seem prepared to listen for Latin American initiatives and advice.

Unfortunately, however, we all seem to share one thing: though we live in an increasingly interdependent modern world, we have lost our vision of what that world should be. Or perhaps it would be more accurate to say that as we have begun to shed our parochial world views, we have yet to replace them with a new one. The decline of the "Western Hemisphere ideal" is complete. Unless we and others like us can come up with a new vision, we shall in the interim simply stumble along together in interdependent—but separate—ways.

SUPPLEMENTARY READING

Luigi R. Einaudi

This book interprets the present with an eye to the future. The authors have relied heavily on personal experience, interviews, and ongoing research to complement published materials. The frequently elusive nature of contemporary documentation and the book's generally "futuristic" focus make it difficult to suggest additional references beyond those already furnished in the text.

But the past can be documented even if the future cannot. The notes that follow combine older classics and newer works to offer an introduction to Latin America's varied traditions and contemporary history. Only books in English on general subjects are included. Many important works are omitted. Readers seeking specialized information, or analyses of specific countries, will find references in the books listed below. More advanced students with a working knowledge of Spanish or Portuguese should, of course, rely principally on the growing body of research and commentary published in Latin America.

Reference Works

A good brief bibliography is R. A. Humphreys, *Latin American History, A Guide to the Literature in English*, Oxford University Press, London, 1966. The more recent Charles C. Griffin, Editor, *Latin America, A Guide to the Historical Literature*, University of Texas Press, Austin, 1971, contains extensive references to works in Spanish and Portuguese. Claudio Véliz, Editor, *Latin America and the Caribbean: A Handbook*, Frederick A. Praeger, New York, 1968, is an indispensable survey, with nearly one hundred articles on a wealth of topics. The standard geography is Preston E. James, *Latin America*, Fourth Edition, The Odyssey Press, New York, 1969. Statistical materials are brought together by the Latin American Center, University of California at Los Angeles, *Statistical Abstract of Latin America*, issued annually, with occasional supplements.

History

A fact-filled single-volume introduction in English is Hubert Herring, *A History of Latin America from the Beginnings to the Present*, Third Edition, Alfred A. Knopf, New York, 1968. The best analysis of the colonial system is C. H. Haring, *The Spanish Empire in America*, Oxford University Press, New York, 1947. For social history, John J. Johnson, *Political Change in Latin America*, Stanford University Press, Stanford, California, 1958, documents the emergence of middle-class groups in the twentieth century and has an excellent bibliography.

For intellectual history, W. Rex Crawford, *A Century of Latin-American Thought*, Revised Edition, Harvard University Press, Cambridge, Massachusetts, 1961, provides a useful synthesis to World War II, while Harold Eugene Davis, *Latin American Social Thought*, Second Edition, The University Press of Washington, D.C., 1966, contains a sampling of major writings by Latin American leaders.

The Social and Cultural Background

Frank Tannenbaum, *Ten Keys to Latin America*, Alfred A. Knopf, New York, 1962, provides an opinionated and readable primer, now somewhat dated. Richard N. Adams and others, *Social Change in Latin America Today*, published for the Council on Foreign Relations by Harper, New York, 1960, present some of the views underlying the reformist orientations of the Alliance for Progress. Charles Wagley, *An Introduction to Brazil*, Columbia University Press, New York, 1963, and Gilberto Freyre, *New World in the Tropics*, Alfred A. Knopf, New York, 1959, give thoughtful perspective to Brazil, virtually a continent apart. Eric R. Wolf and Edward C. Hansen, *The Human Condition in Latin America*, Oxford University Press, New York, 1972, and Oscar Lewis, *Five Families: Mexican Case Studies in the Culture of Poverty*, Basic Books, New York, 1962, vividly portray popular living conditions.

For literature, Germán Arciniegas, *The Green Continent: A Comprehensive View of Latin America by its Leading Writers*, Eighth Edition, Knopf, New York, 1967, combines arts and learning. Selden Rodman, *South America of the Poets*, Hawthorn Books, Inc., New York, 1970, records interviews in a haphazard but stimulating travelogue. Many excellent Latin American novels in translation, including Gabriel García Márquez, *One Hundred Years of Solitude*, and Mario Vargas Llosa, *Time of the Hero*, as well as older classics by Jorge Icaza, Carlos Fuentes, Miguel Angel Asturias, and others, provide general perspective as well as cultural enrichment.

Contemporary Problems

Douglas A. Chalmers, Editor, *Changing Latin America, New Interpretations of its Politics and Society,* Proceedings of the Academy of Political Science, Vol. 30, No. 4, New York, 1972, contains thirteen essays representative of recent American social science.

For politics, Kalman H. Silvert, *The Conflict Society,* Revised Edition, American Universities Field Staff, Inc., New York, 1966, offers a varied collection of original essays. Jacques Lambert, *Latin America: Social Structures & Political Institutions,* University of California Press, Berkeley and Los Angeles, 1967, provides a general analysis by a French scholar with a strong Brazilian background. Paul E. Sigmund, Jr., *Models of Political Change in Latin America,* Praeger, New York, 1970, is a useful reader. The growing importance of institutions and bureaucratic norms gives considerable importance to works such as Russell H. Fitzgibbon, Editor, *The Constitutions of the Americas,* University of Chicago Press, Chicago, 1948, which could profitably be updated.

Irving Louis Horowitz, Josué de Castro and John Gerassi, Editors, *Latin American Radicalism,* Random House, New York, 1969, present a comprehensive introduction to Latin American radical views, also well represented in James Petras and Maurice Zeitlin, Editors, *Latin America: Reform or Revolution? A Reader,* Fawcett Premier Books, Greenwich, Conn., 1968. C. Wright Mills, *Listen Yankee,* McGraw-Hill, New York, 1960, reflects the mood and views of the Cuban revolutionaries at their euphoric peak in the summer of 1960.

The interplay between economics and politics is the theme of both Charles W. Anderson, *Politics and Economic Change in Latin America,* D. Van Nostrand Company, Inc., Princeton, New Jersey, 1967, and Albert O. Hirschman, *Journeys Toward Progress,* The Twentieth Century Fund, New York, 1963. William P. Glade, *The Latin American Economies: A Study of Their Institutional Evolution,* American Book Co.-Van Nostrand, New York, 1969, focuses on economic history, also treated by Stanley Stein and Barbara Stein, *The Colonial Heritage of Latin America: Essays on Economic Dependence in Perspective,* Oxford University Press, New York, 1966.

Two additional readers containing materials on contemporary issues are: Rodolfo Stavenhagen, Editor, *Agrarian Problems & Peasant Movements in*

Latin America, Doubleday & Company, Inc. (Anchor Books), Garden City, New York, 1970, and Karl M. Schmitt, Editor, *The Roman Catholic Church in Modern Latin America,* Knopf, New York, 1972.

International Relations

Yale H. Ferguson, Editor, *Contemporary Inter-American Relations: A Reader in Theory and Issues,* Prentice-Hall, Inc., Englewood Cliffs, New Jersey, 1972, is a useful sampler. Federico G. Gil, *Latin American-United States Relations,* Harcourt Brace Jovanovich, New York, 1971, and Edward J. Williams, *The Political Themes of Inter-American Relations,* Duxbury Press, Belmont, California, 1971, are recent introductory surveys. Two major historical works on U.S. policy are Dana G. Munro, *Intervention and Dollar Diplomacy in the Caribbean, 1900–1921,* Princeton University Press, Princeton, New Jersey, 1964, and Bryce Wood, *The Making of the Good Neighbor Policy,* Columbia University Press, New York & London, 1961. The Alliance for Progress is reviewed in Jerome Levinson and Juan de Onís, *The Alliance that Lost its Way,* Quadrangle Books, Chicago, 1970. More recent materials will be found in *The Rockefeller Report on the Americas,* Quadrangle, New York, 1969, in pamphlets like Colin I. Bradford, Jr., *Forces for Change in Latin America: U.S. Policy Implications,* Overseas Development Council, Monograph Number Five, Washington, D.C., 1971, and in government documents and congressional hearings. The activities of non-Latin American countries are chronicled in Herbert Goldhamer, *The Foreign Powers in Latin America,* Princeton University Press, Princeton, New Jersey, 1972. J. F. Normano, *The Struggle for South America,* George Allen & Unwin Ltd., London, 1931, is a minor classic, emphasizing recurring patterns of foreign economic activity.

Recent Case Studies

An abridged list of recent case studies, many of which reveal broader processes of Latin American life, might include:

On Mexico: John Womack, *Zapata and the Mexican Revolution,* Knopf, New York, 1968, and David Ronfeldt, *Atencingo, The Politics of Agrarian Struggle in a Mexican Ejido,* Stanford University Press, Stanford, California, 1973.

On Brazil: Ralph Della Cava, *Miracle at Jōaseiro,* Columbia University Press, New York, 1970 (social protest in historical perspective); Alfred

Stepan, *The Military in Politics: Changing Patterns in Brazil,* Princeton University Press, Princeton, 1971; Philippe C. Schmitter, *Interest Conflict and Political Change in Brazil,* Stanford University Press, Stanford, California, 1972; and Nathaniel H. Leff, *Economic Policy-making and Development in Brazil, 1947–1964,* John Wiley, New York, 1968.

On Argentina: José Luis de Imaz, *Los que mandan (Those Who Rule),* State University of New York Press, Albany, 1970 (a translation by Carlos Astiz of an excellent local study of the Argentine elite); Carlos Díaz Alejandro, *Essays in the Economic History of the Argentine Republic,* New Edition, Yale University Press, New Haven, 1970, and Robert Potash, *The Army and Politics in Argentina, 1918–1945,* Stanford University Press, Stanford, California, 1969 (the first of a projected two-volume set).

On other countries: Richard L. Maullin, *Soldiers, Guerrillas, and Politics in Columbia,* D. C. Heath, Lexington, Mass., 1973, and Edward Gonzalez, *Cuba Under Castro: The Limits of Charisma,* Houghton Mifflin, Boston, 1974.

On inter-American relations: Abraham F. Lowenthal, *The Dominican Intervention,* Harvard University Press, Cambridge, 1972, and Riordan Roett, *The Politics of Foreign Aid in the Brazilian Northeast,* Vanderbilt University Press, Nashville, Tennessee, 1972.

Current Events and Research

Major U.S. newspapers cover Latin American news in a maddeningly erratic fashion. *The Times of the Americas,* Woodward Building, Washington, D.C. 20005, publishes a weekly summary of rather conventional news and notes. The best news analysis is furnished by *Latin America,* a weekly political and economic newsletter published at 6/7 New Bridge Street, London EC4V 64R. *Business Latin America,* available from Business International Corporation, 757 Third Avenue, New York, New York 10017, is a useful source of developments affecting foreign business operations. The monthly *Latin American and Empire Report,* published by the North American Congress on Latin America (NACLA), Box 57, Cathedral Station, New York, New York 10025, concentrates on radical news and analysis, and is a counterweight to complacency.

The contemporary journalism tradition of Carleton Beals, John Gunther, and Tad Szulc is upheld by Swedish journalist Sven Lindqvist, *The Shadow: Latin America Faces the Seventies,* Pelican Latin American Library, Penguin Books, 1972, which, however, reflects the excessive pessimism of the late 1960s.

The Latin American Research Review, Sid W. Richardson Hall, University of Texas, Austin, Texas 78712, is precisely what its name implies: an essential means of keeping up with current research, including critical reviews, bibliographies, and notes on meetings.

The Best Way

Of course, the best way to learn about Latin America is to go there. In the English tradition of observant travel, Howell Davies, Editor, *The South American Handbook,* Trade and Travel Publications, Ltd., Bath, England, annually publishes information on the countries of the Caribbean and Central as well as South America.

INDEX

SELECTED RAND BOOKS

Bagdikian, Ben H. *The Information Machines: Their Impact on Men and the Media.* New York: Harper and Row, 1971.

Cohen, Bernard, and Jan M. Chaiken. *Police Background Characteristics and Performance.* Lexington, Mass.: D.C. Heath and Company, 1973.

DeSalvo, Joseph S. (ed.) *Perspectives on Regional Transportation Planning.* Lexington, Mass.: D. C. Heath and Company, 1973.

Downs, Anthony. *Inside Bureaucracy.* Boston, Mass.: Little, Brown and Company, 1967.

Garthoff, Raymond L. *Soviet Military Doctrine.* Glencoe, Illinois: The Free Press, 1953.

George, Alexander L. *Propaganda Analysis: A Study of Inferences Made From Nazi Propaganda in World War II.* Evanston, Illinois: Row, Peterson and Company, 1959.

Goldhamer, Herbert, and Andrew W. Marshall. *Psychosis and Civilization.* Glencoe, Illinois: The Free Press, 1953.

Goldhamer, Herbert. *The Foreign Powers in Latin America.* Princeton, New Jersey: Princeton University Press, 1972.

Hammond, Paul Y., and Sidney S. Alexander. *Political Dynamics in the Middle East.* New York: American Elsevier Publishing Company, 1972.

Hitch, Charles J., and Roland McKean. *The Economics of Defense in the Nuclear Age.* Cambridge, Mass.: Harvard University Press, 1960.

Horelick, Arnold L., and Myron Rush. *Strategic Power and Soviet Foreign Policy.* Chicago, Illinois: University of Chicago Press, 1966.

249

Kecskemeti, Paul. *The Unexpected Revolution*. Stanford, California: Stanford University Press, 1961.

Leites, Nathan, and Charles Wolf, Jr. *Rebellion and Authority: An Analytic Essay on Insurgent Conflicts*. Chicago, Illinois: Markham Publishing Company, 1970.

Maullin, Richard L. *Soldiers, Guerrillas, and Politics in Colombia*. Lexington, Mass.: D. C. Heath and Company, 1973.

Melnik, Constantin, and Nathan Leites. *The House Without Windows: France Selects a President*. Evanston, Illinois: Row, Peterson and Company, 1958.

Moorsteen, Richard, and Morton I. Abramowitz. *Remaking China Policy: U.S.-China Relations and Governmental Decision Making*. Cambridge, Mass.: Harvard University Press, 1971.

Nelson, Richard R., T. Paul Schultz, and Robert L. Slighton. *Structural Change in a Developing Economy: Colombia's Problems and Prospects*. Princeton, New Jersey: Princeton University Press, 1971.

Novick, David (ed.) *Current Practice in Program Budgeting (PPBS): Analysis and Case Studies Covering Government and Business*. New York: Crane, Russak & Company, Inc. 1973.

Pascal, Anthony H. (ed.) *Racial Discrimination in Economic Life*. Lexington, Mass.: D. C. Heath and Company, 1972.

Quade, Edward S., and Wayne I. Boucher. *Systems Analysis and Policy Planning: Applications in Defense*. New York: American Elsevier Publishing Company, 1968.

Quandt, William B. (ed.) *The Politics of Palestinian Nationalism*. Berkeley, Calif.: University of California Press, 1973.

Stepan, Alfred. *The Military in Politics: Changing Patterns in Brazil*. Princeton, New Jersey: Princeton University Press, 1971.

Williams, John D. *The Compleat Strategyst: Being a Primer on the Theory of Games of Strategy*. New York: McGraw-Hill Book Company, 1954.